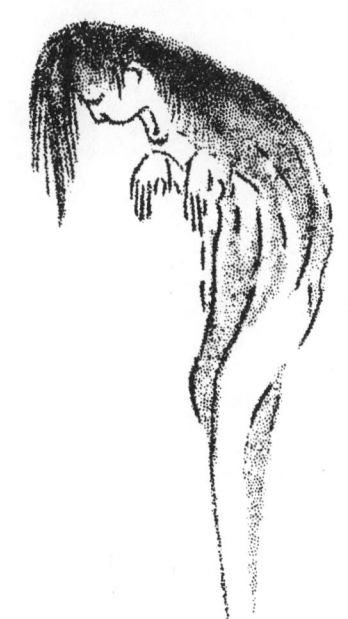

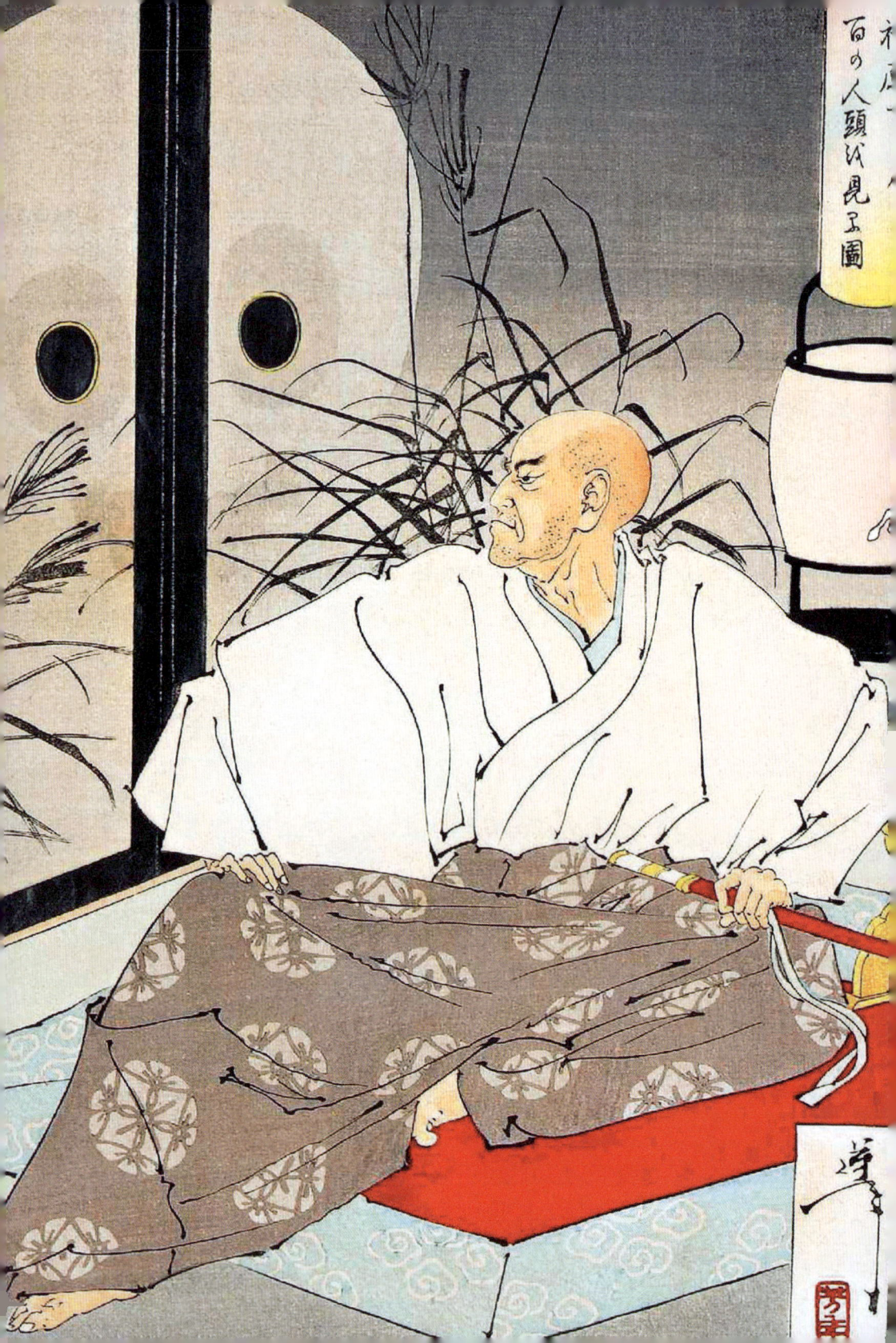

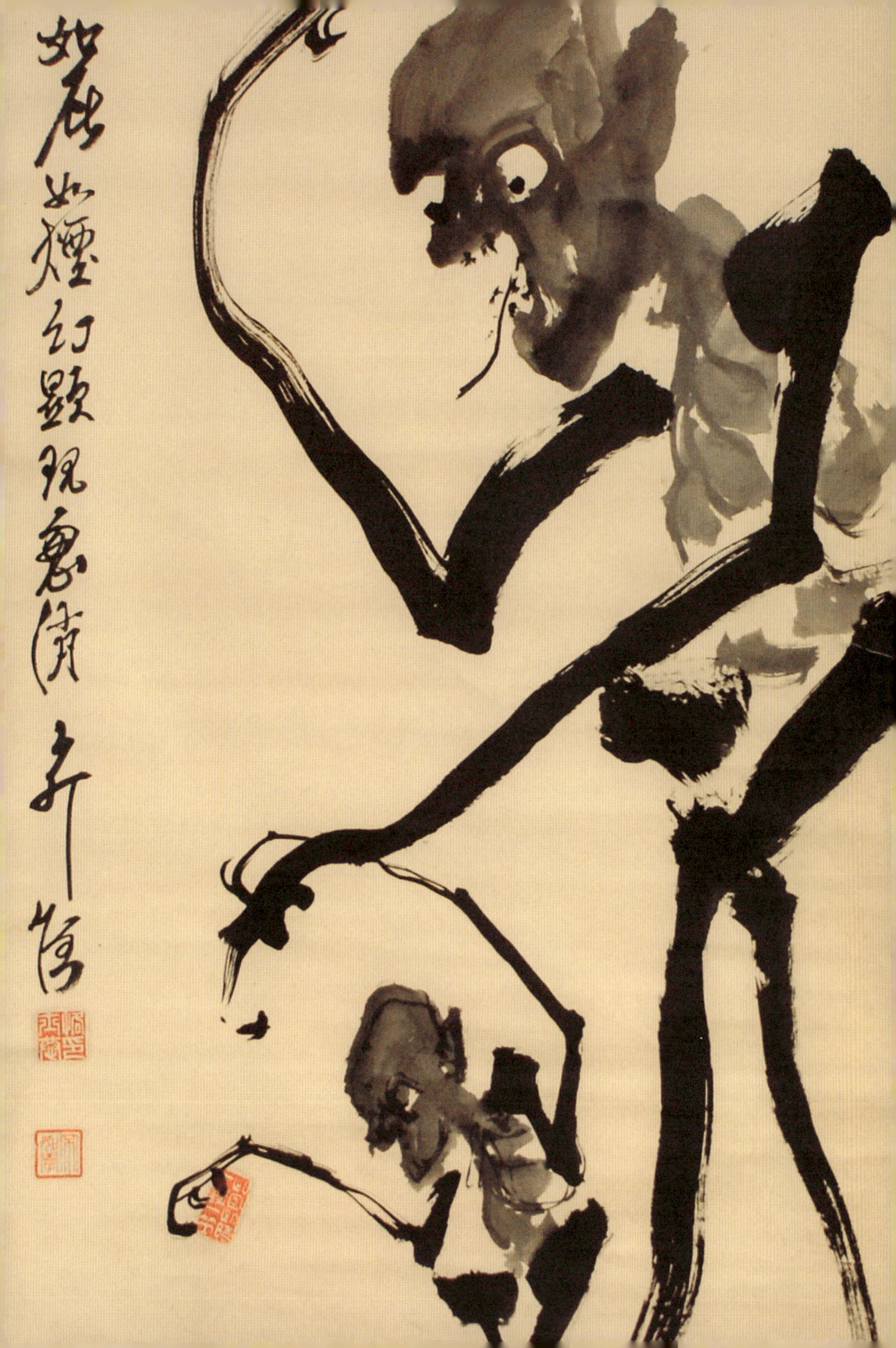

YŌKAI
GHOSTS

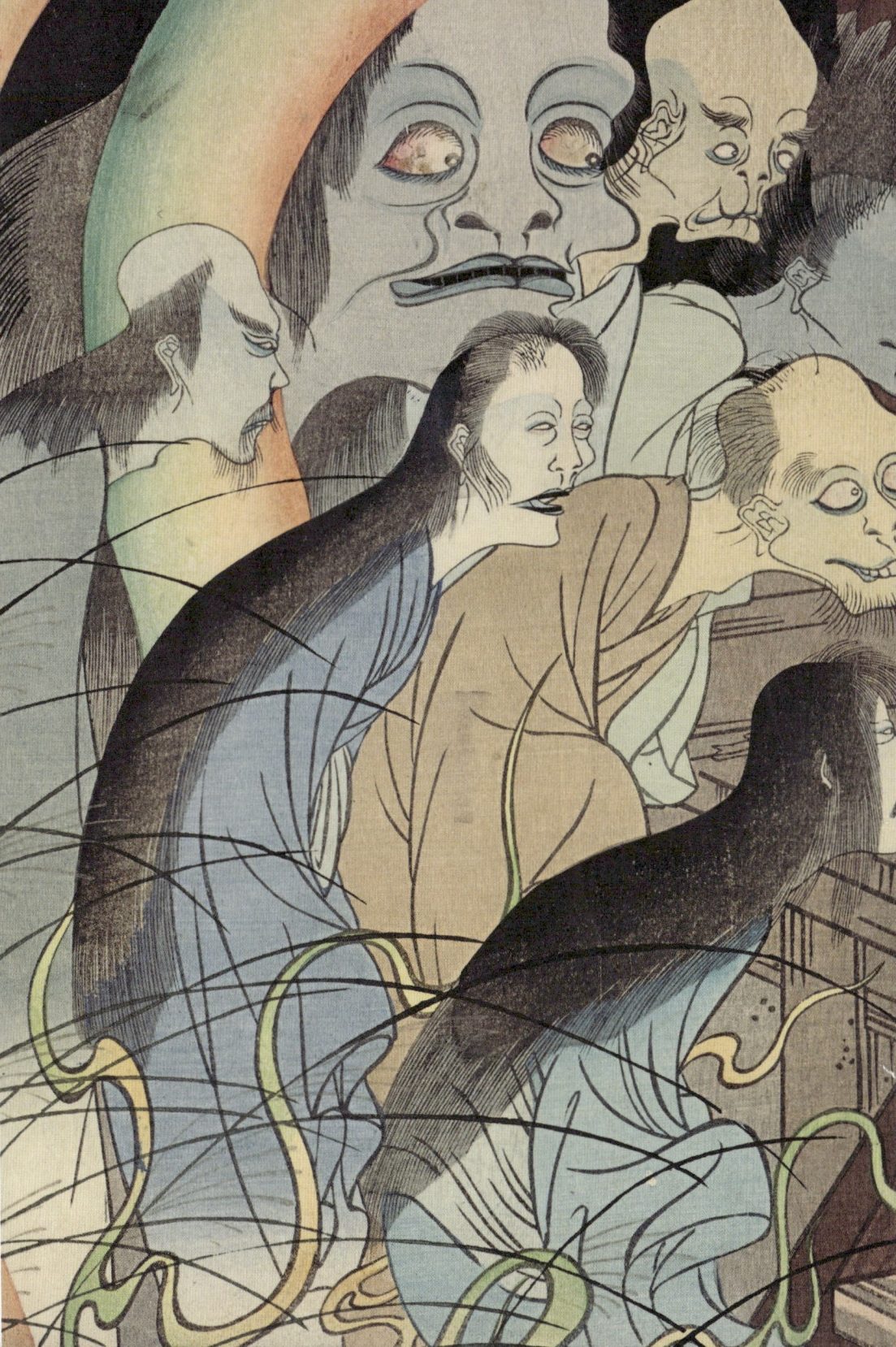

YŌKAI
GHOSTS

By the Great Masters of Japanese
Woodblock Printing

PRESTEL
MUNICH · LONDON · NEW YORK

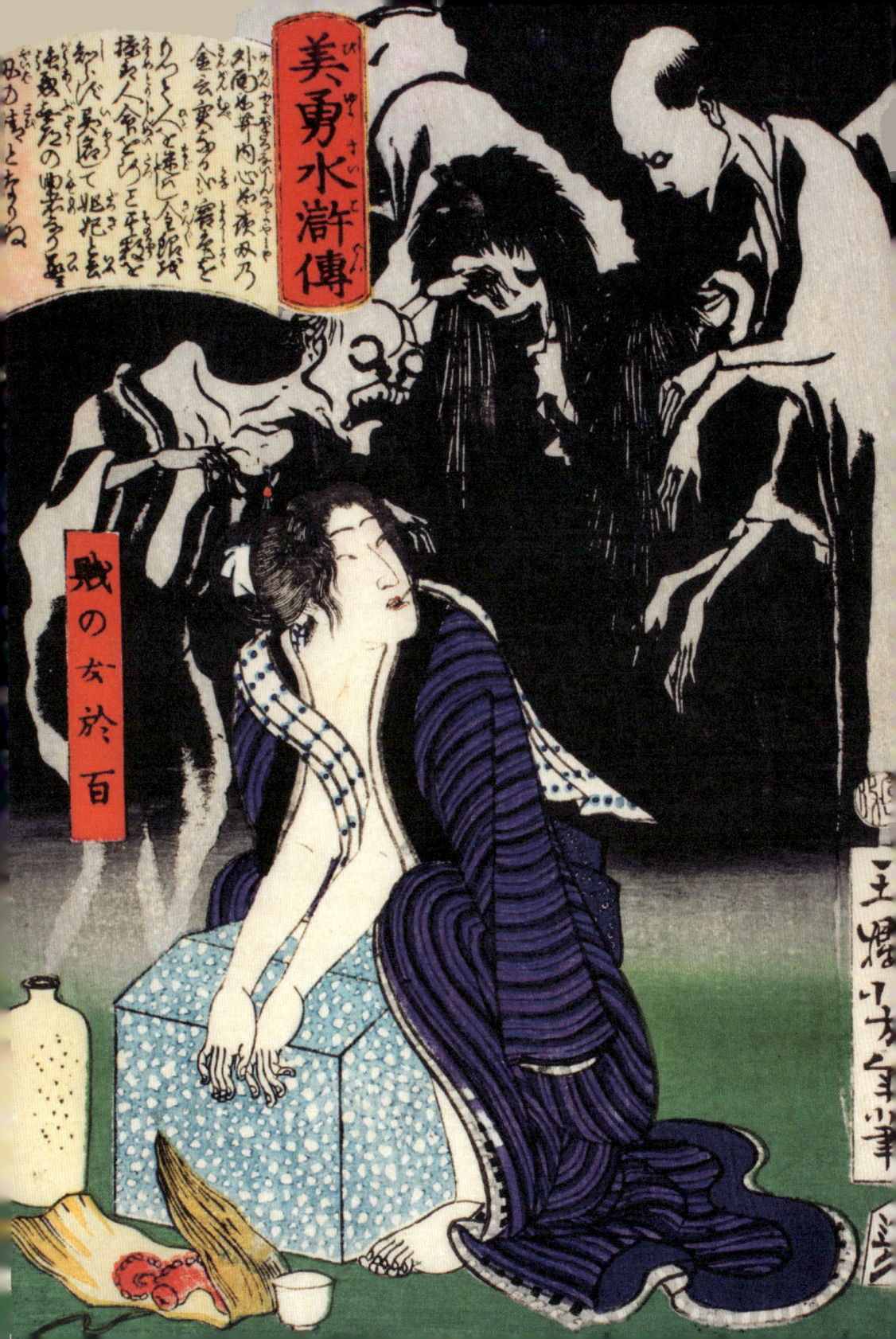

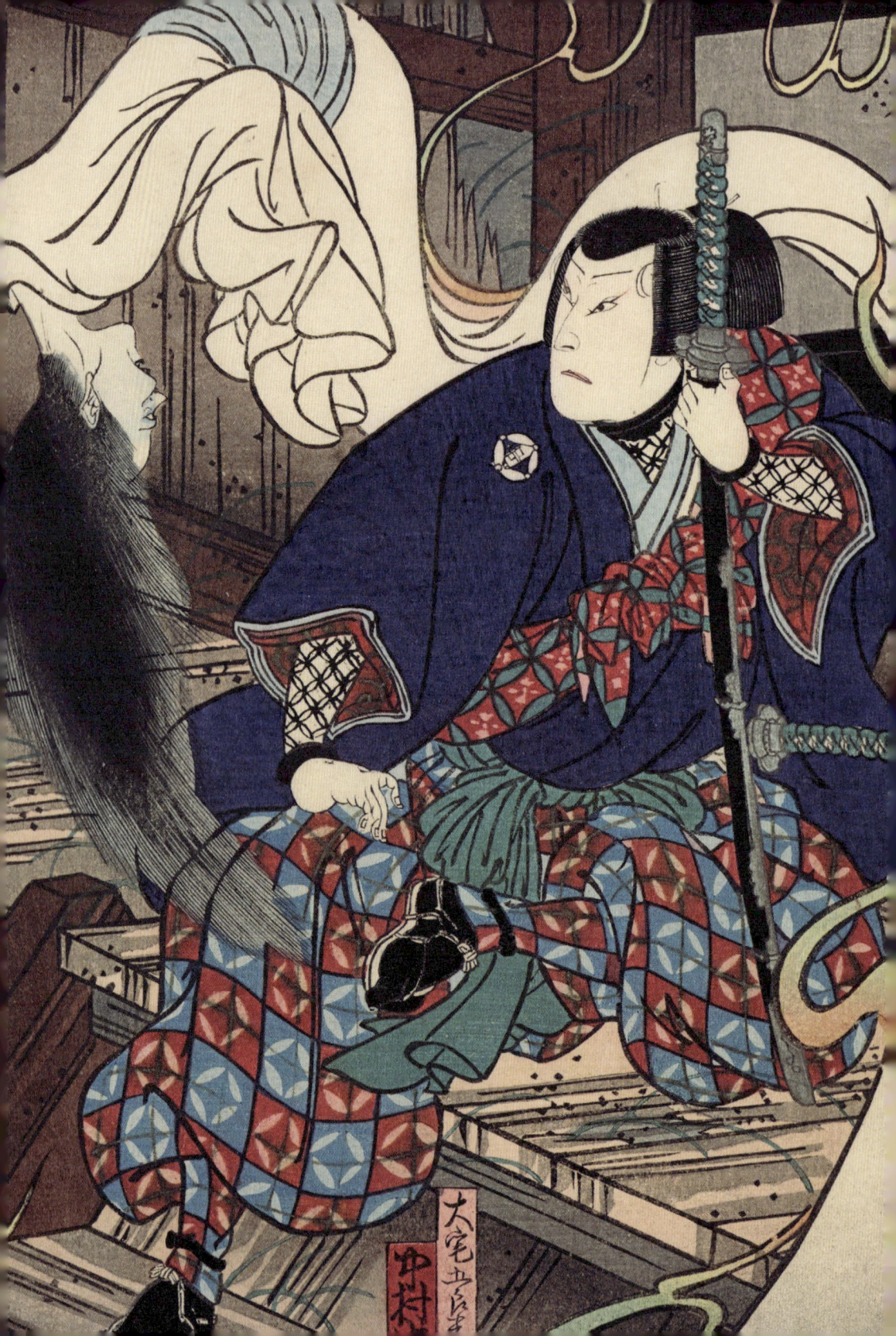

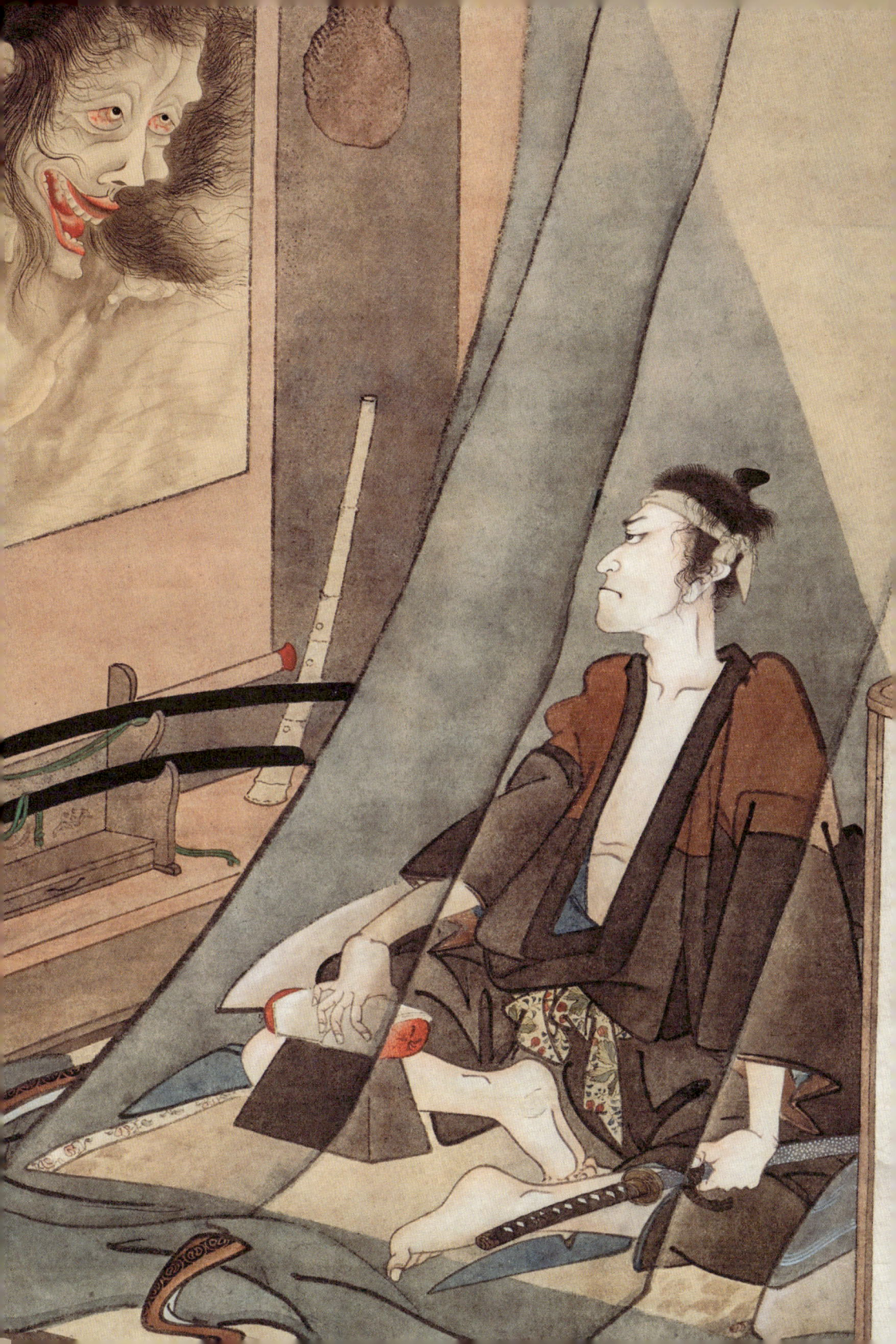

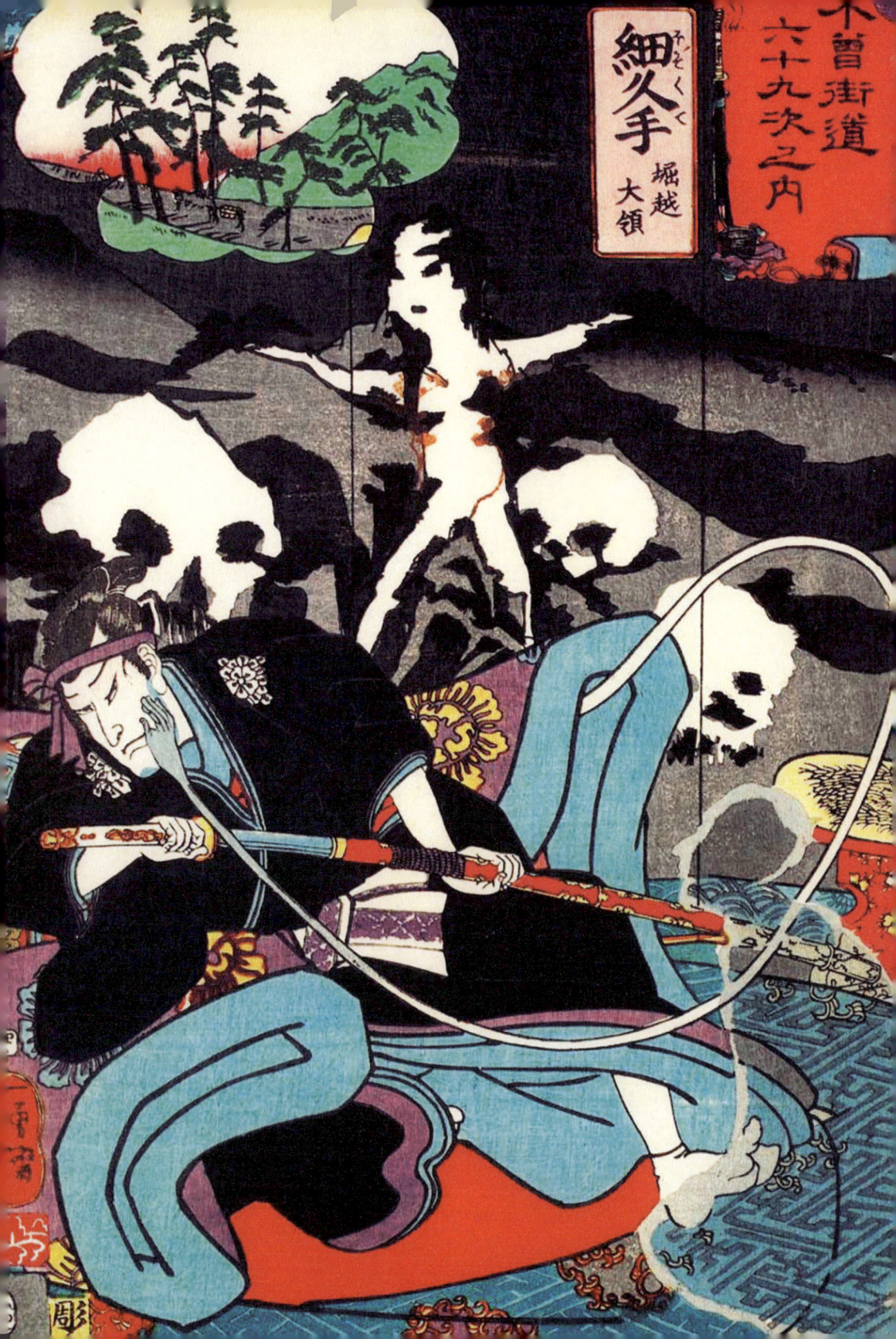

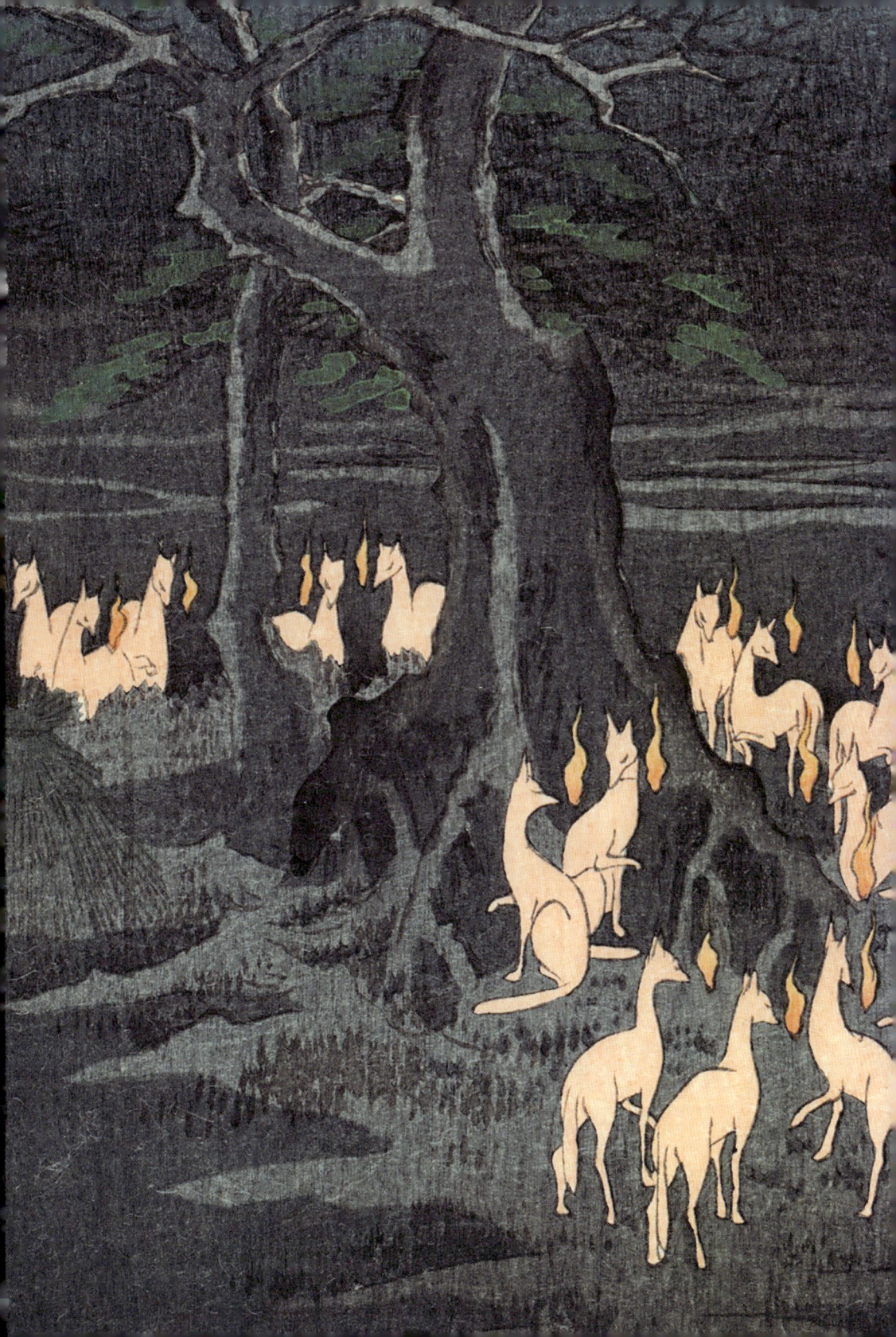

GATE TO THE UNDERWORLD 18

AUTOPSY ON A REVENANT 28

OKIKU 45

OTSUYU 57

UBUME 67

NOH 77

FUNAYŪREI 87

YUKI-ONNA 99

OIWA, THE FACE OF DEATH 109

KASANE 121

HEADS THAT FLY 127

THE SMILE OF DEATH 137

HANNYA 143

DEMONS OF THE BATTLEFIELD 151

KOHADA KOHEIJI 163

IMAGES OF TWO INTERLACED
WORLDS 173

List of Illustrations 183

Bibliography 189

Inside cover: Hirabayashi Shūsai, *Ghost of a Courtesan (Yūrei oiran)*, detail, ca 1926–1940 Courtesy of Galerie Mingei, Paris
p. 2: Tsukioka Yoshitoshi, *Taira Kiyomori Sees Skeletons at Fukuhara*, detail, 1865

p. 4: Doi Gōga, *Skeleton Father and Son Doing the Bon Dance*, detail, second half of the 19th century Minneapolis Institute of Art
pp. 6–7: Utagawa Yoshitaki, *Soharto Tangondaki Nakamura Sojuro as Otake Goro Mitsokuni (Ghosts)*, detail, date unknown Philadelphia Museum of Art

p. 8: Tsukioka Yoshitoshi, *Shizunome Ohyaku and Four Hungry Ghosts*, detail, 1866 Philadelphia Museum of Art
p. 9: Utagawa Kuniyoshi, *Hosokute Lord Horikoshi*, detail, 1852
p. 10: Utagawa School, *Ghost Story*, detail, late 19th century Minneapolis Institute of Art

pp. 12–13: Utagawa Hiroshige, *New Year's Eve Foxfires at the Changing Tree, Ōji*, detail, ca 1857 New York, The Metropolitan Museum of Art
pp. 14–15 Katsukawa Shun'ei, *Once Upon a Time (Imawa mukashi)*, detail, 1790 New York, The Metropolitan Museum of Art

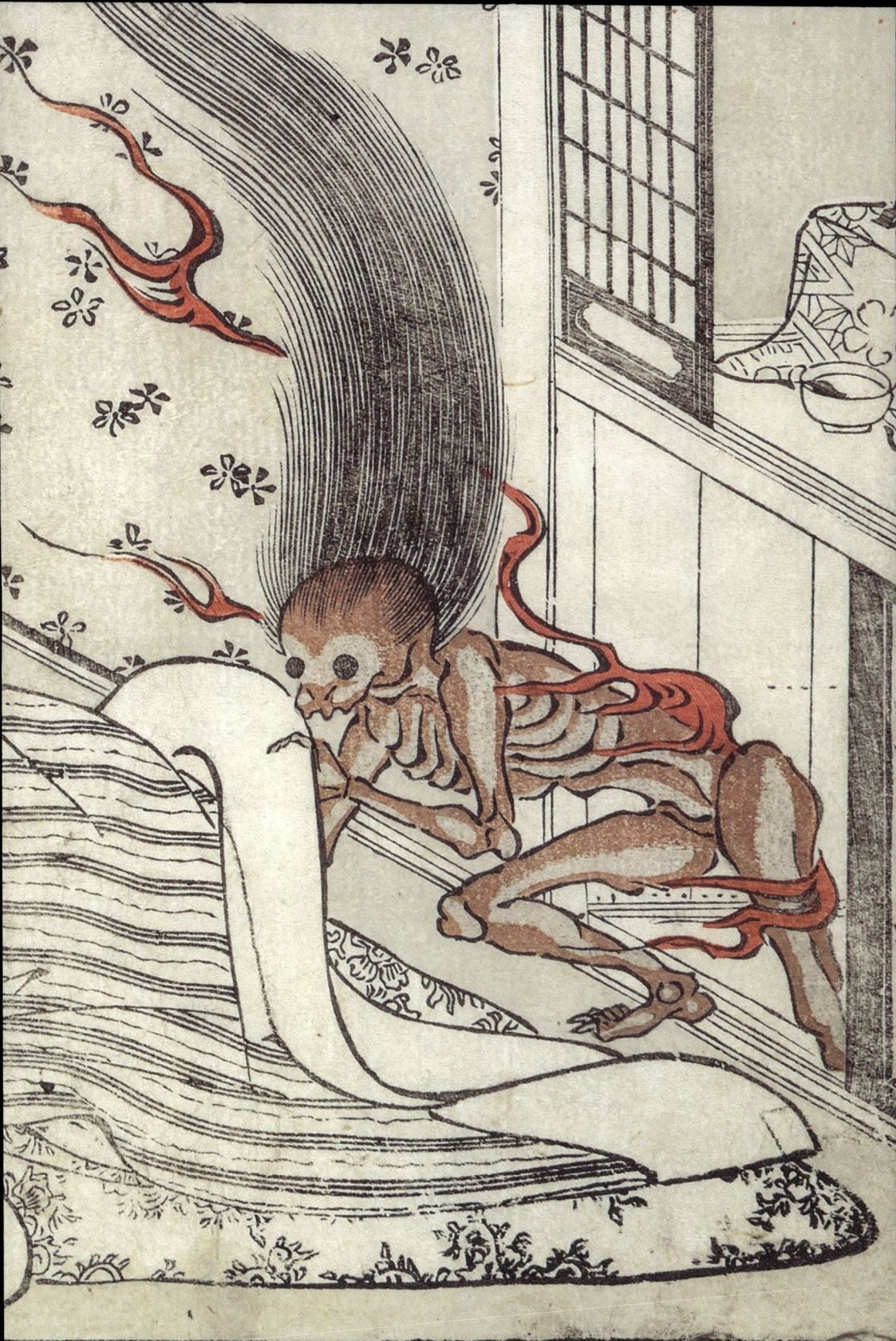

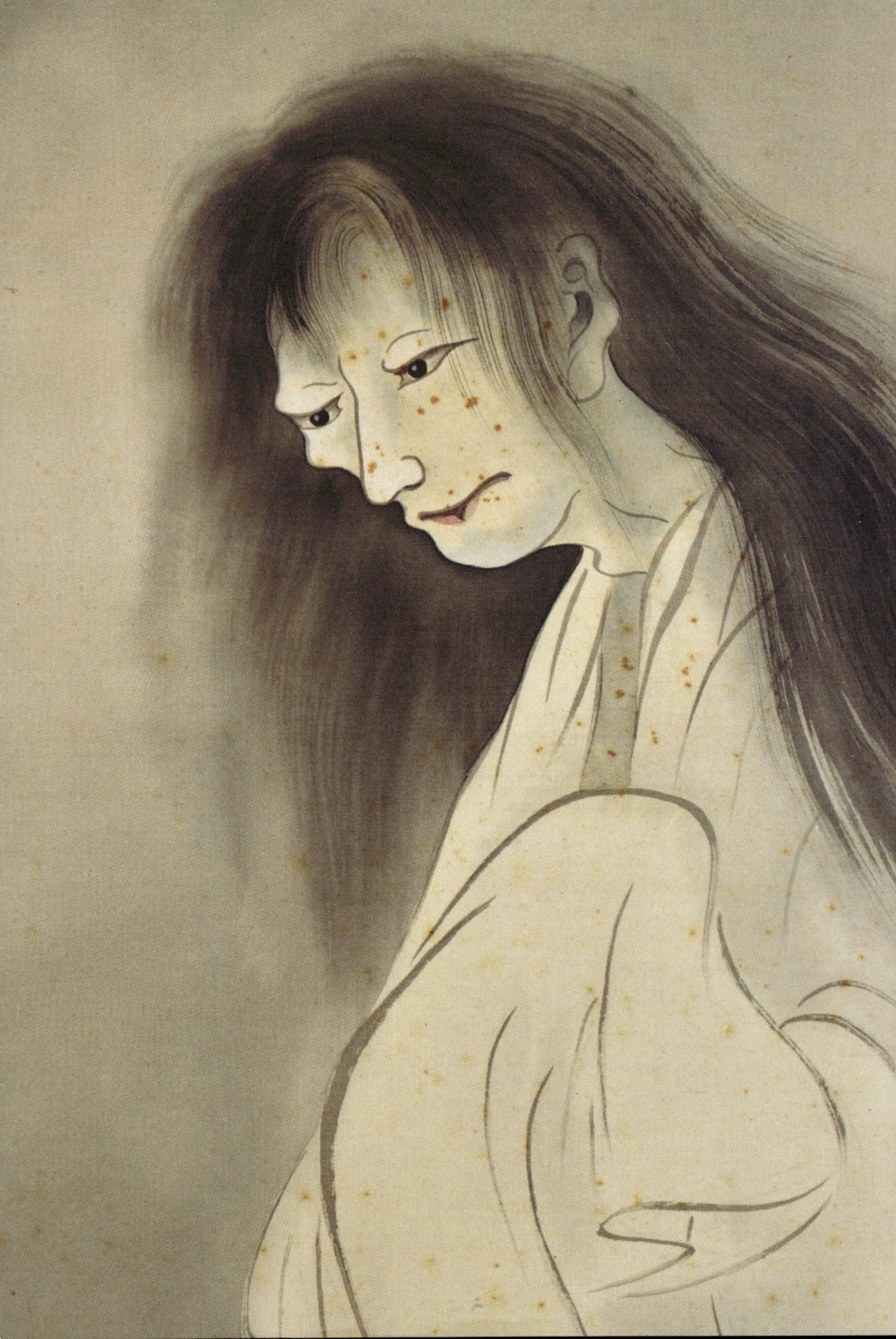

YŪREI

*Stories of Love and Death
in Traditional Japan*

PHILIPPE CHARLIER

•

We see that all things animate must die
When from the body the soul does part
I am the body, you the better part
Where are you then, O beloved soul?

Louise Labé (ca 1524–1566)

Though I am without shape, I am light.
I am light inside a transparent body . . .
This light is my soul . . .
Very different to the souls you possess,
My naked soul roams the world . . .
The light can burn a body,
But my soul, it is burning too . . .

Yukio Mishima, 'Yoroboshi'

Your curse does not scare me!
I am strong, because I have been loved . . .

Yukio Mishima, 'Yoroboshi'

GATE TO THE UNDER- WORLD

•

It is the same story, again and again. The same legend, repeating itself from generation to generation. A woman is abandoned, driven to suicide, or cravenly murdered. A wife or mistress with no escape but death, she is starved and subjected to morbid jealousy, petty cruelty, harassment and humiliation. Everything conspires against her until she dies in the prime of her life. But even death brings no end, for when the soul departs prematurely, there is no possibility of eternal rest or swift reincarnation – quite the opposite: This is the start of a long period of wandering for the wrathful spirit, which will, as the centuries pass, continue to associate with humans, inciting fear and pity alternately.

While these stories are centuries old (and sometimes older), graphic representations of them have been produced only relatively recently. We owe that to one man, Ōkyo Maruyama. Born in 1733, this painter was confronted one evening with the ghost of the love of his life, Oyuki. Were his eyes deceived by whisps of steam from his teapot, or by a draft of air fluttering the edges of a flowery kimono or snuffing out a lantern? Whatever his inspiration, he created more than just a technique; he found a means of capturing these immaterial beings in images and ultimately enabled them to make an appearance in the world of the living. With his paintings of Japanese ghosts (*yūrei-ga*), drawn meticulously on human-sized canvases (*kakemono*), he opened supernatural gates that now allow communication between the living and the dead.

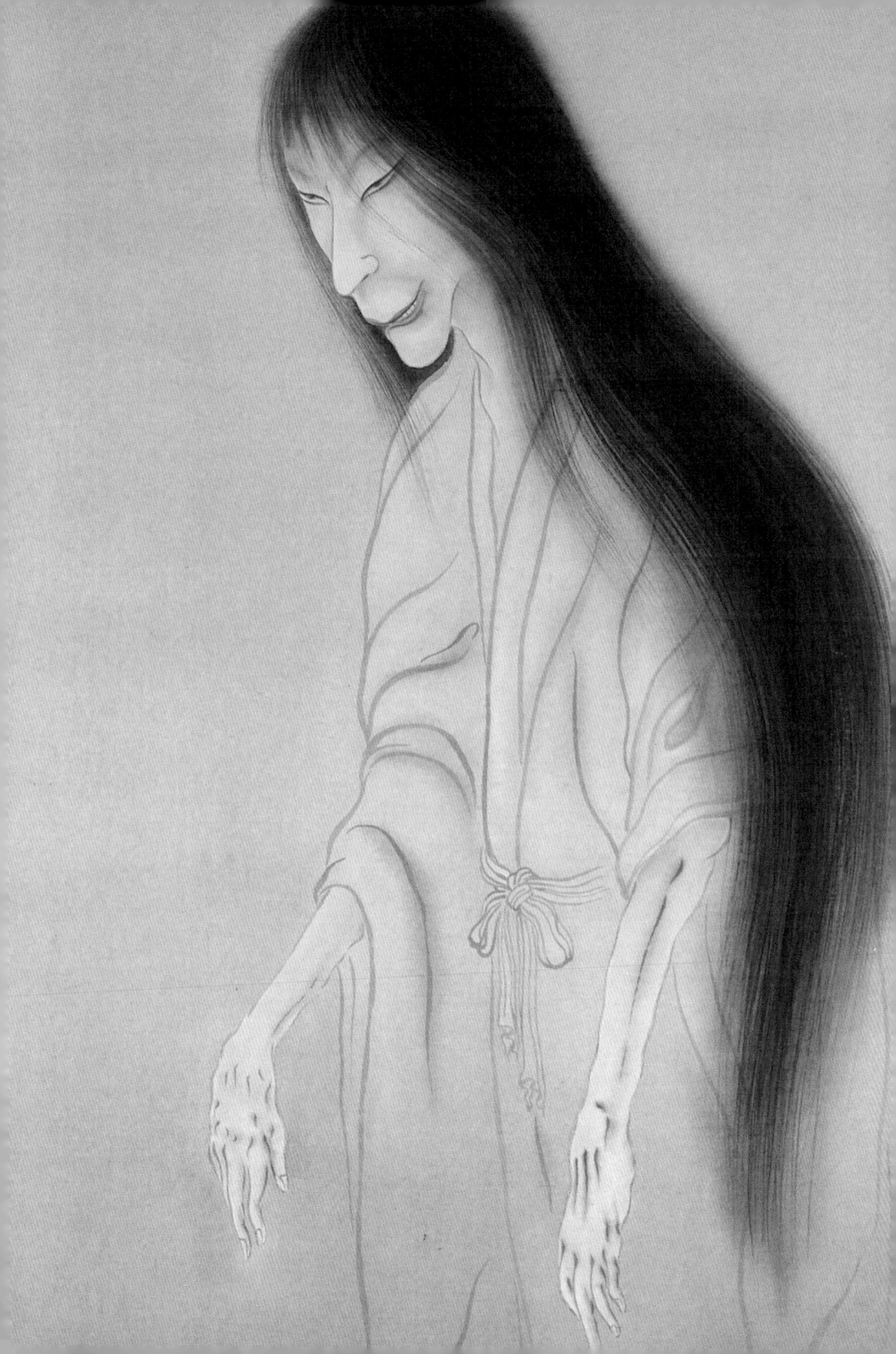

During the Edo period (1603–1867), men of the cultural and literary elite – or those who claimed to be – would organise night-time vigils, a kind of 'game of death' in which spectres and ghosts were summoned. These 'vigils by one hundred candles' (*hyaku monotogari*) always followed the same pattern: men (no women were permitted) would meet in the back room of a temple or home, an alcove of some kind. On the wall would hang a *yūrei-ga*, freshly unrolled from its white wooden box. On the floor, tatamis, a teapot, a few cups and bottles of sake. And, most importantly, one hundred candles, all lit, arranged in a circle. As soon as the sun set, one of the guests would position himself in the centre of the circle, facing the painting – that is, facing the ghost painted on the life-size canvas, literally at its feet, supplicant and adoring.

Then, the man begins to read in a low voice, audibly, but respectfully, as if in semi-silence. It is no ordinary text that he is reading: these are fantastical stories (*kaidan*), collections of age-old tales, anecdotes about monsters and hybrid creatures (*yōkai*), haunted castles and wells from which gruesome spectres emerge . . . Once the story ends, the teller allows a few minutes of silence to pass, then stands up slowly and blows out a candle. And so it continues. Each story read is a trail into the darkness, like a long path of initiation. Shortly before dawn – the vigil ever constant and unbroken – the one hundred stories have been told, and the last candle is blown out. An inky blackness then engulfs the alcove. This accumulation of tales has amply prepared minds for marvelling. And it is in this near-perfect obscurity that, slowly, the phantom will be drawn out from the canvas, to engage with the living according to their wishes. What will they do? Drink some tea or sake? Discuss the many worlds? Or lie down on a tatami and abandon themselves to lascivious caresses? One thing is certain: this ghost is not going to return to the beyond on its own. It has taken great effort to open the gate to the underworld, and the ghost will require a guide to accompany it back to its realm. In compensation for its passing that forbidden gate, it may even claim the guide as spoils.

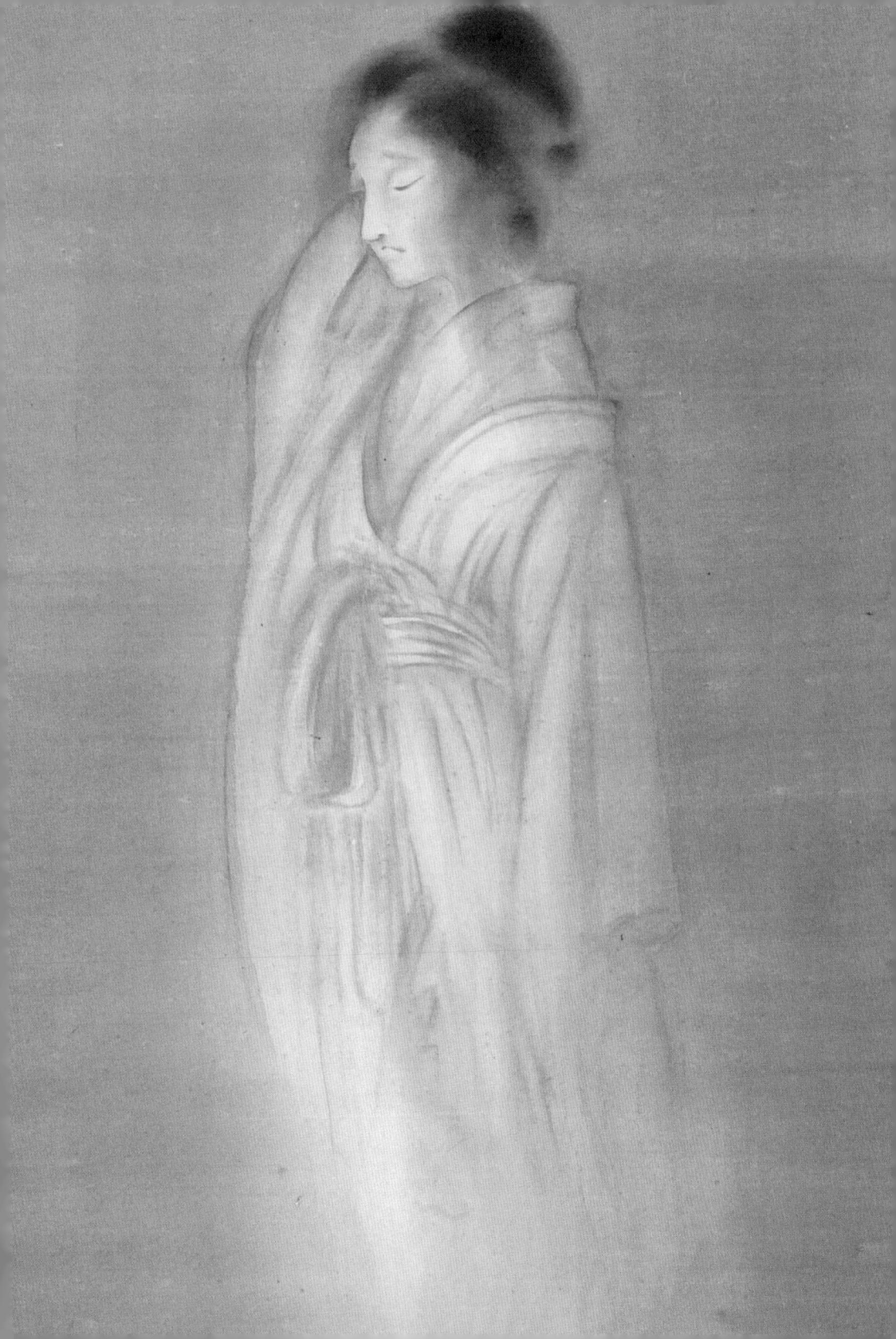

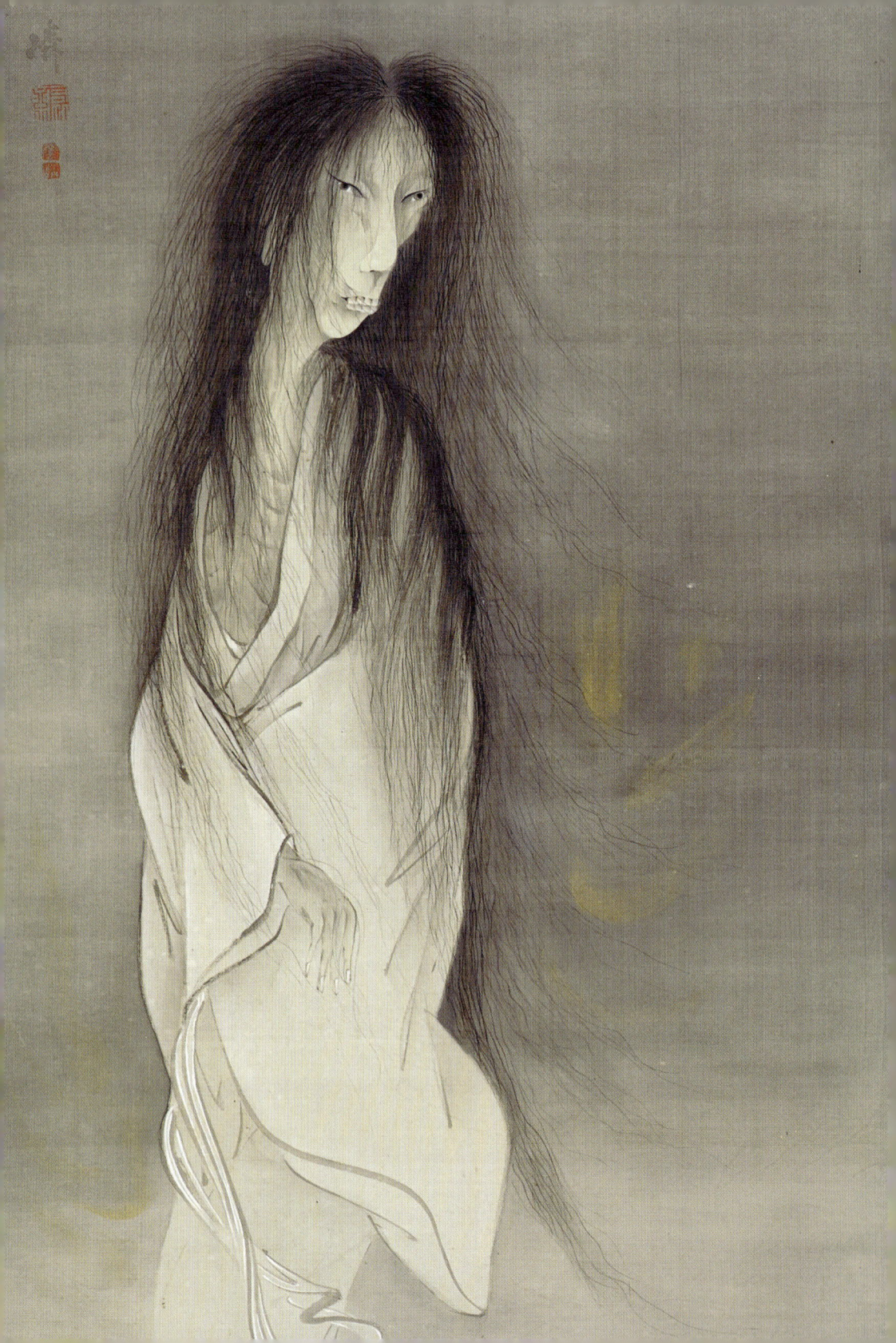

Summoning spectres is a dangerous game, and it can cost lives.

Meanwhile, we have these paintings, and each one is a story of love and death. Pictures at an exhibition, where death and resentment reign.

p. 16: Anonymous 19th century master, *Ghost*, detail
Paris, Collection of Philippe Charlier
p. 19: Iguchi Kashu, *Ghost*, detail
Paris, Musée du quai Branly – Jacques Chirac

p. 21: Terasaki Kōgyō, *Ghost*, right-hand scroll of a diptych, detail, July 1900
Minneapolis Institute of Art
p. 22: Kaitu Unrin, *Ghost*, detail, 1882
Paris, Musée du quai Branly – Jacques Chirac

pp. 24–25: Tsukioka Yoshitoshi, *The Priest Sōgi Notices a Pair of Ghosts in an Abandoned House*, detail, 1902
Philadelphia Museum of Art
pp. 26–27: Utagawa Kunisada I (aka Toyokuni III),

The Ghost of Kamata Matahachi, the Servant, Kamata Matahachi and the Former Mistress of His Brother Tied to a Tree, detail, 1855
Paris, Musée du quai Branly – Jacques Chirac

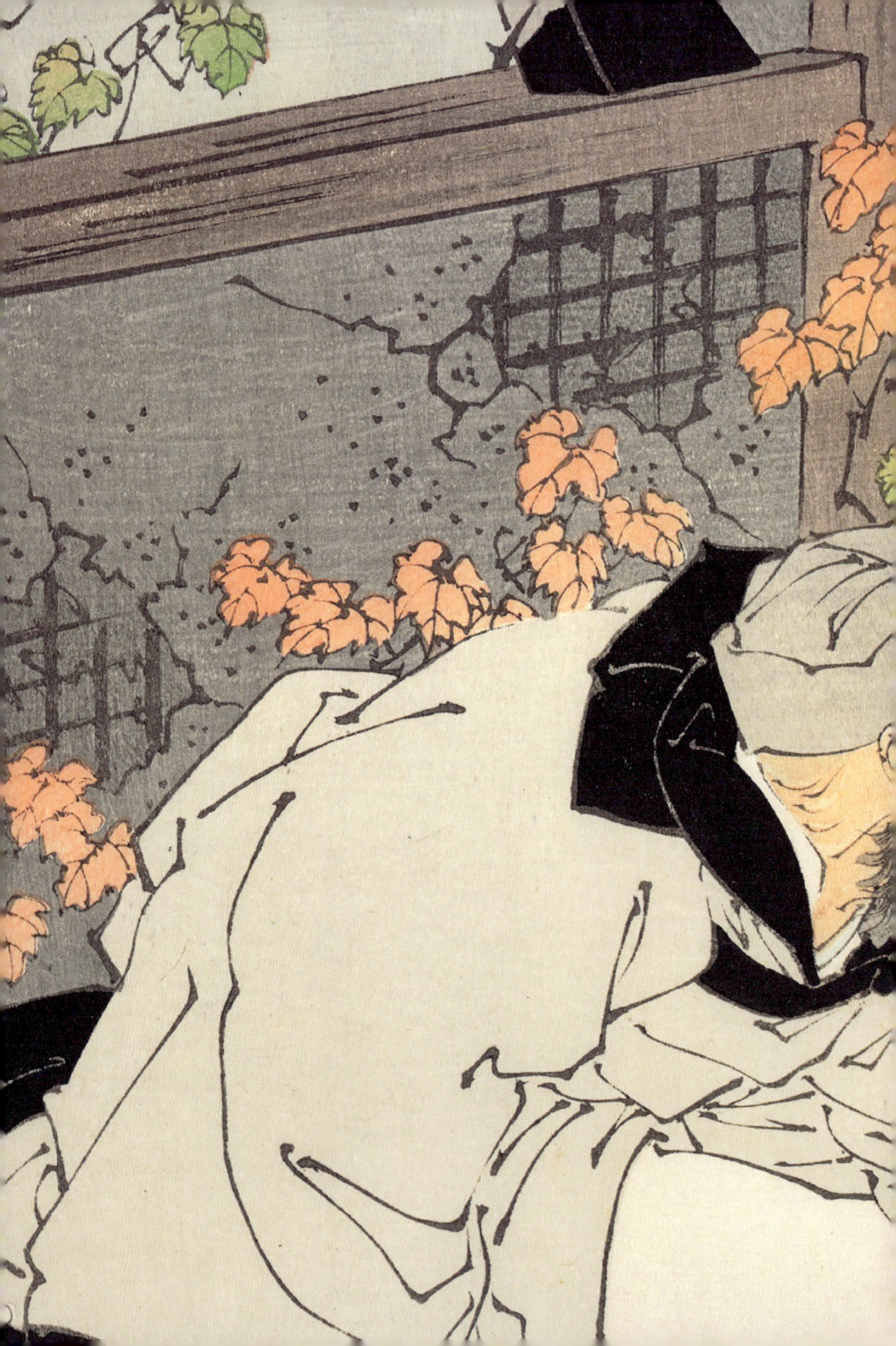

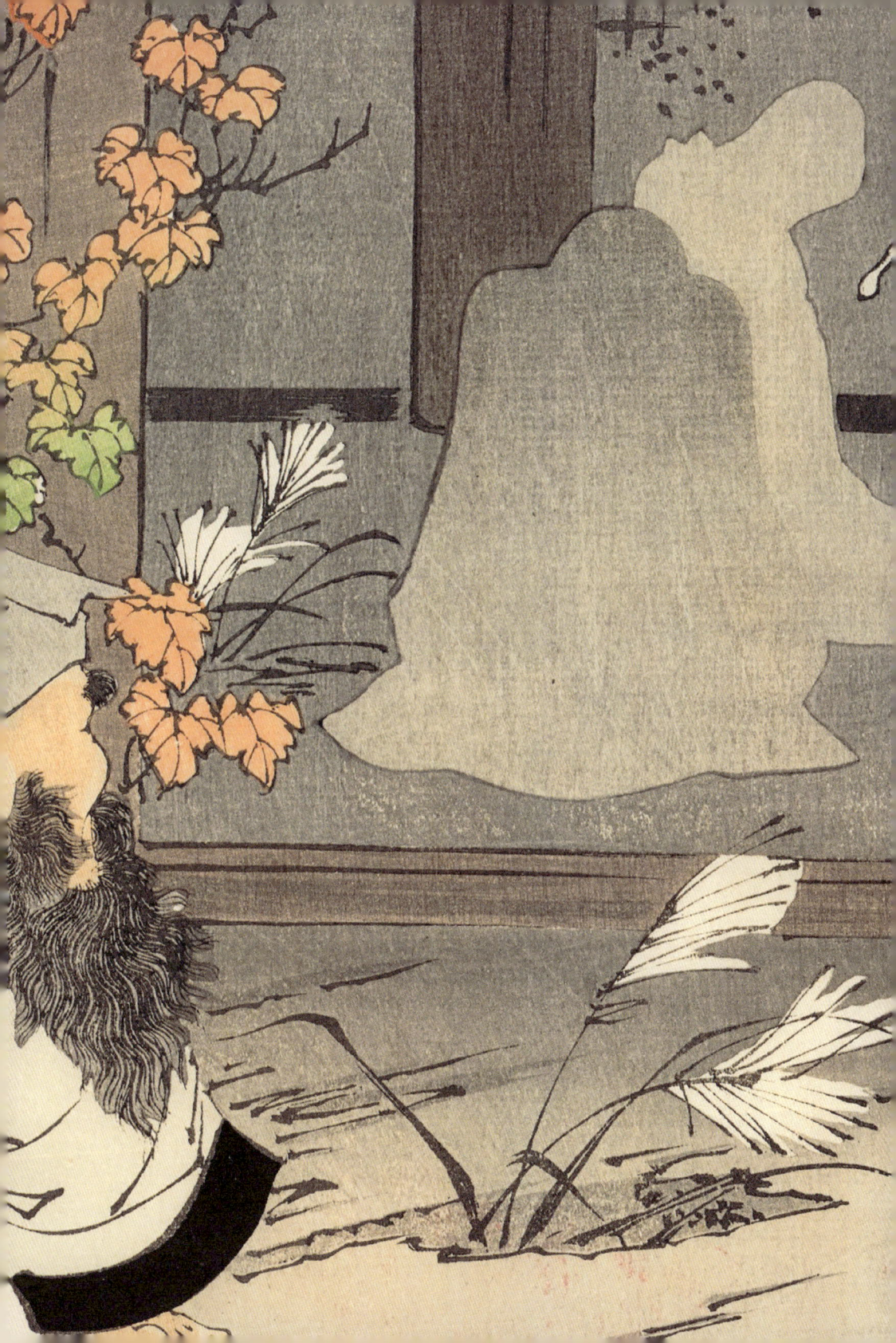

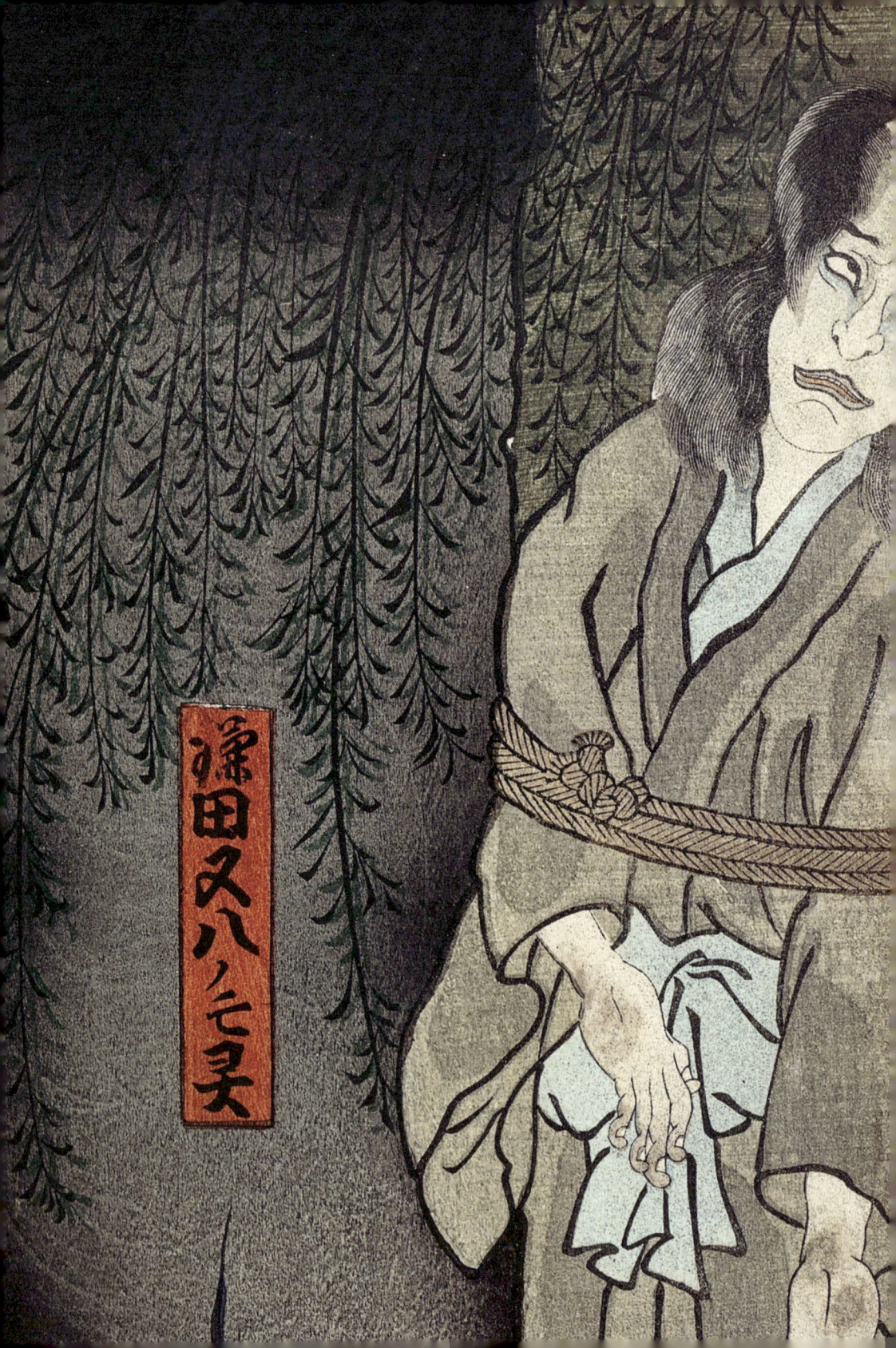

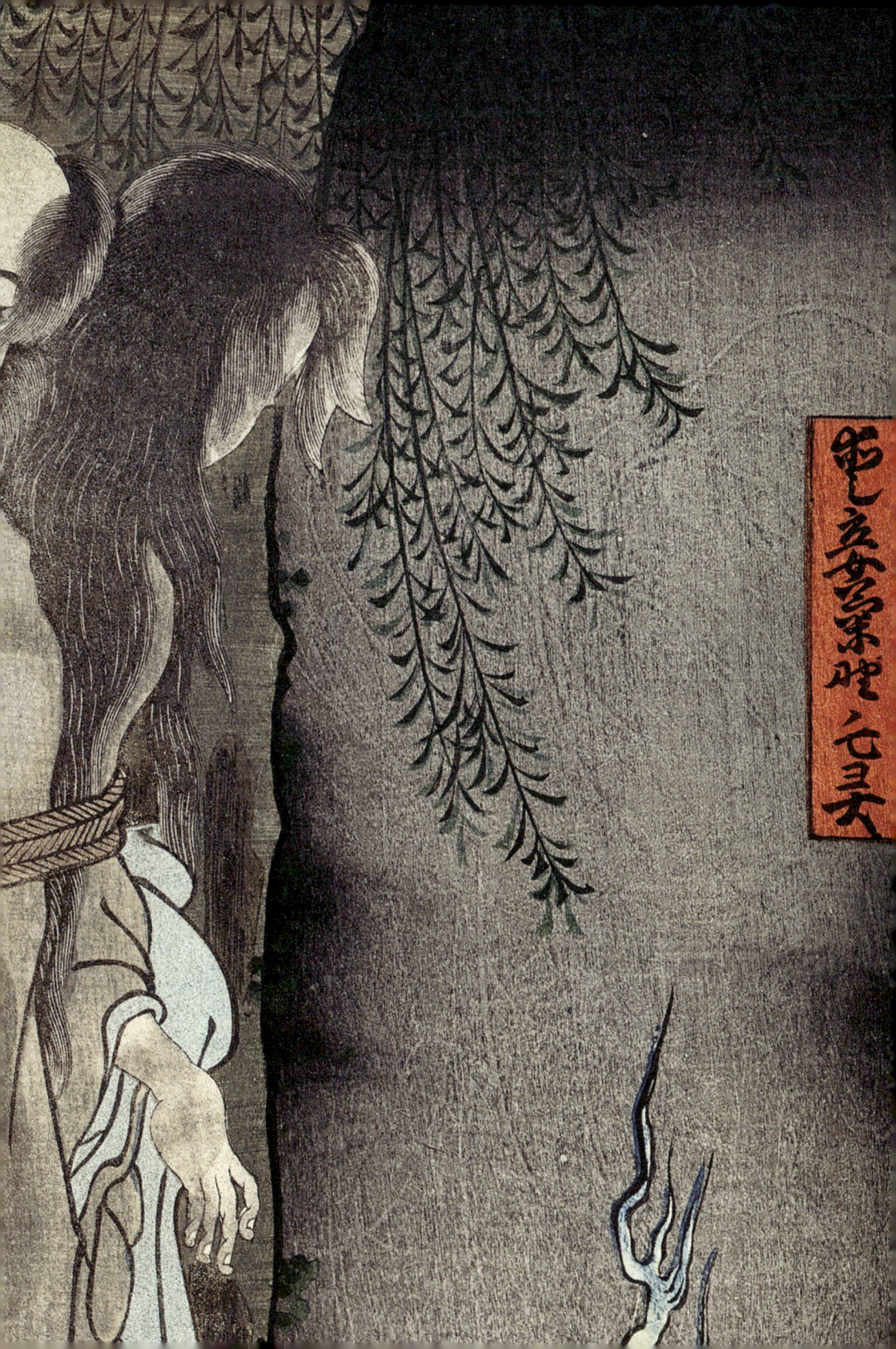

AUTOPSY
ON A
REVENANT

•

There is no ghost without grief, without fury, without resentment or regret. Such are the emotions that drive the deceased's refusal to leave the Earth – and the living – behind. These dead are not 'gone', they are merely less easily seen. And they choose whom they appear to with precision, as their own interests dictate.

What do the spirits of the dead look like? First of all, they are almost all women, as though men have the monopoly on cruelty – maybe that is true? – and women monopolise the thirst for vengeance – which, surely, is false.

Yūrei have no legs; their body generally stops at the knees. Is this a way of depicting their ethereal, gliding aspect? Does not the word *yūrei* itself, after all, mean evanescent (*yū*) spirit (*rei*)? A voluminous, white garment flutters on their emaciated body – though this is less a garment than a shroud, a funeral kimono all in white (for white is the colour of death in Buddhism). Sometimes it is a solid colour (*katabira*); other times it is inscribed with sutras in black ink (*kyôkatabira*). Everything about a phantom's appearance is lugubrious. It is like a set of physical signs testifying to the malignancy of this supernatural being. Its hair is loose, sometimes tousled; always in disarray, as is common at funerals or during periods of mourning.

It is the moment of death that is decisive: When the final breath leaves the body, the soul (*reikon*) accompanies it and arrives at an intermediate space, a kind of purgatory where it waits until its destiny is decided. Its ultimate fate

28

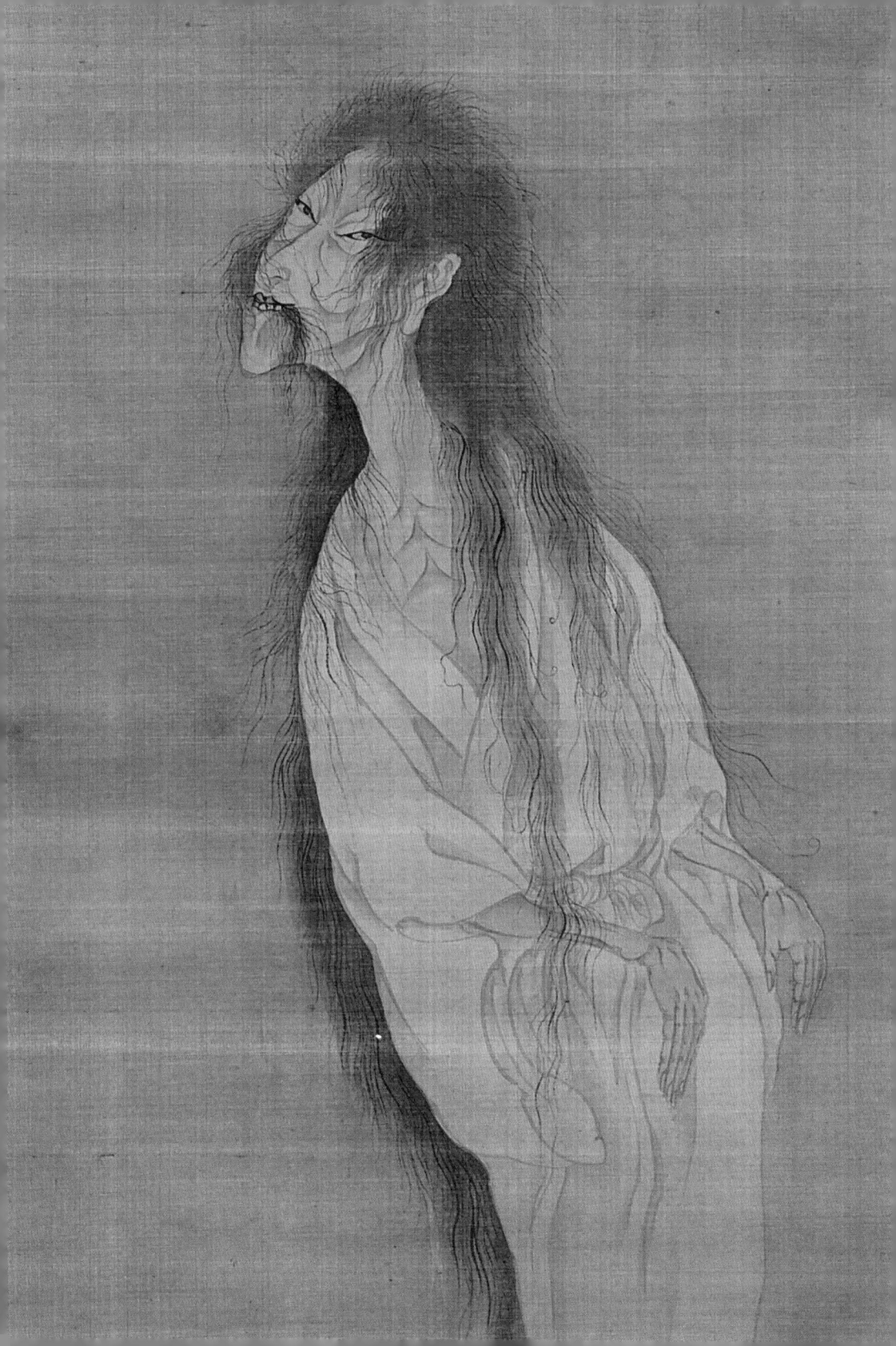

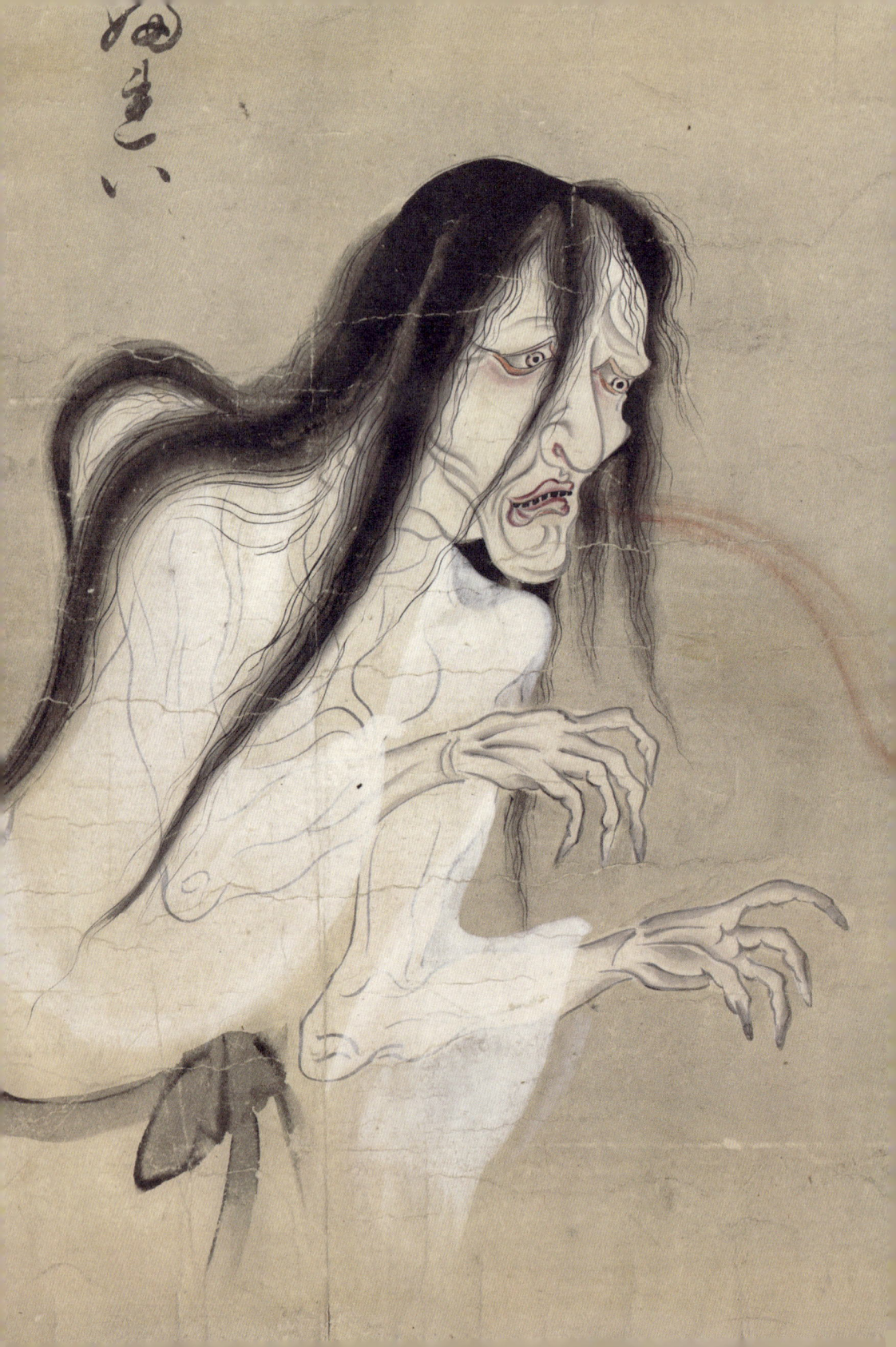

depends on the community of the living and on the deceased herself. If the death was violent or bloody (through murder, assassination, suicide or accident), if the funerary rites were not properly observed, or if the person was consumed by negative emotions (unrequited love, hatred, jealousy, grief, thirst for vengeance, and the like), then their soul is damned. It does not join the community of ancestors and does not acquire the status of family protector. Instead, its path leads towards the world of the living, where it reassumes – in part – its physical form and haunts places and persons until it achieves equanimity: funeral rituals impeccably completed, or its emotional turmoil fully resolved.

Sometimes, pale lights float all around the *yūrei*, attenuated flames or strange wills-o'-the-wisp. They signify the imminence of the spectre and its thirst for vengeance (*urami*) against the living.

The cruder the manner of the condemned's death, the greater the *yūrei*'s malignant force. Every ghost carries its history like a burden, like a weight that hinders – or delays – its redemption, its ultimate liberation. The great diversity of ghost-paintings (*yūrei-ga*) show so many stories of betrayal, abandonment, and depravity, passed on from generation to generation. All Japanese children know not just what happened to Oiwa (how poison disfigured her face), but also the dramas surrounding the deaths of Okiku, Ubume or Yuki-onna. Each tale is an example not to be followed, but also a means of spiritual edification, a chance to learn how to prevent the catastrophe of a bad death and its disastrous consequences for the community of the living.

Yūrei paintings are collected by a handful of private individuals, but also by Buddhist sanctuaries, which show them to the faithful at Obon, the festival of the dead, in late August when the heat is stifling. Probably the largest collection of them in Japan is held in Zenshoan temple, in Tokyo. It is believed to play a role in the cult of the bodhisattvas Kannon and Jizo, the 'savers of souls' who are miraculously able to bestow merits upon the deceased so that they can be saved

from perdition and reintegrated into the cycle of reincarnation.

There is a ghost for every time of life and every circumstance. Whatever the particular situation may be, an established narrative exists that can accommodate it: There is the mother (*ubume*) whose death during or after childbirth causes her to 'abandon' the child; she returns to haunt the little one and bring it sweets, or takes an excessively close interest in the children of others, to the point of doing them harm through the mere nearness of her toxic presence; there are mischievous child ghosts (*zashiki warashi*) who tease and play tricks on people; their presence in a home is considered to be more of a good omen; there are spirits consumed by resentment and hatred (*onryō*), often aristocrats or men of culture (*goryō*) brought down by disgrace, epidemic or revolt; the spirits of the drowned (*funayūrei*) who slowly become half-human, half-fish hybrids; spirits attached to a precise locality (*jibakurei*), protecting it against inopportune visitors or perpetuating the gloomy legend surrounding it; floating spirits with no precise human shape (*fuyūrei*), whose already indistinct physical form is now totally disintegrated . . . Nothing is impossible in this culture where everyday objects – brooms, teapots, lanterns (not to be confused with phantom lanterns, *chōchin obake*), sake jars, kimonos, sandals, futons, mirrors, gongs, etc. – are said to come alive and act on their own once they have been in service for a hundred years (*tsukumogami*).

Yūrei are driven by a precise, specific desire and are linked to a certain place – for example, the well of Himeji castle, in the case of Okiku; or, for the ghosts of the forest of Aokigahara, the foot of Mount Fuji, the scene of countless suicides every year. They focus on a single objective, which they will not relinquish until they have obtained justice (or until Shintoist and/or Buddhist rites – like complex exorcisms – liberate this soul in pain). There are, though, beings with almost infinite abilities to metamorphose, and they are not to be confused with ghosts. The *obake* – that is their name – come and go from

32

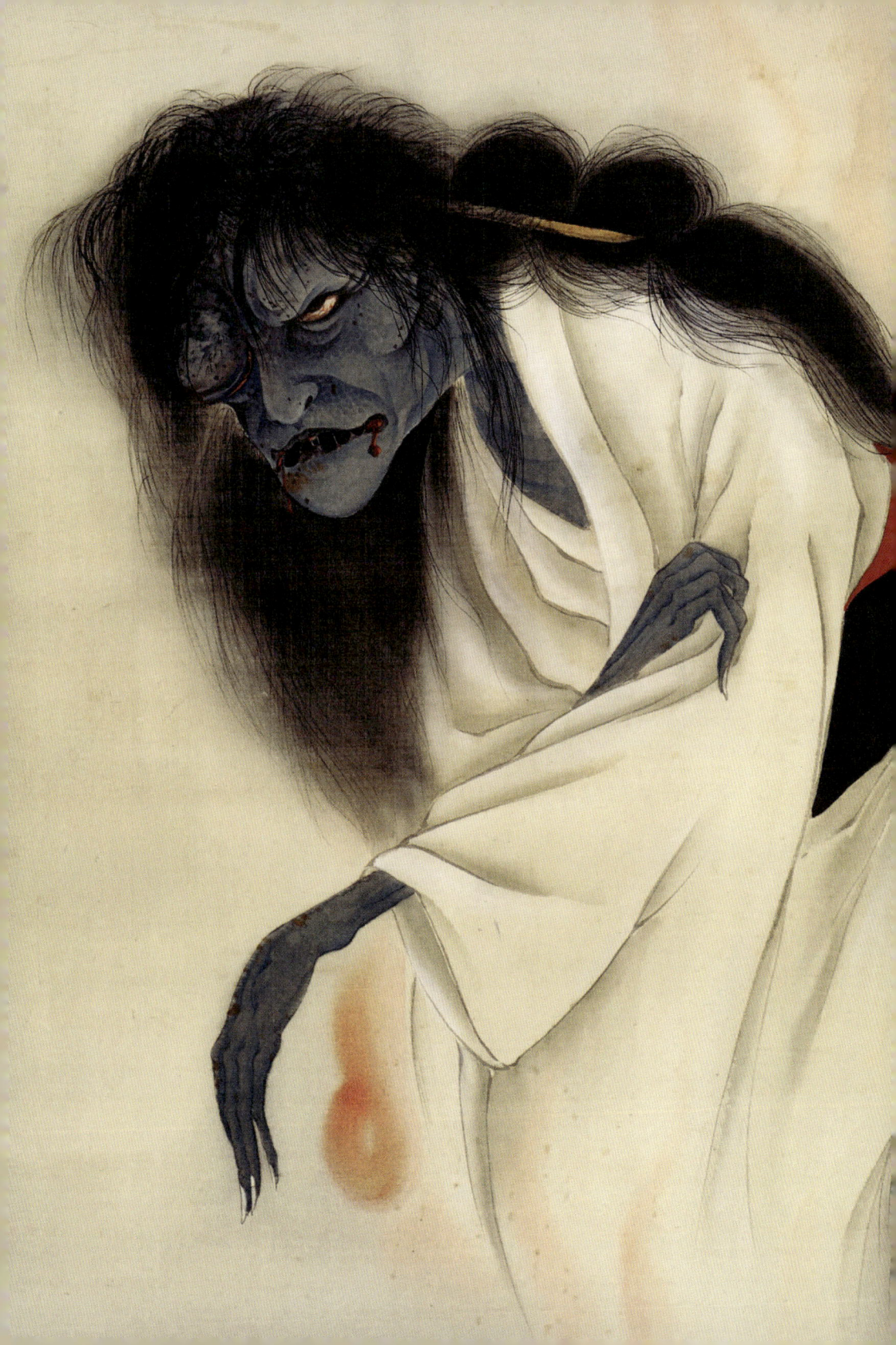

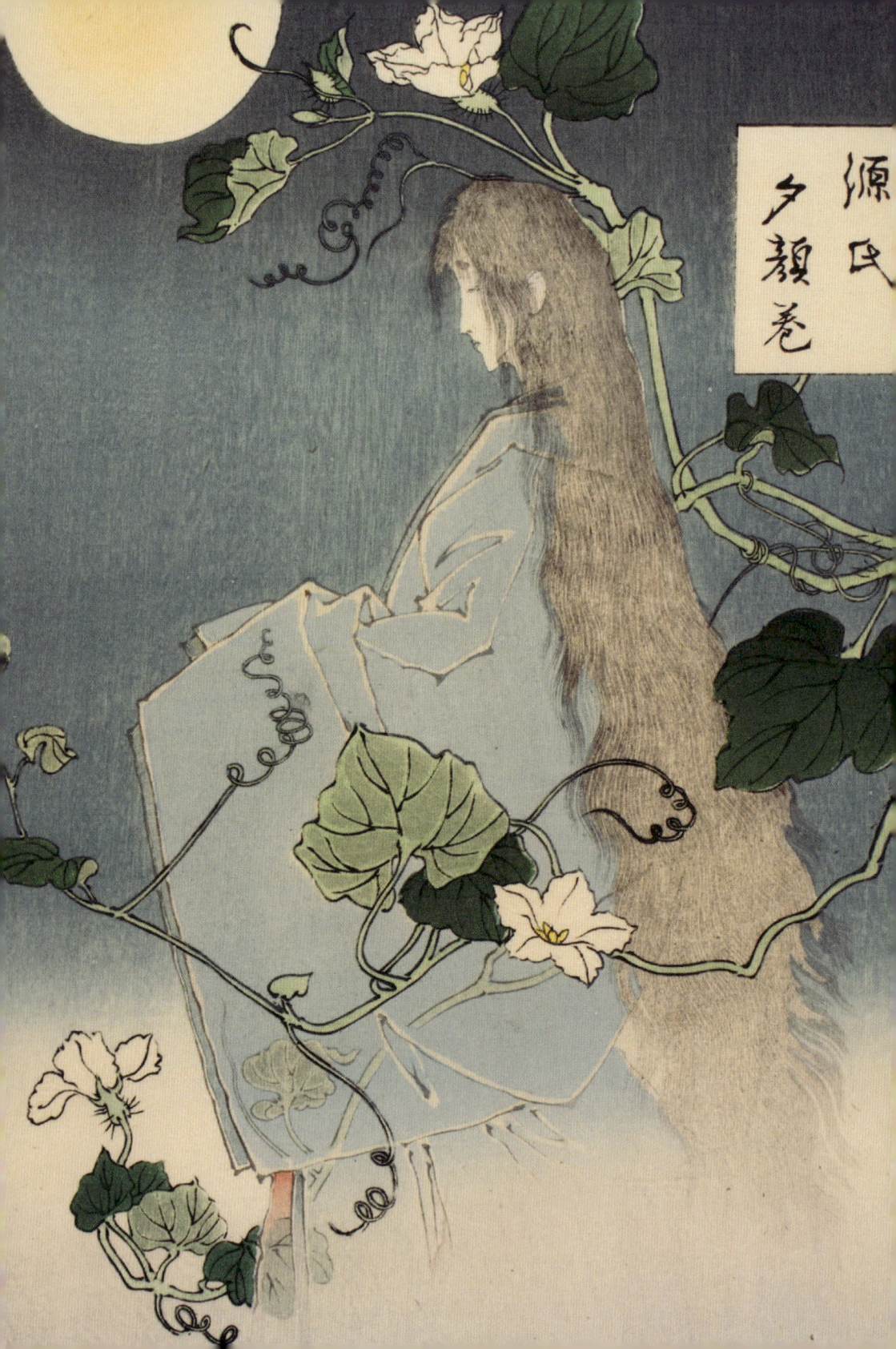

源氏
夕顔
巻

one place to the next, with no specific history or predestined victim.

Ghosts and supernatural beings are at liberty to appear at any hour of the day or night. Space and time are at their unlimited disposal. But, for those condemned souls – the *yūrei* – one time is more favourable than others: the 'hours of the cow', deep in the night, which, for Westerners, corresponds to 2:00, 2:30 a.m.

But make no mistake: ghosts do not have the monopoly over haunting. Even in the living, a part of the soul can leave the body and take on the form of a ghost (*ikiryō*) which, driven by intense rage or jealousy, will haunt a place with a vigour comparable to that of a genuine *yūrei*. In *The Tale of Genji*, the eleventh-century classic of Japanese literature attributed to Murasaki Shikibu, we find one such story of infernal partition of the soul: Rokujo, a woman of boundless ambition brutally thwarted by her husband's unexpected death, falls in love with Genji, who rejects her. Her jealousy and resentment slowly transform her into a kind of demon which goes on to haunt Genji and then to possess his pregnant wife, ultimately causing her demise. Rokujo comes to realise the evil she has done. She shuts herself away in a cloister to atone for her crimes and limit her wicked deeds, but her *ikiryō*, now set free, continues to act malevolently. Only the rituals performed by Genji's own daughter will permanently restore peace and harmony.

There are many ways to end the existence of a *yūrei*: interring its mortal remains if it has been deprived of a burial; bidding the family of the person who caused the demise of the 'wrongly dead' to pray intensely and sincerely; deifying the *yūrei* (though this is somewhat artificial, similar to an alchemist transforming lead into gold); placing holy Shinto papers (*ofuda*) on the spectre's forehead or body; or allowing the fateful destiny of physical union between a ghost and a human to take its course. Some of these methods are more effective than others, and some *yūrei* are especially resistant. Despite the repeated efforts of countless generations, the spectre of Oiwa unceasingly haunts

35

and frightens the living, to the point of threatening to kill actors who dare to embody her cursed spirit in Noh theatre or in films.

p. 29: Ōkyo Maruyama, *Ghost*, detail, 1793 Paris, Musée du quai Branly – Jacques Chirac
p. 30: *Yūrei*, detail from the *Bakemono no e*, late 17th – 18th century Provo, Brigham Young University Library
p. 33: Ikkyo, *Ghost of Oiwa*, detail, late 19th – early 20th century Paris, Musée du quai Branly – Jacques Chirac
p. 34: Tsukioka Yoshitoshi, *The Ghost of Yūgao from The Tale of Genji*, detail, 1886

Philadelphia Museum of Art
p. 37: Tsukioka Yoshitoshi, *Samanosuke Mitsutoshi with Fox Fires*, detail, 1865 Los Angeles County Museum of Art
p. 38: Utagawa Toyokuni I, *Onoe Matsusuke I as the Ghost of the Wet-Nurse Iohata and Matsumoto Kojiro as Mokuemon in Tokubei of India: Tales of Strange Lands (Tenjiku Tokubei ikoku banashi)*, detail, 1799–1809 The Art Institute of Chicago

p. 39: Katsukawa Shunshō, *Man Falling Backward, Startled by a Woman's Ghost over a River*, detail of the ghost, ca 1782 The Art Institute of Chicago
p. 40: Utagawa Toyokuni I, *Onoe Shoroku as a Ghost*, detail, date unknown Washington DC, Arthur M. Sackler Gallery, Smithsonian Institution

p. 41: Kitagawa Utamoro, *Child's Nightmare of Ghosts*, detail, ca 1800/01 The Art Institute of Chicago
pp. 42–43: Katsukawa Shunshō, *Ichikawa Danjuro V as a Skeleton, Spirit of the Priest Seigen* (left), *and Iwai Hanshiro IV as Princess Sakura* (right), detail, 1783 The Art Institute of Chicago

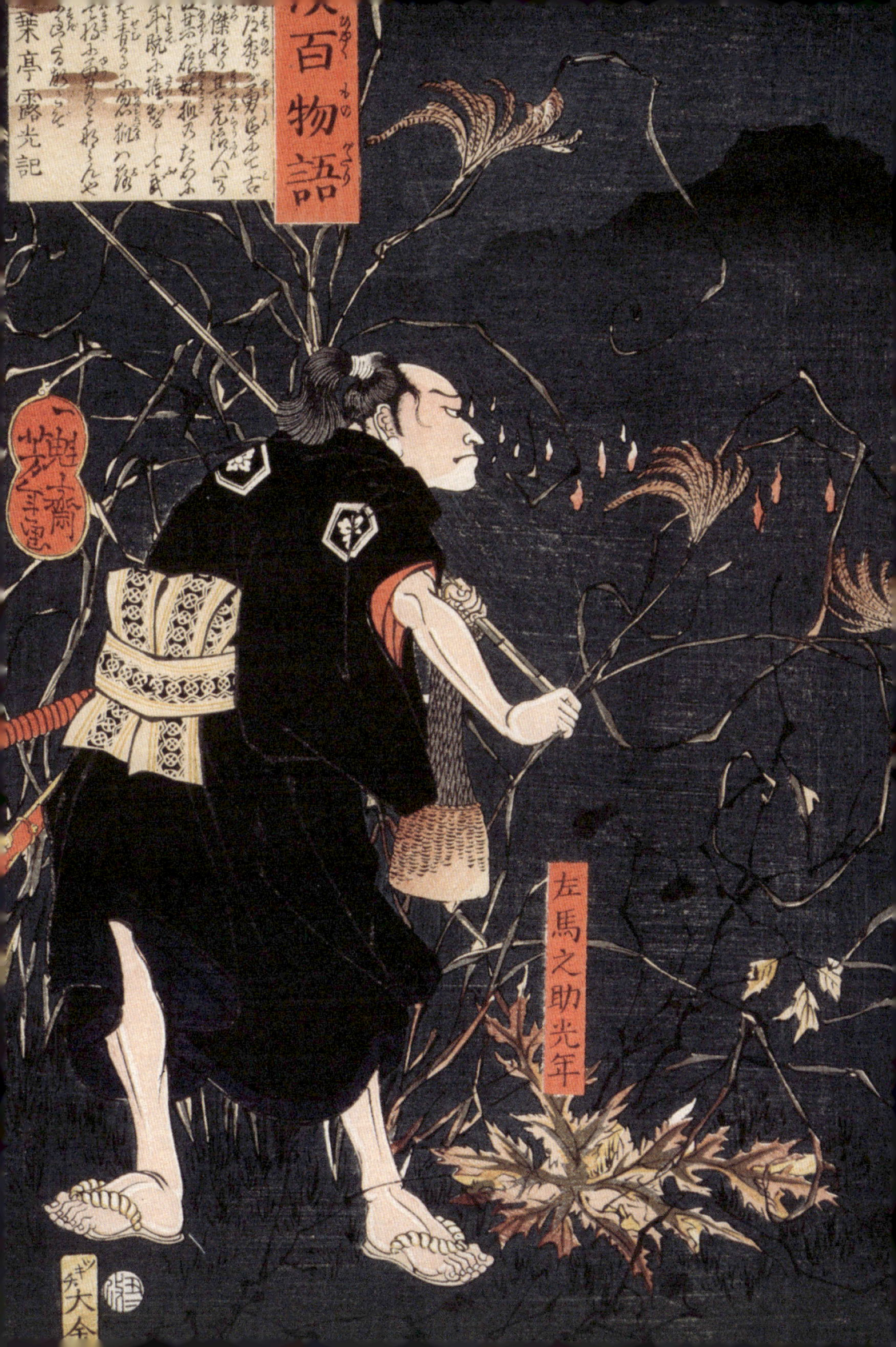

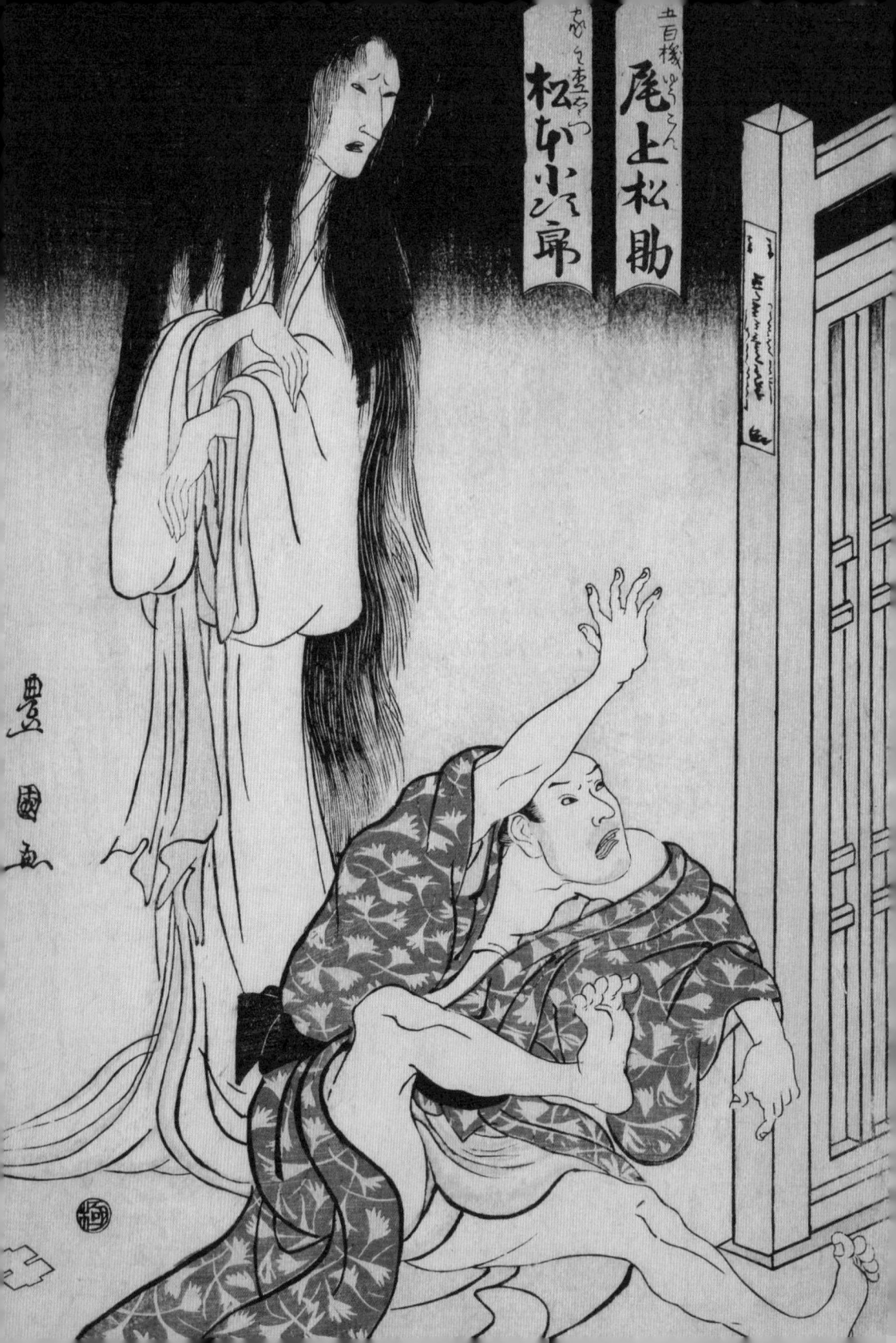

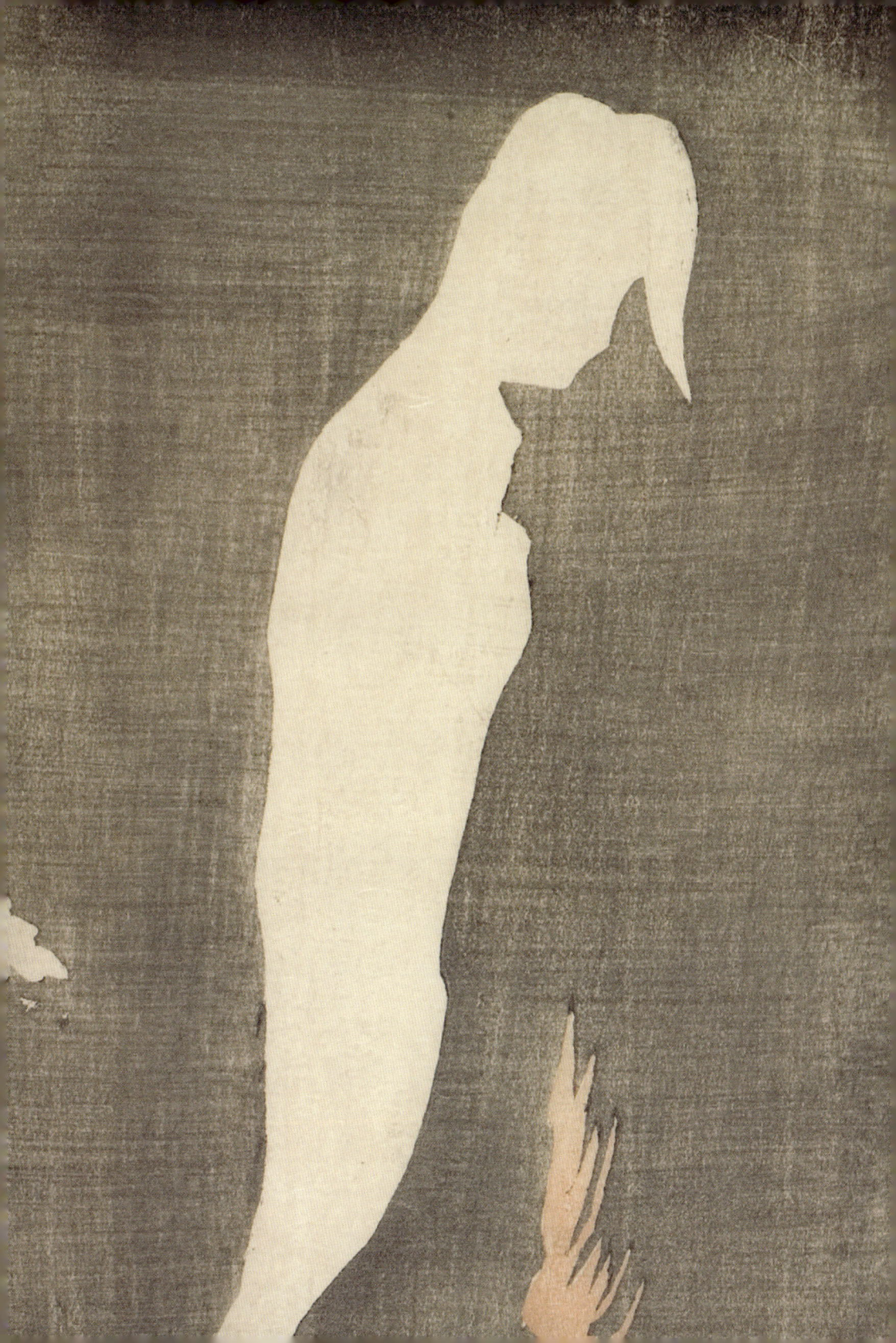

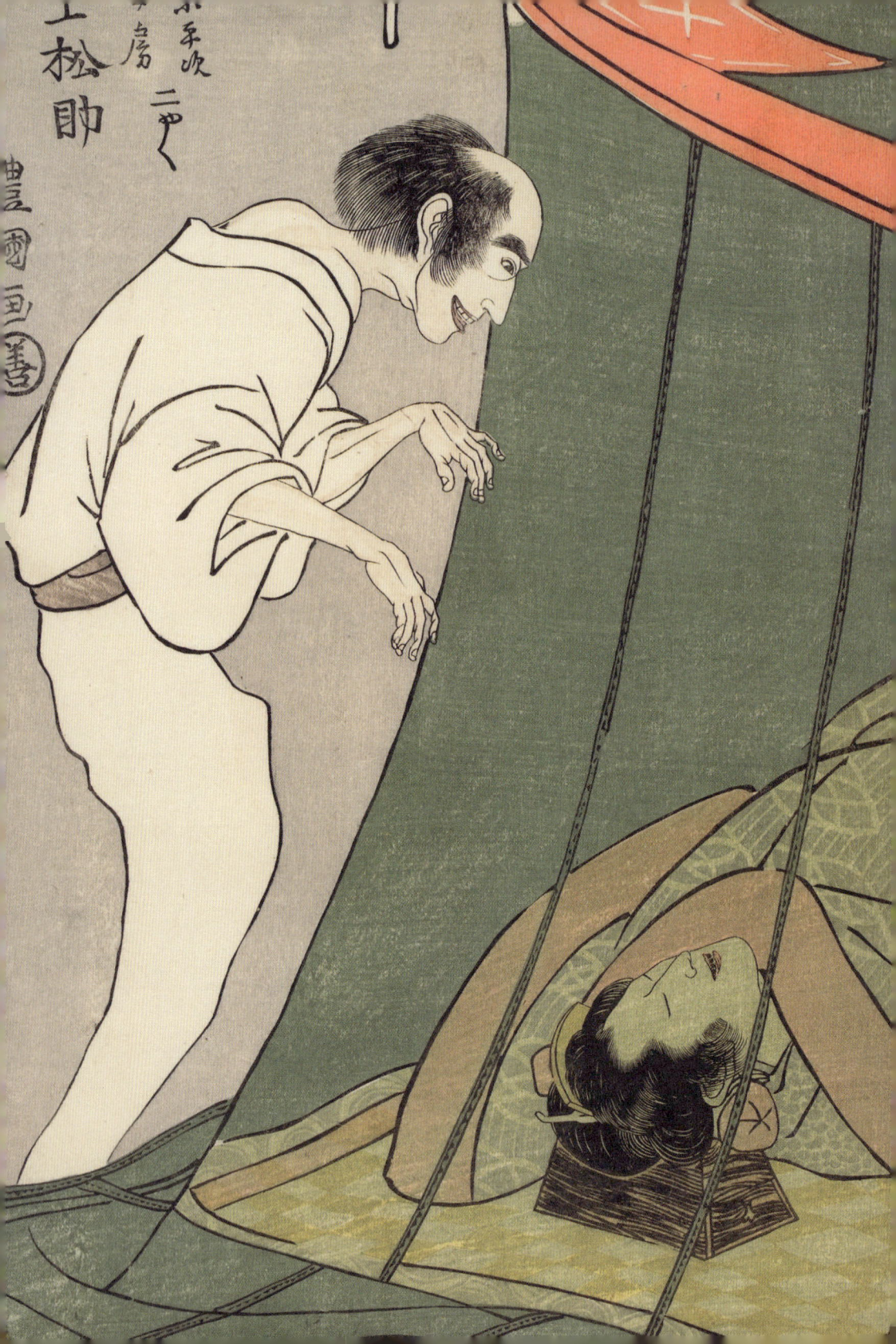

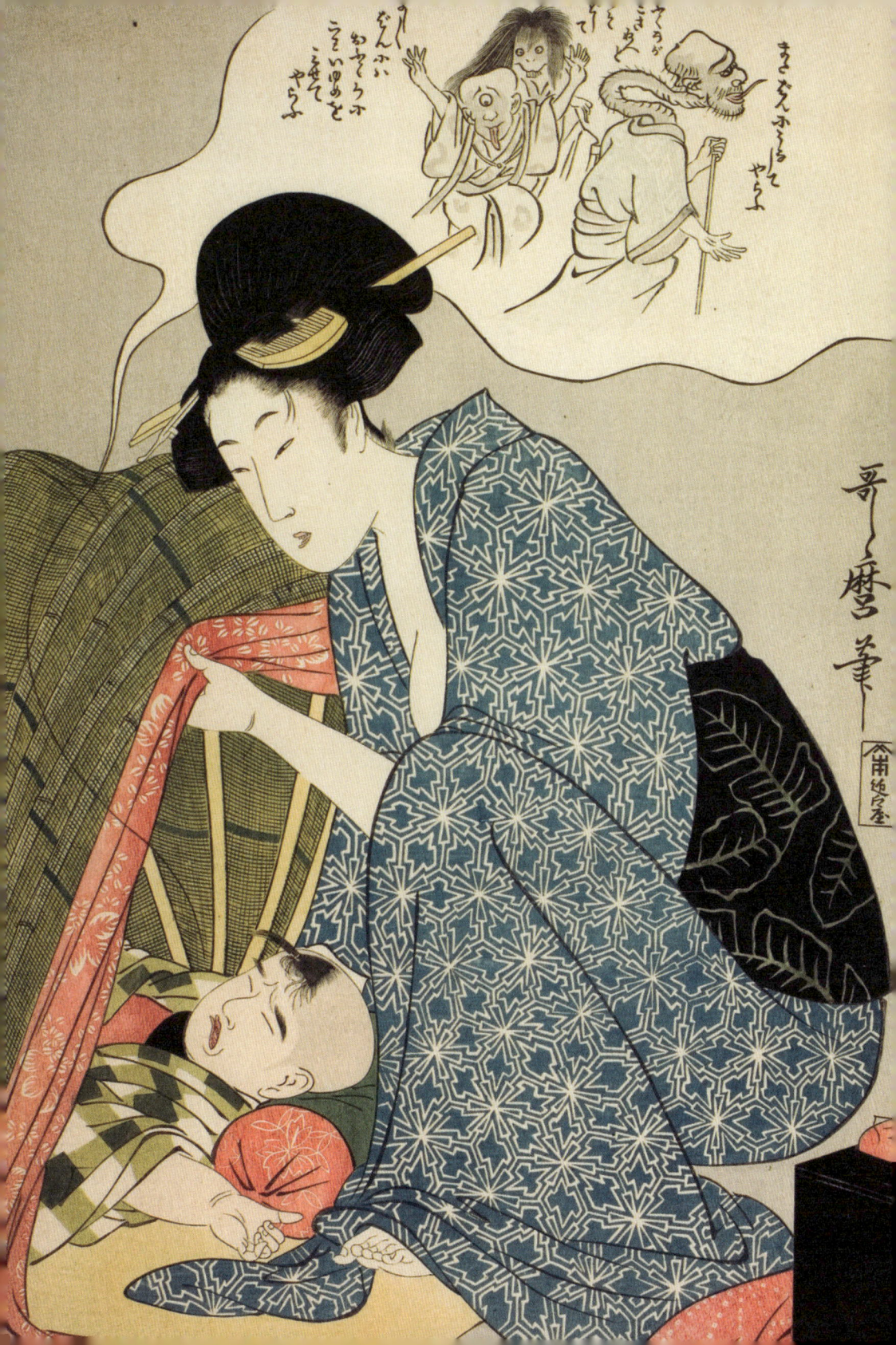

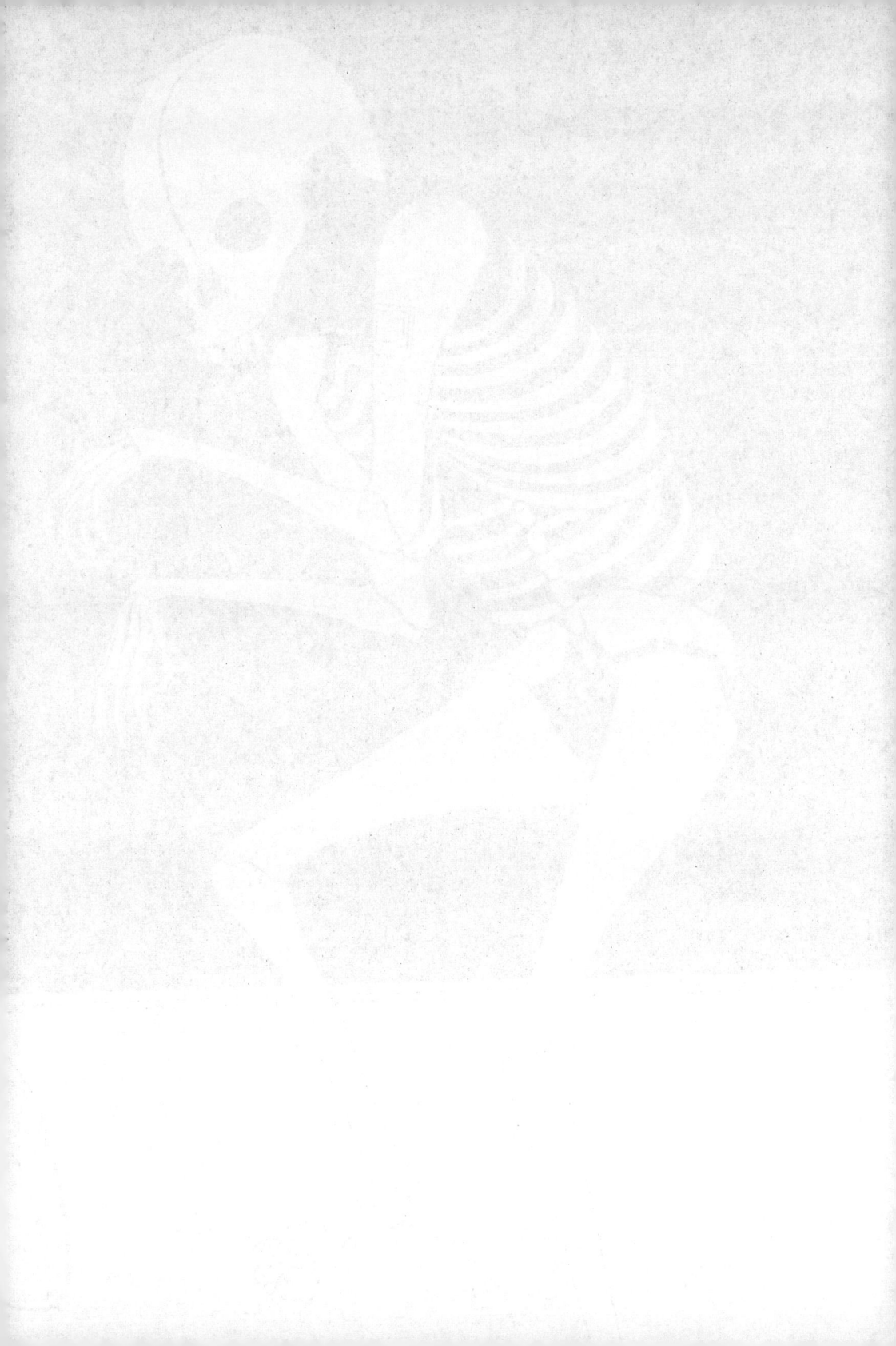

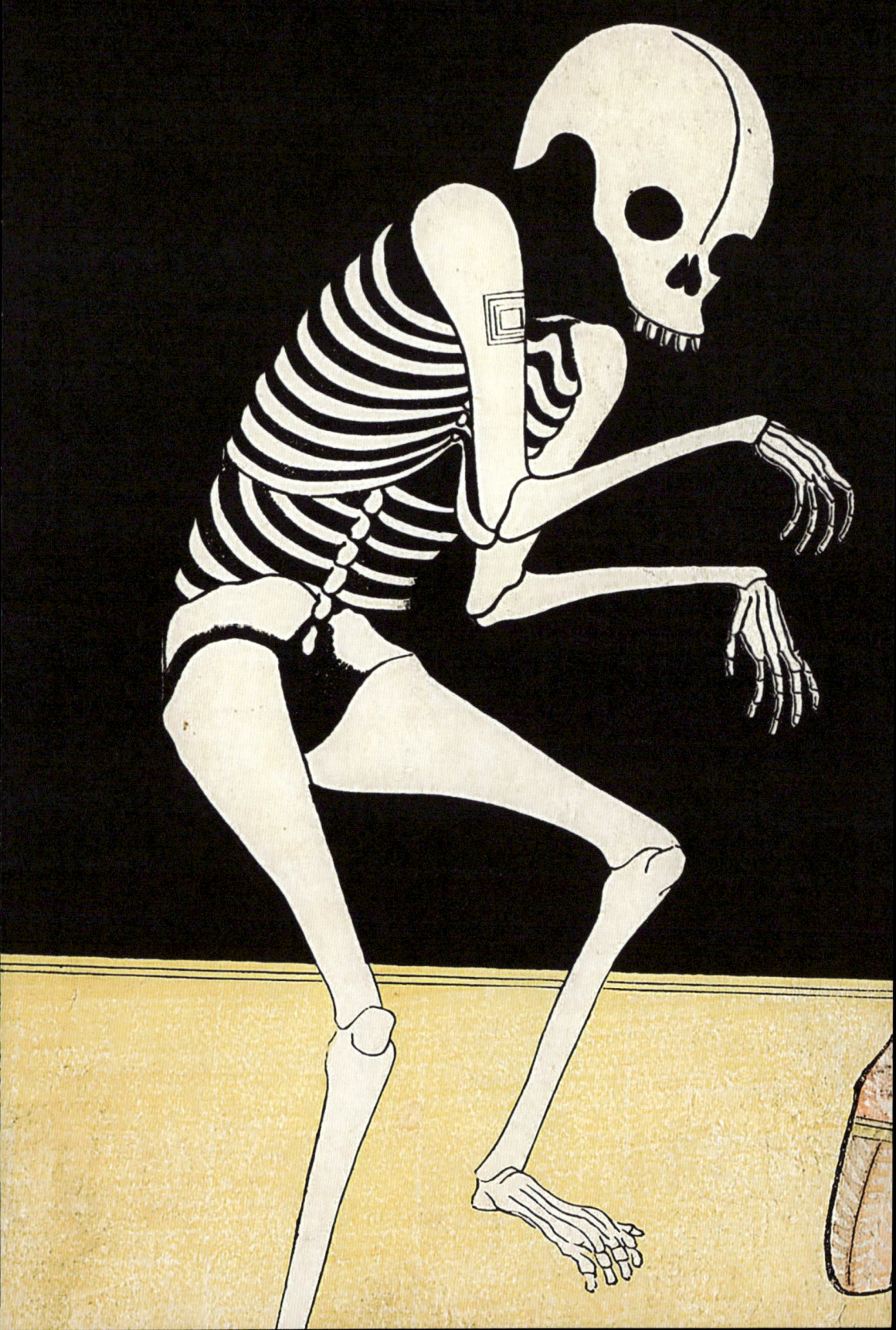

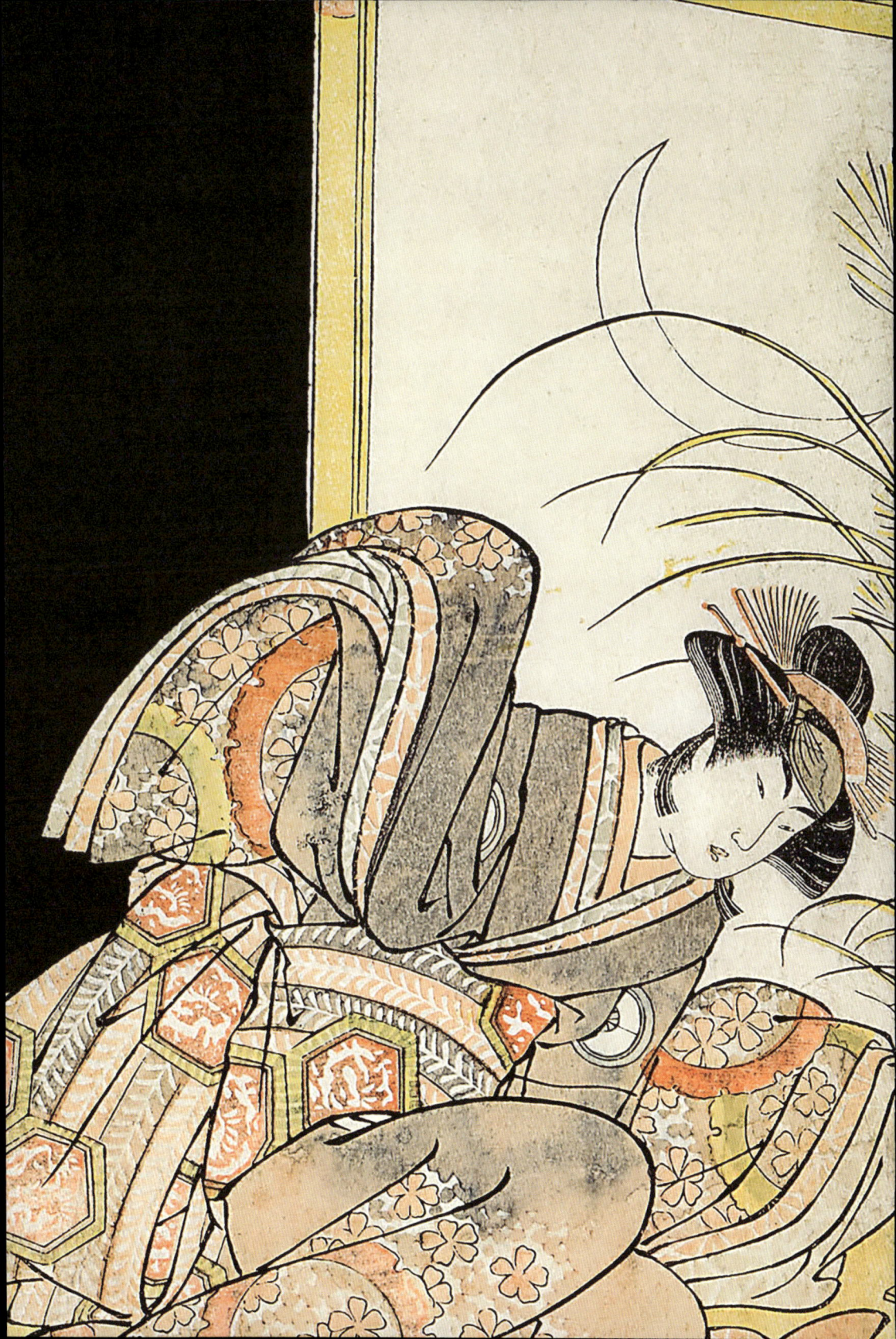

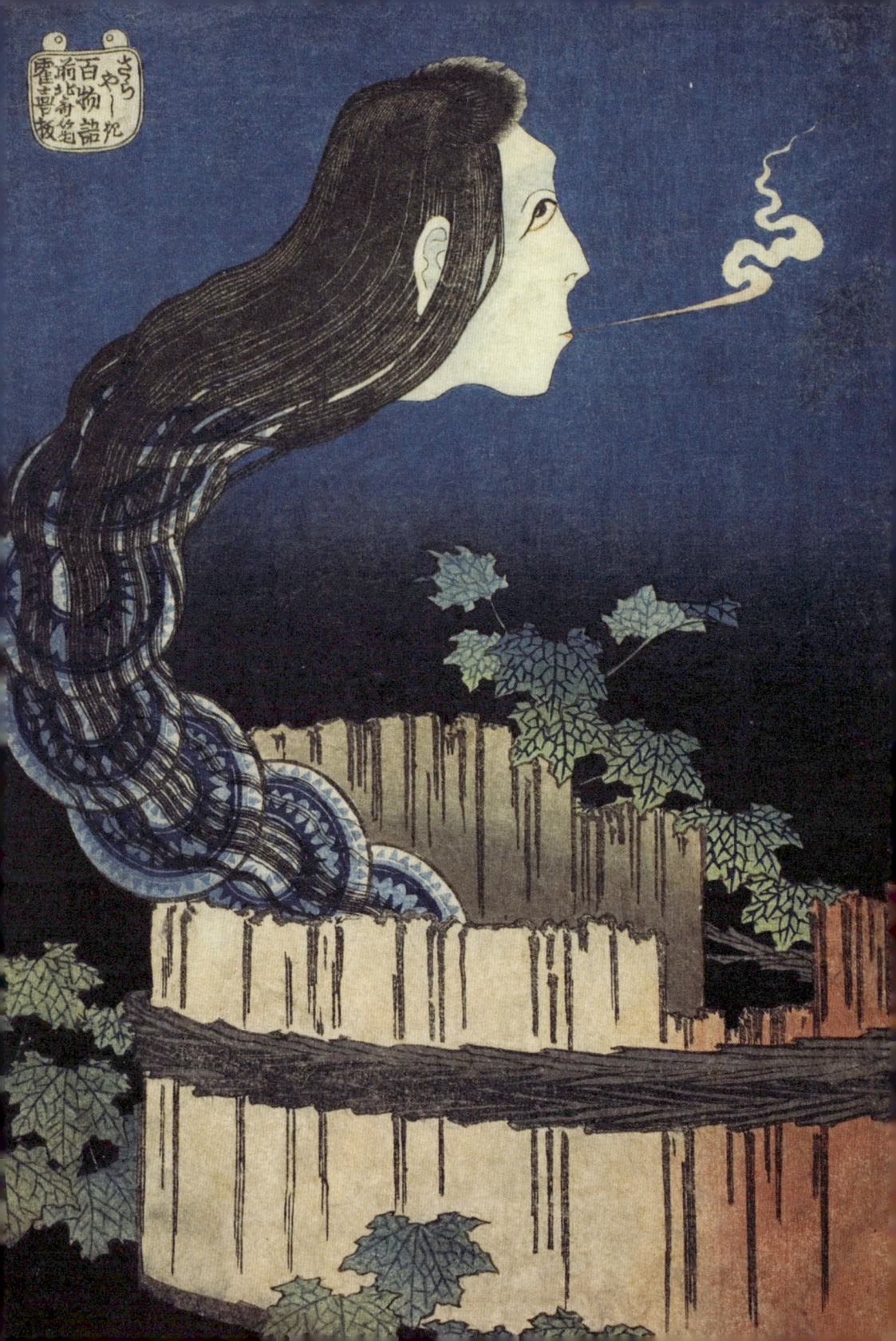

OKIKU

•

The first time the ghost of Okiku was revealed was in July 1741, during a *bunraku* show at Toyotakaza Theatre in Osaka, in the play *The Dish Mansion at Banchō* (*Banchō Sarayashiki*). Since then, there have been many retellings of the story, always featuring a scullery maid who dies too soon and comes back to haunt the castle where she works. In the original version, the young woman is subjected daily to the advances of her master, the steward of Himeji Castle, who wishes to make her his mistress. One evening, consumed with impatience and agitated by her repeated refusals, he plays a trick: he hides one of the dishes that she is responsible for, summons her and asks, 'Where is the tenth dish?' She counts the remaining nine in front of him, unable to understand what has happened. The man, a samurai named Aoyama, then proposes to 'wipe the slate clean' if she agrees to sleep with him, but she rejects him once again. Losing all sense of propriety, he has the other servants beat her, tie her up and suspend her above a well at the castle. 'Final warning, Okiku. Love or death?' She remains obstinate, whereupon he draws his sword and cuts the rope. She falls in, her bones breaking as she lands on the bottom of the well, and drowns.

The violence of Okiku's death prevents her from returning to the cycle of reincarnation, and she becomes a *yūrei*, emerging from her well to torment first Aoyama and then his descendants, proclaiming her innocence and imploring that justice be done. The cursed well (*Okiku-ido*) can be seen at Himeji Castle, where it is the object of popular curiosity and morbid fascination equally.

Periodically, she emerges from this dark hole to count to nine (without ever getting to ten) or futilely roams the corridors, lanes and courtyards in search of the tenth dish. People try to placate her, whispering a quiet 'ten . . .' when she finishes

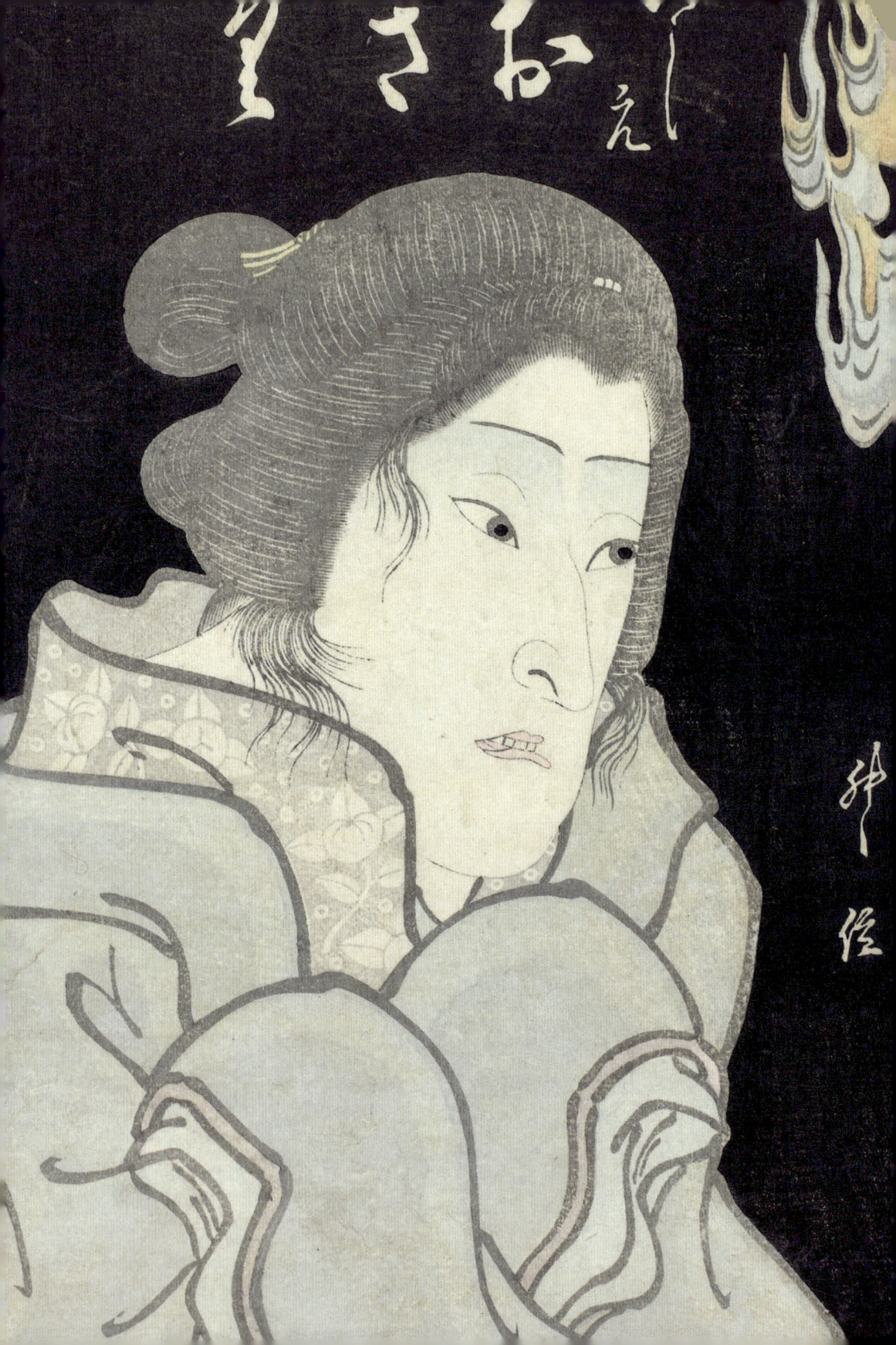

counting, but her peace of mind never lasts, since she soon realises that the dish is still missing.

Other versions exist, adding various details or alternative storylines. In one, Okiku, refusing to participate in a plot against the shogun, ends up being thrown into the well by a man named Tetsuzan. In another, the ghost first appears when cruel Aoyama wipes his sword in a fold of his kimono. In a further version, the samurai is initially pledged in marriage to Okiku but, wishing to wed another woman, he breaks the tenth dish, knowing that the penalty in the event of its loss or damage is death by decapitation. He then offers 'to wipe the slate clean' and finally, when she refuses to give in, breaks all of the dishes in a rage and throws Okiku into the well. An additional storyline has it that Aoyama, when confronted with the *yūrei* of Okiku, sees not a horrible and repulsive ghost (as others do who see her) but a vision of infinite beauty and serenity; to join her forever in death, he commits hari kari. In one last example, Okiku is the servant of a noblewoman and subject to the jealousy of her mistress, who pushes her to commit suicide by jumping into a castle well (the mistress then goes mad and dies shortly after).

Wells have long been viewed as gateways between the worlds of the dead and the living, and ghosts were sometimes thought to dwell there. This idea gained even greater currency following the story of Okiku, and in 1795, as though to prove it, there was a widespread infestation of wells by caterpillars covered in whitish filaments that prompted residents to nickname the creatures 'Okiku insects', as though the fibres on their surface were elements of her funeral shroud. More recently, Kōji Suzuki's 1991 novel *Ring* and Hideo Nakata's 1998 film of the same name take up the theme of a 'madwoman' (*kyōjo-mono*) named Sadako, who becomes a *yūrei* and emerges from a cursed well where her unburied body remains deprived of funerary rites.

p. 44: Katsushika Hokusai, *The Mansion of the Plates*, detail, 1831/1832 The Art Institute of Chicago
p. 46: Kiyosada, *Arashi Rikaku II as the Ghost of Okiku*, detail, August 1848 Amsterdam, Rijksmuseum

p. 49: Tsukioka Yoshitoshi, *The Ghost of Okiku in the Play 'The Dish Mansion' (Sarayashiki)*, detail, 1902 Philadelphia Museum of Art
p. 50: Kawanabe Kyōsai, *Manga*, detail of Okiku, 1881 New York, The Metropolitan Museum of Art

p. 51: Toyohara Kunichika, *The Samurai Aoyama with the Ghost of Okiku*, detail, 1892 Amsterdam, Rijksmusem
pp. 52–53: Utagawa Kunisada I (aka Toyokuni III), *Actors with the Ghost of Okiku in the Play 'The Dish Mansion' (Sarayashiki)*, detail, 1857 Amherst College, Mead Art Museum

pp. 54–55: Utagawa Kunisada I (aka Toyokuni III), *Ichikawa Kodanji IV as the Ghost of Iwafuji (Iwafuji no bōrei)* (right) and *Iwai Kumesaburō III as Second Onoe (Nidai no Onoe)* (left), detail, 1860 Boston, Museum of Fine Arts

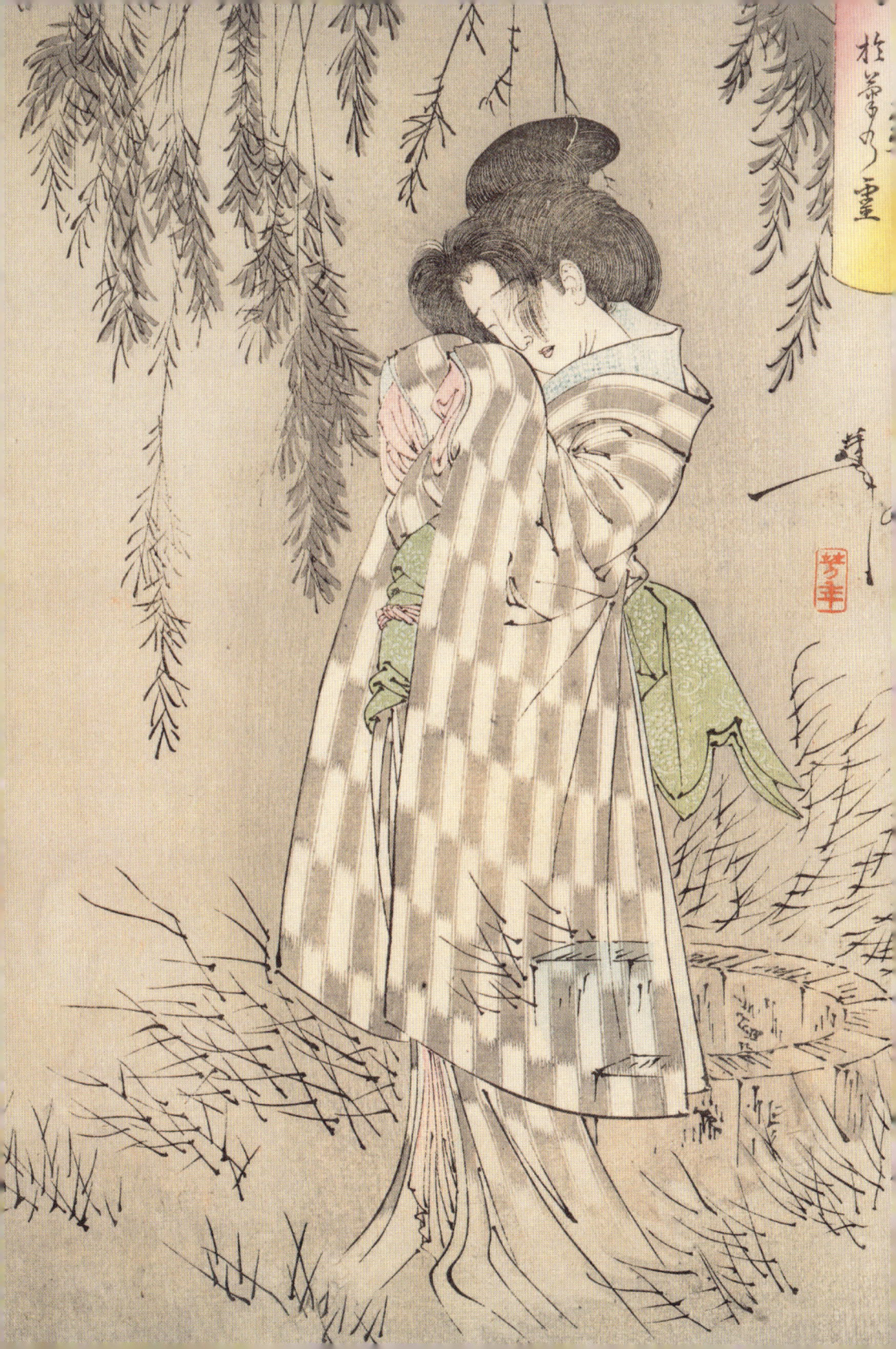

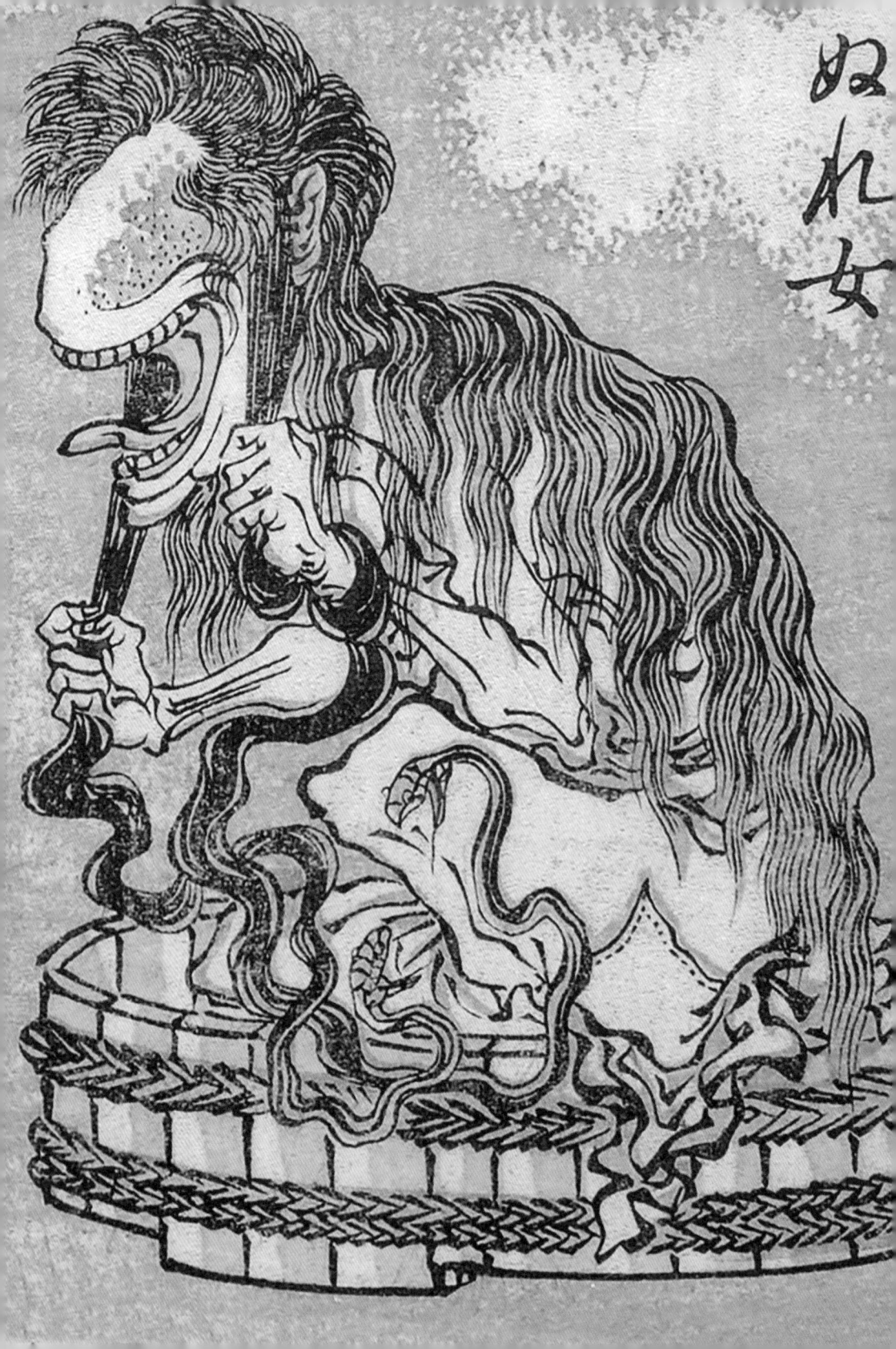

ぬれ女

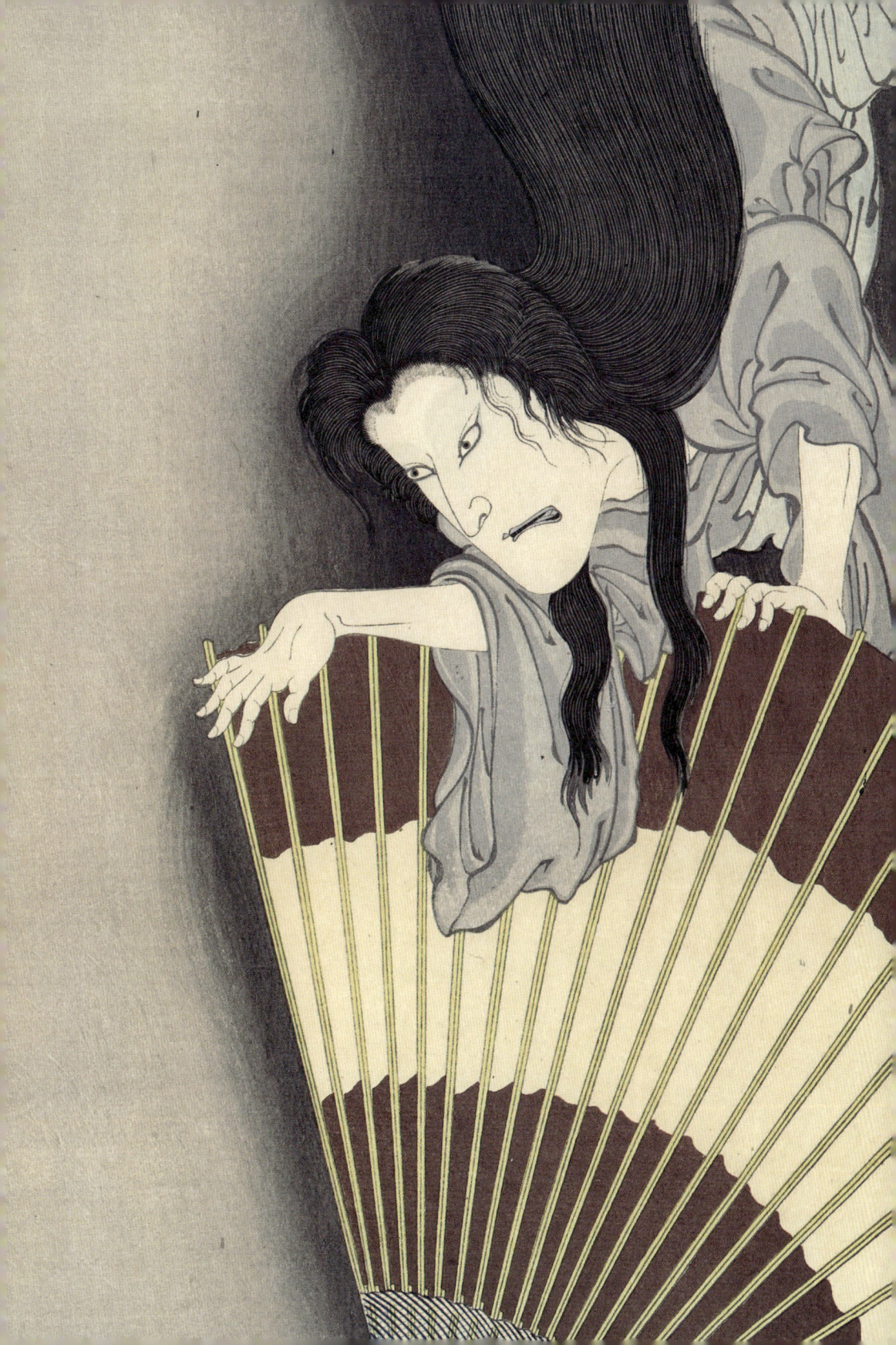

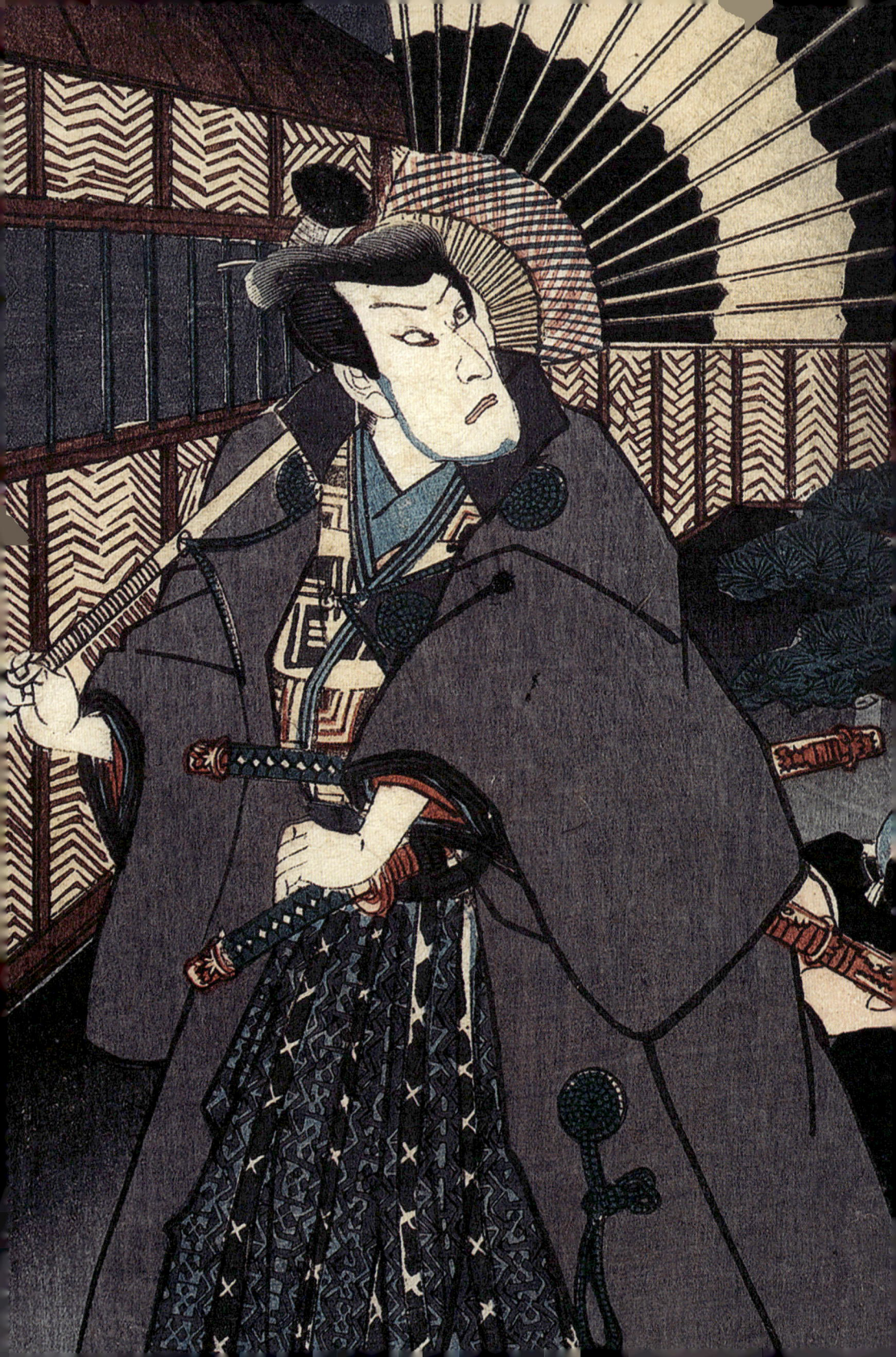

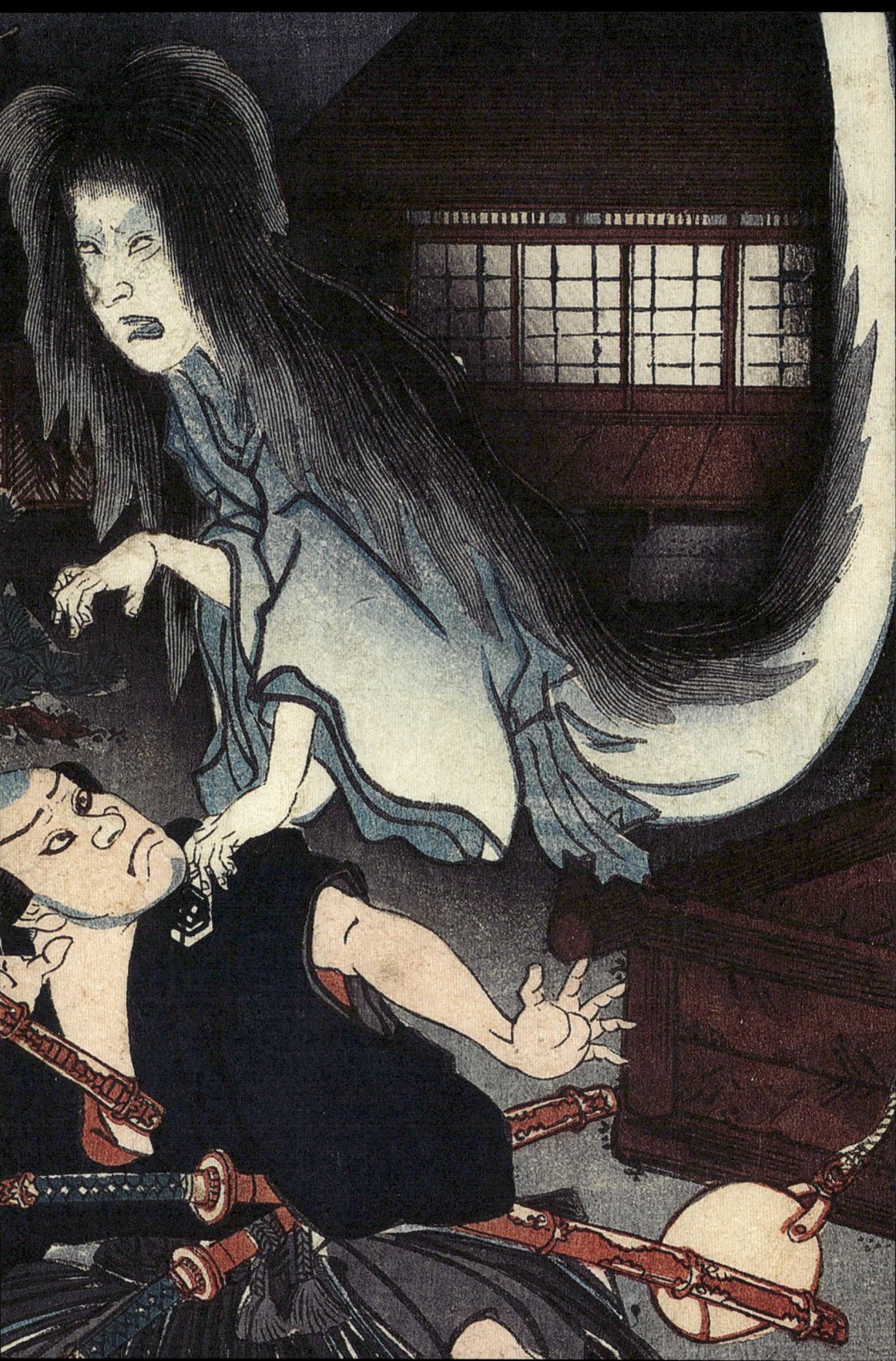

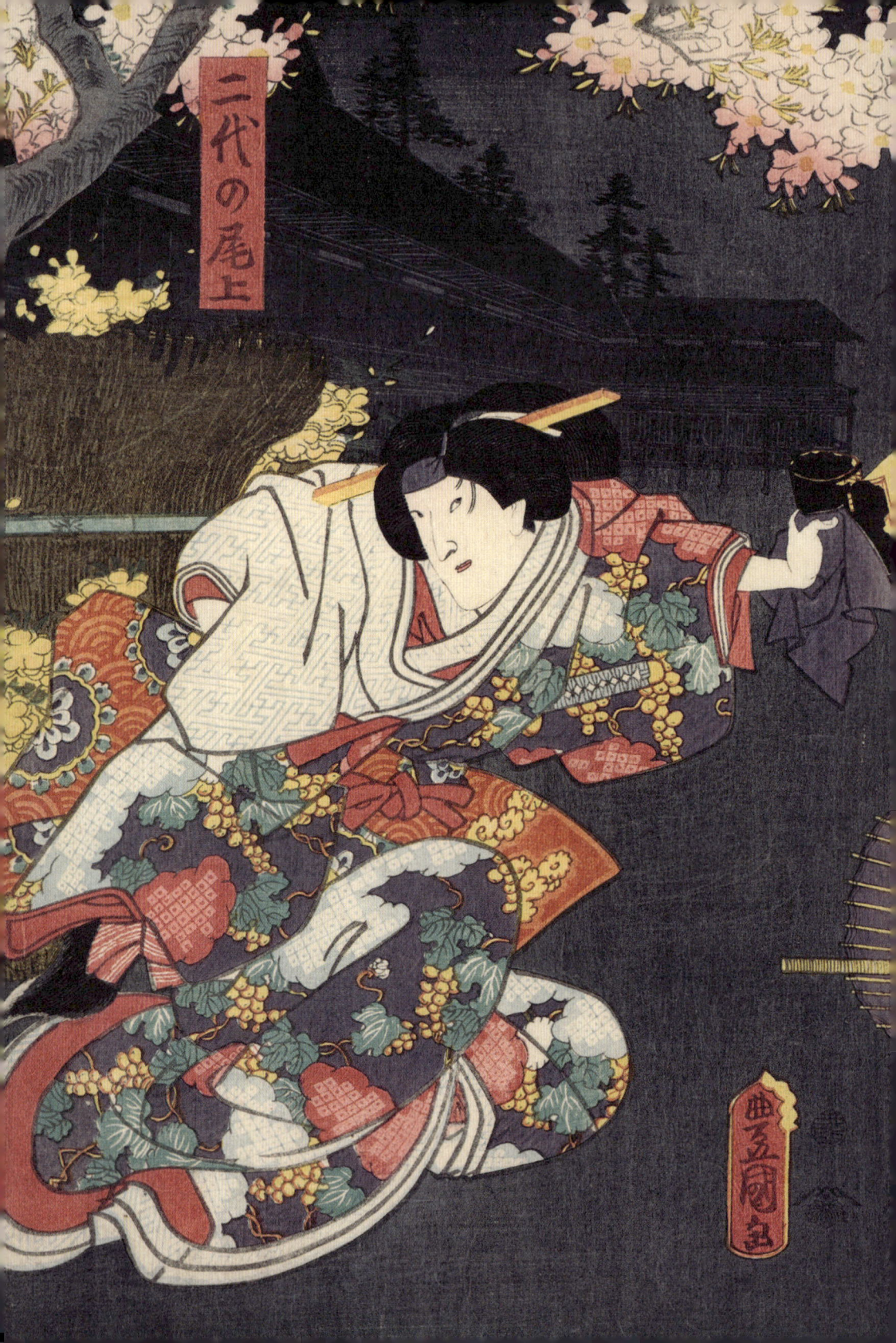

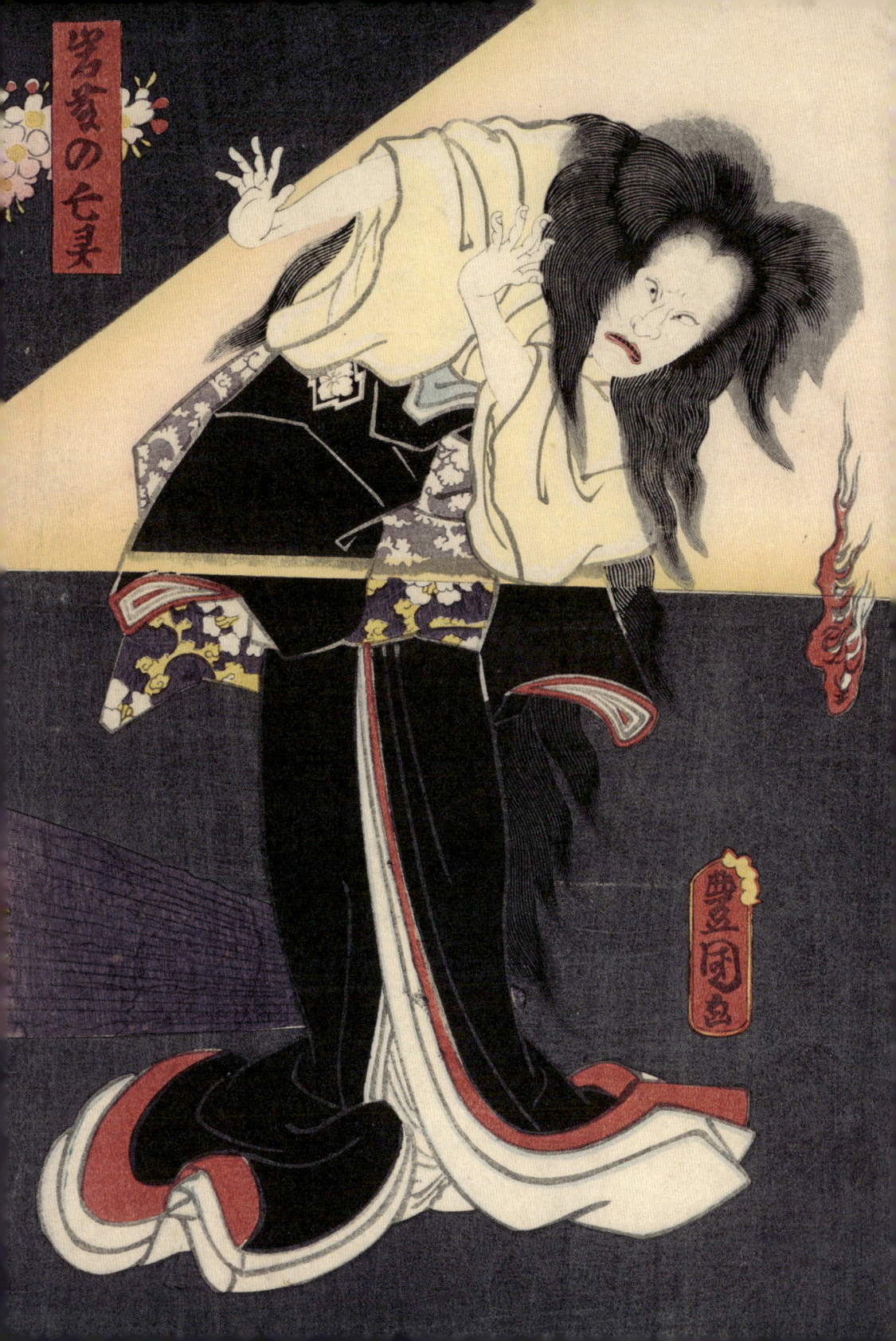

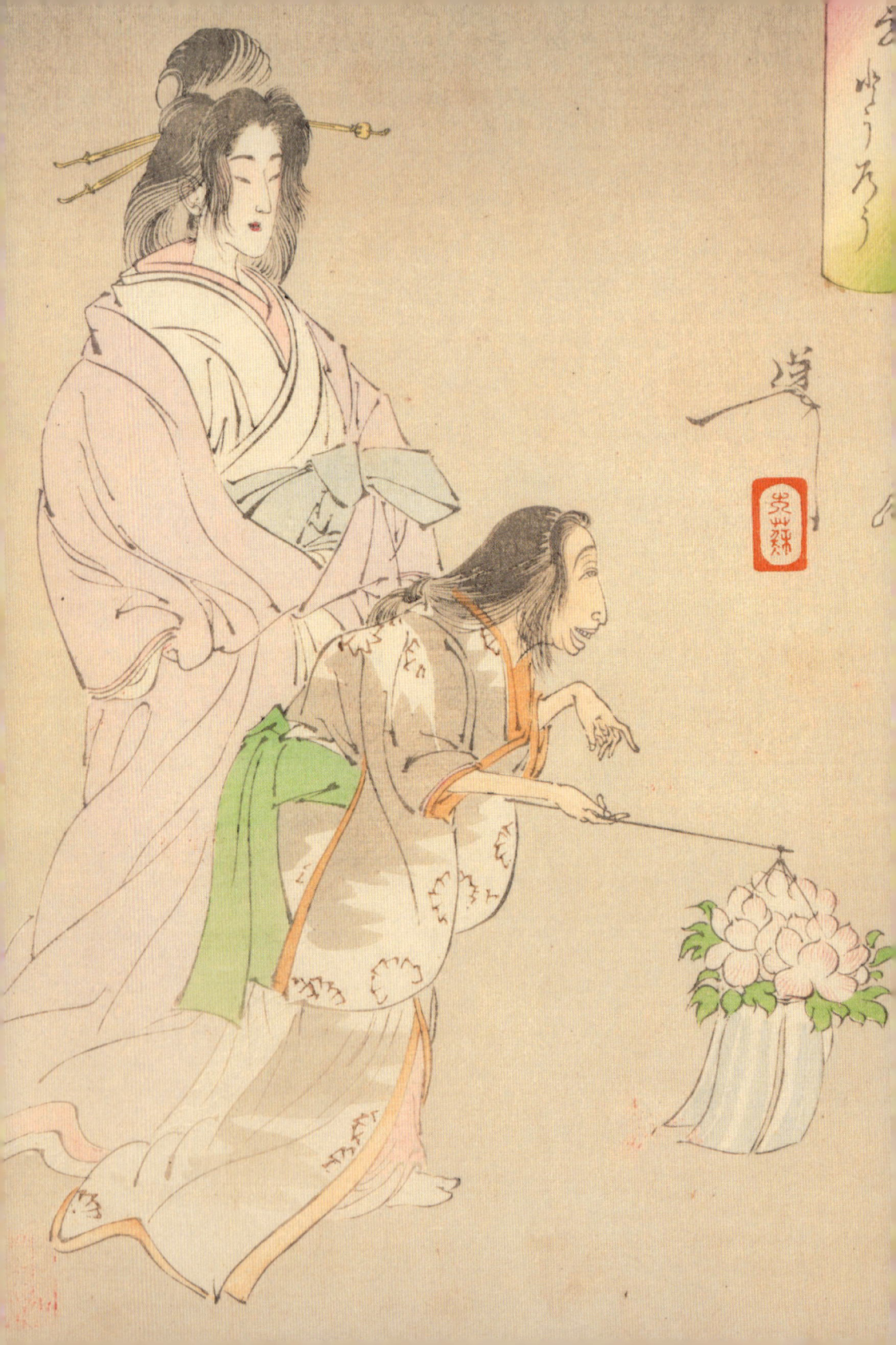

OTSUYU

•

Love stories often end badly, especially when they involve ghosts. We might come to this conclusion when we read collections of popular tales handed down across China, Korea or Japan. Numerous classic works celebrate the porosity between the world of the living and the world of the dead. The three most famous are Qu You's *New Stories after Snuffing the Lamp* (1378), Li Zhen's *More Tales Told by Lamplight* (1433), and Pu Songling's *Strange Tales from a Chinese Studio* (1740). In each, ghosts and fox-spirits mete out a kind of parallel, post-mortem justice, as they unite carnally with high-ranking men, sometimes to corrupt them, sometimes out of genuine love.

Otsuyu's destiny is drawn from a tale from these collections, *The Peony Lantern* (*Botan Dōrō*). On the first night of the month of the ghosts (*Obon*), a gorgeous lady walks in the street accompanied by her very young servant, who carries a lantern decorated with peonies. They stop outside the home of a widowed samurai, Ogiwara Shinnojo. He glimpses the woman and is instantly enchanted, swearing eternal love. Every night from then on, this beautiful stranger joins Ogiwara, always accompanied by her servant. She offers herself to him, and then leaves the house before sunrise. One evening, noticing these ever less discreet comings and goings, a neighbour sneaks a look between the panels of the samurai's sleeping-room and is astounded to catch him lying alongside a skeleton. Later, when Ogiwara talks with a Buddhist priest, he learns that he has been enchanted by a *yūrei* and that his life is in danger: carrying on this venomous relationship will very soon drive him to his grave. The priest lends him a protective talisman, which Ogiwara places at the entrance to his house. At nightfall, the mysterious woman is unable to cross the threshold and so she calls to Ogiwara, urging him to join her outside

57

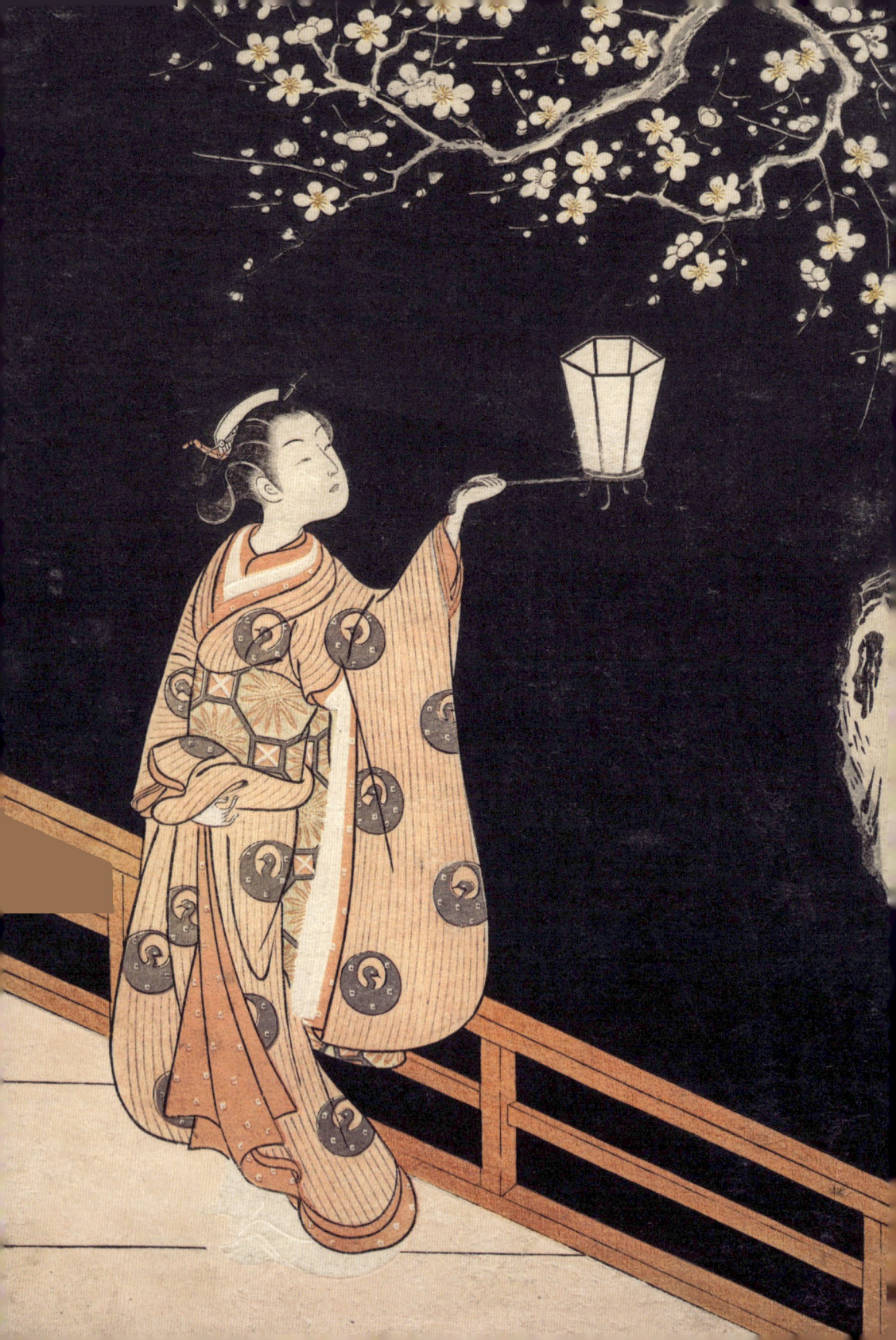

and come and sleep at her home. Enfeebled by desire, the samurai exits his house and follows his ghost-mistress and her servant. By the light of the magic lantern, they walk through the lanes and out of the town. Reaching the suburbs, they come upon a temple garden where, on a derelict tomb, the woman offers herself to him for the last time. At first light, when the rising sun has just begun to shine on the lovers, only the corpse of Ogiwara is found, lying on a female skeleton.

This classic version, set down by the writer Asai Ryōi in 1666, was overlaid, palimpsest-like, by a more modern legend adapted to Kabuki theatre in the late nineteenth century. The later tale tells of a young student, Saburo, who is in love with the daughter of his father's best friend, a beautiful woman named Otsuyu. They court each other, declare their love, and swear to remain faithful and to marry. Unfortunately, Saburo, suddenly falling ill, is unable to meet Otsuyu for several weeks. When he finally leaves his home and hurries to Otsuyu's house to see her again, he learns that she is dead and buried. In desperation, Saburo rushes off to pray for the repose of his beloved's soul. But, at the temple – it is the month of the ghosts, Obon – he runs straight into Otsuyu and her young servant. Are they spectres? Absolutely not! It turns out that her aunt, opposed to the marriage and determined to put a stop to any union between the two lovers, started rumours that Otsuyu and Saburo had died. From then on, the two young people meet every night, unnoticed, the young woman guided by her servant who carries a lantern adorned with peonies. They keep up this forbidden relationship for several weeks, until a servant of Saburo spies the lovers through a hole in the oilcloth of a sleeping-room panel. To his horror, he sees his master making love to a skeleton, while a second skeleton holds a peony lantern in a corner of the room. A Buddhist priest is summoned to the house and tries to reason with Saburo, who is blinded by love. Unable to make Saburo see sense, the priest leads him to the cemetery and shows him the graves of Otsuyu and her servant. The reality of the situation forces the young man to grasp that he must give in to destiny and rid himself of this

59

ghost. Covering the doors of his home with protective talismans (*ofuda*), he calls on Amida, the Buddha of salvation, and fervently recites redemption prayers (*nenbutsu*). The talismans and rituals work as they should, but the *yūrei* of Otsuyu and her servant continue to come and knock at the door every night, begging for caresses. Still amorous and incapable of satisfying his passion physically, Saburo begins to see his health decline. The young man's servants, wishing to make their master happy and restore his strength and vigour, tear down the *ofuda* all around the house. The following night, now unimpeded, the two ghosts enter. Otsuyu slides open the side panels of Saburo's sleeping-room, slowly lifts her kimono in front of him, and offers herself fully to the young man. At first light, the servants coming in to tidy the room and put away the tatamis discover their master's corpse wrapped around a skeleton; a smile of ecstasy is still on his face.

What is the message of this 'sexy ghost' story? The two versions, one from the Edo period (1603–1867) and the other from thc Meiji period (1868–1912), differ in meaning substantially, but one theme dominates: the idea of love being stronger than death. In both cases, the lover dares to put love before death, risking death in his determination to savour love to the fullest.

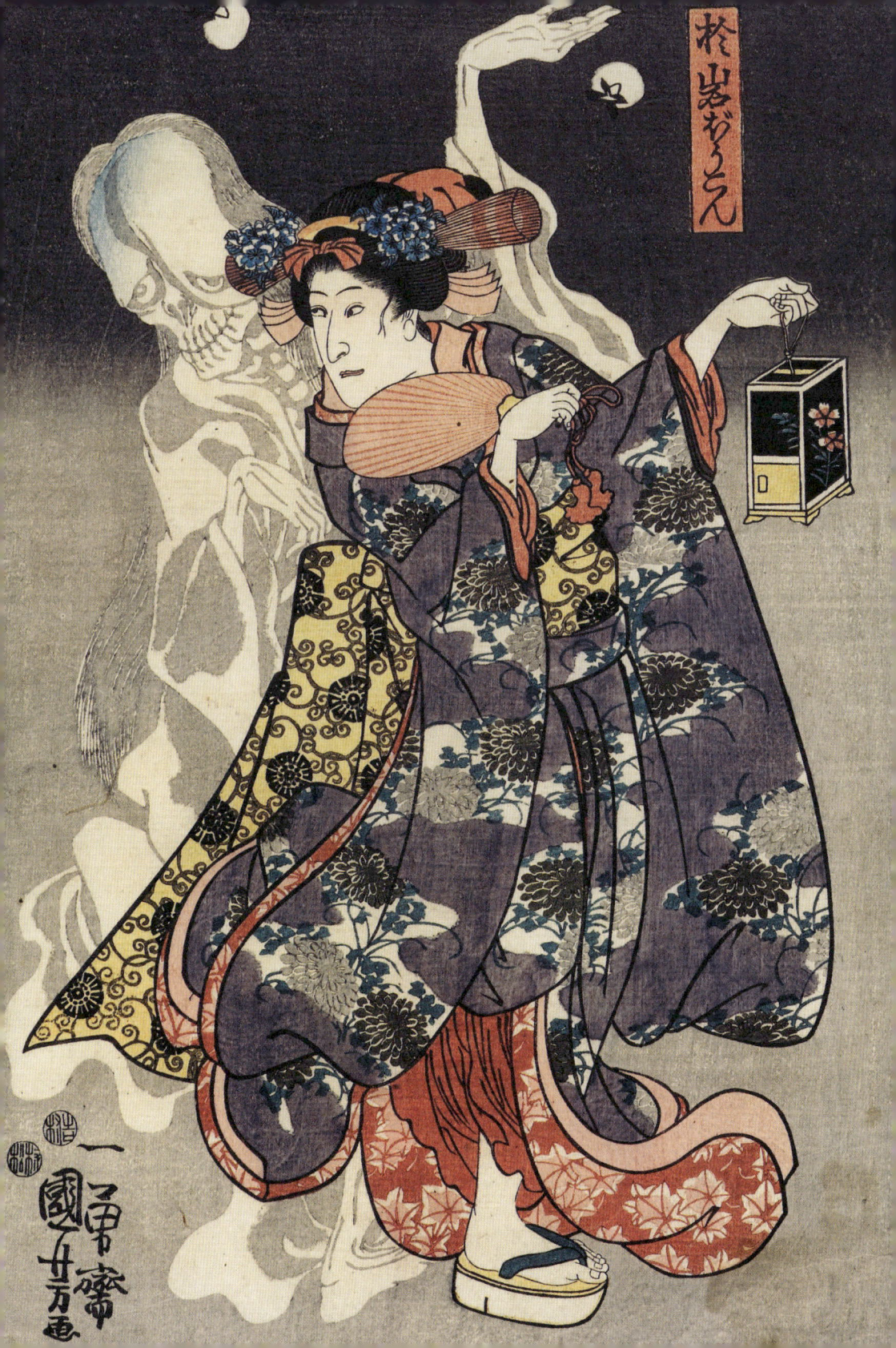

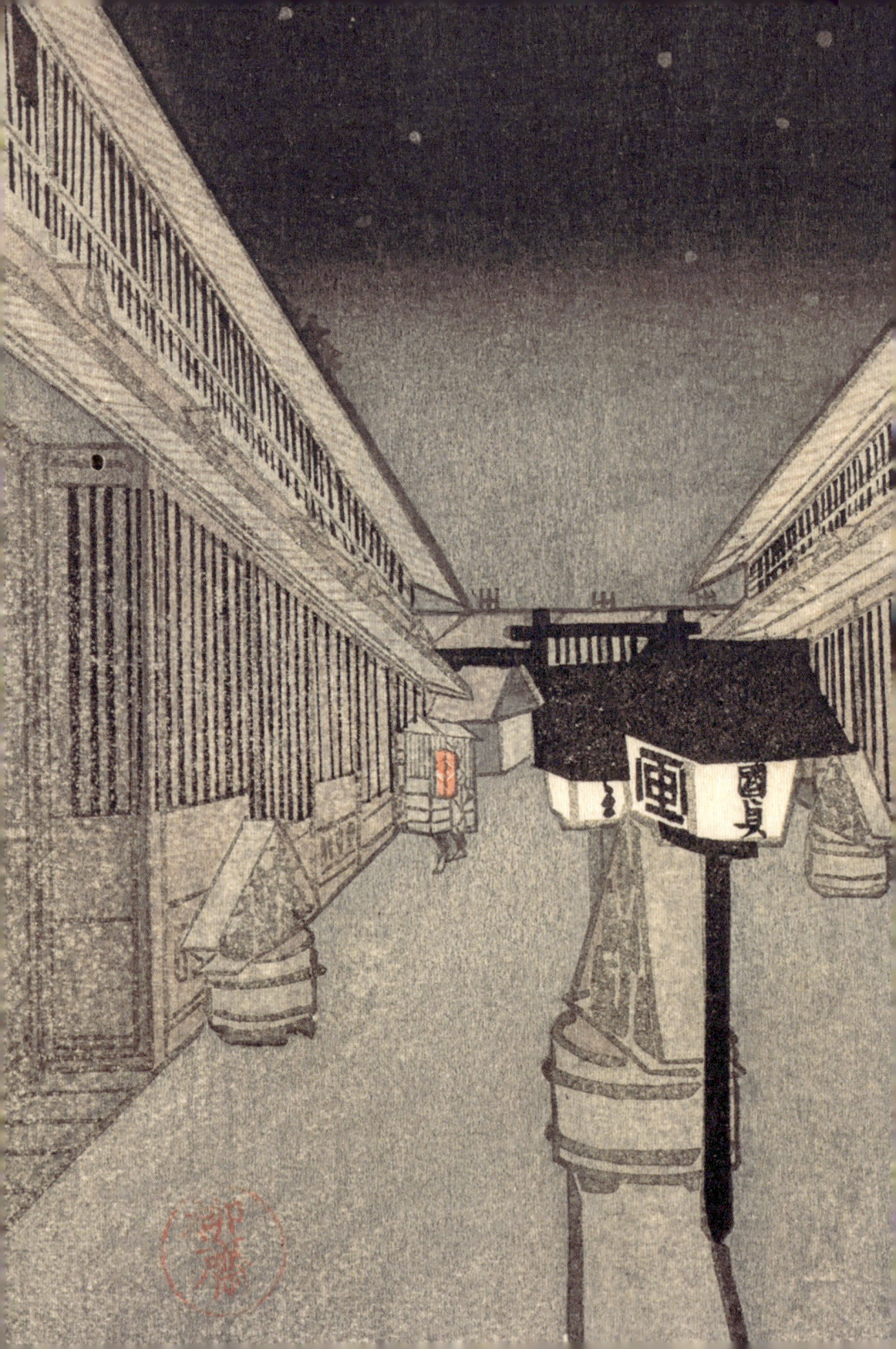

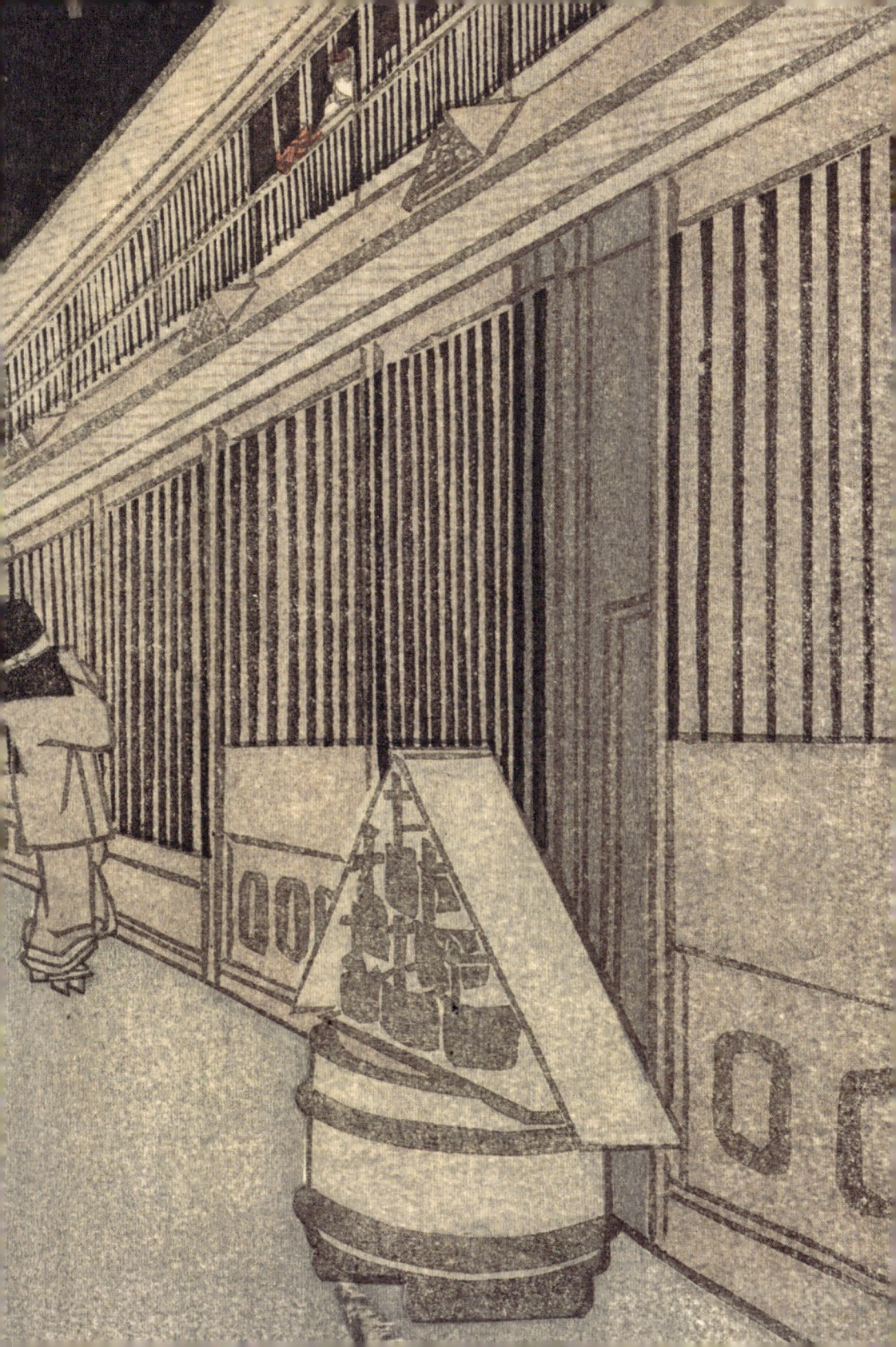

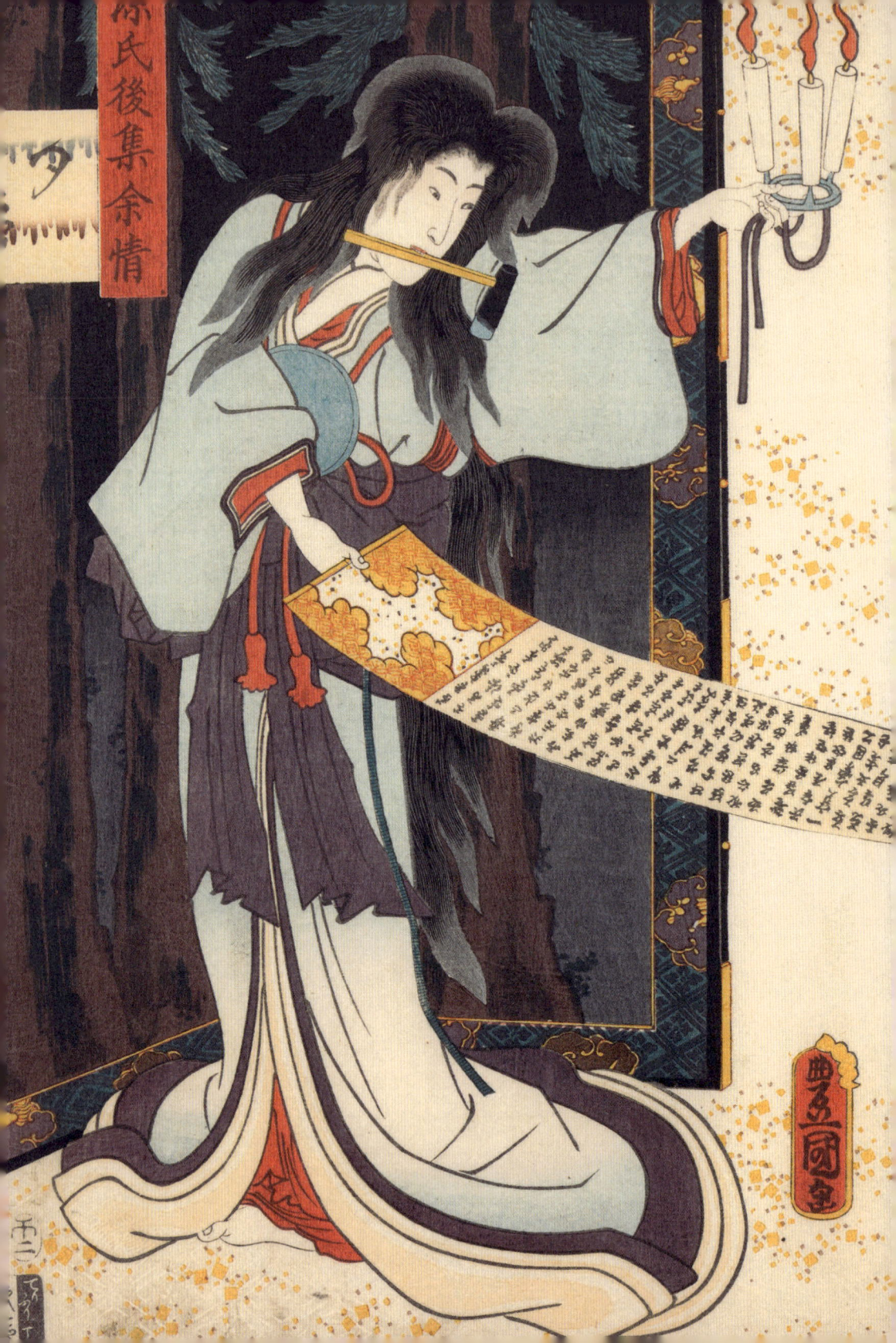

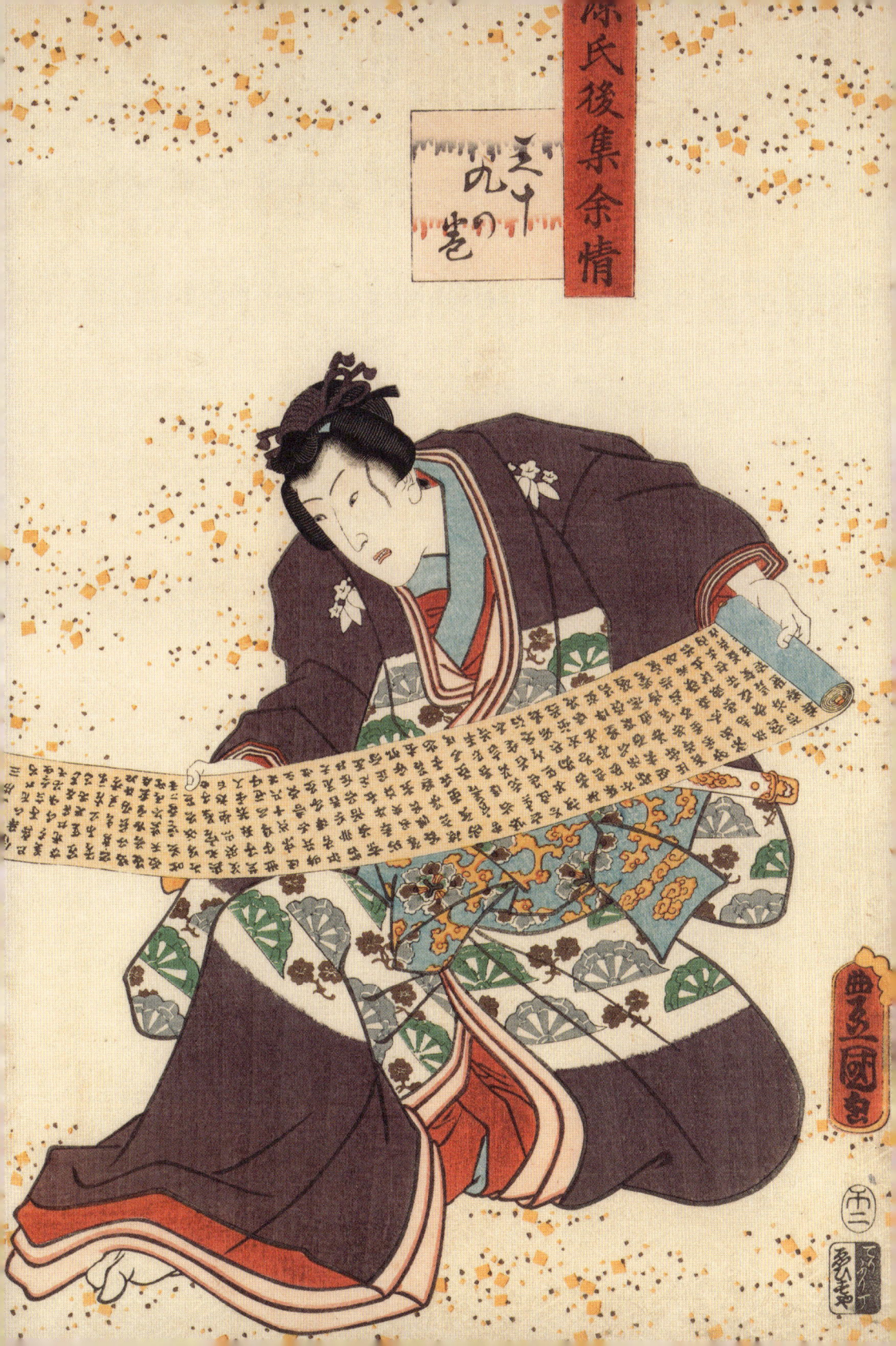

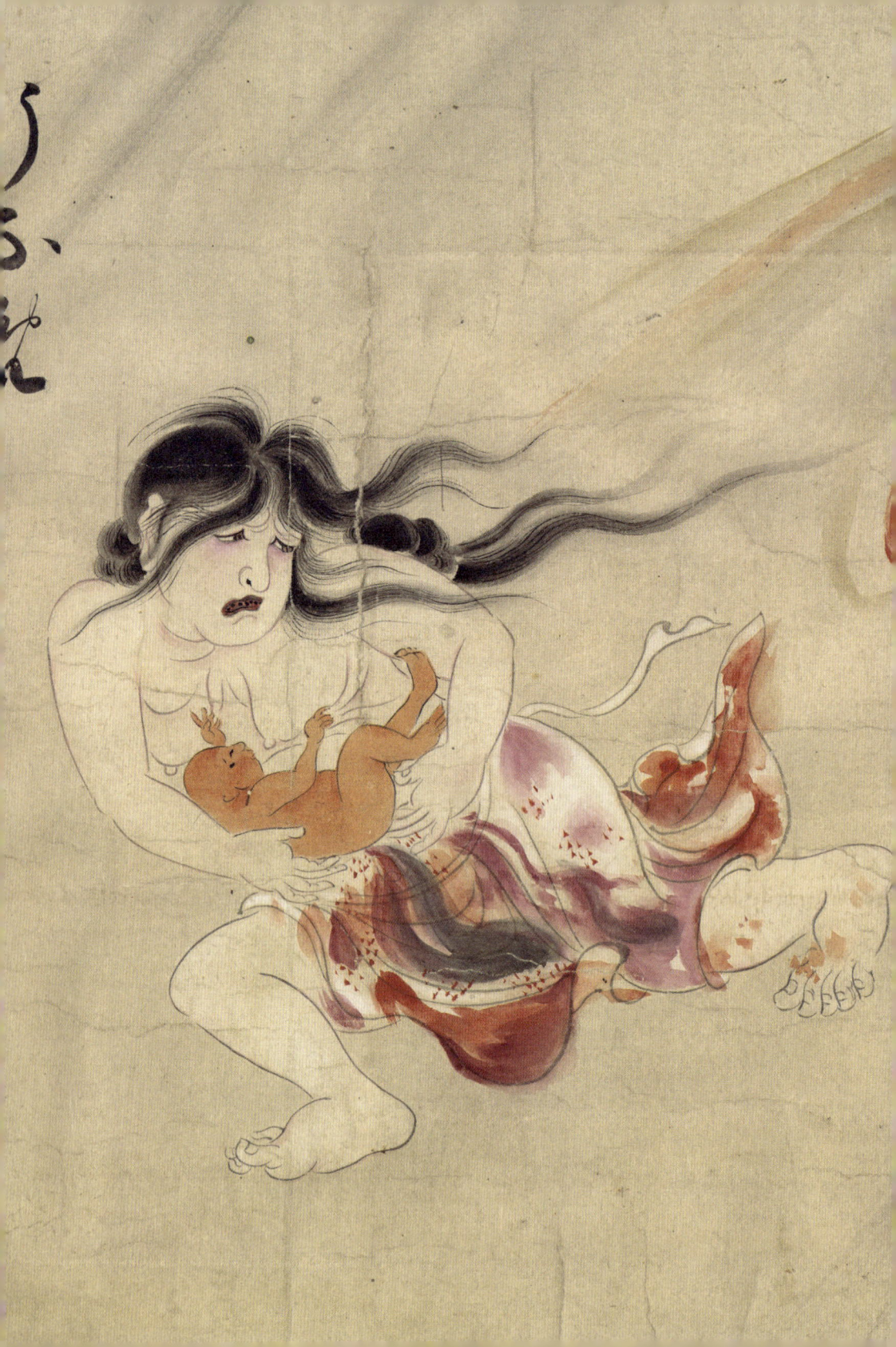

UBUME

•

The death of a woman who is pregnant or giving birth is perhaps more horrific than any other kind of death. This intolerable demise can summon the ghost Ubume, who appears in the night as a young and beautiful woman, her hair dishevelled, her kimono torn and covered in blood. She runs aimlessly through dark alleys or near cemeteries, holding a tightly swaddled new-born which she tries to hand over to passers-by. When she vanishes, the swaddling is revealed to contain only a large stone or a bundle of leaves.

Some stories tell of women who die during childbirth and come back as ghosts, aching for the child who did not accompany them into death and attempting, more or less clumsily, to grab another little one in its place. Ubume may try to tear a child out of its mother's arms, or when she sees a child alone, she may beg for a kiss or a cuddle. In another story, she steals an infant from its bed in order to take it back to the underworld with her. In yet another, she gives a baby her cold breast, from which flows death-bringing milk.

In order to prevent a woman who died before or during childbirth from becoming an *obo*, an *ubu*, or an *ubume* (Ubume's name has come to stand for a whole genre of ghosts), sometimes a doll would be placed on her corpse in the hope this substitute would deceive her. Other, more pragmatic people would pull the dead child out of its mother's body and place it in her arms, in an eternal embrace.

In addition to personifying the pain and disappointment of an irreparable loss, Ubume reflects an evolution in thinking about pregnant women and their unborn children. Once considered to be an extension of their mothers' bodies, children progressively took on ever greater independence until ultimately mothers were seen as 'mere instruments of male reproduction'. Thus, the death

of a woman in childbirth or during pregnancy –
and consequently the death of the unborn child –
became the sole responsibility of the woman, who
bears the burden of guilt after death and into
infinity.

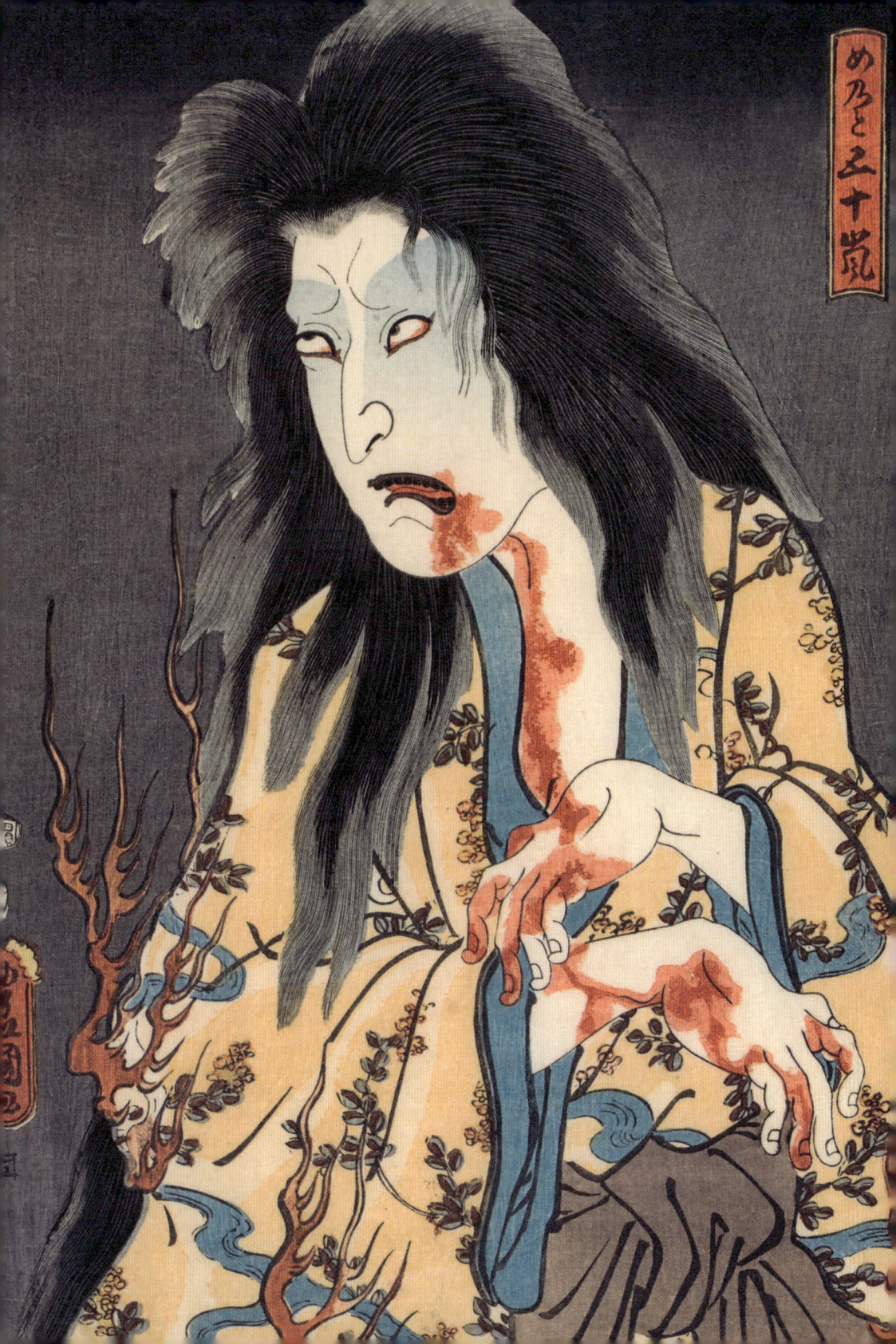

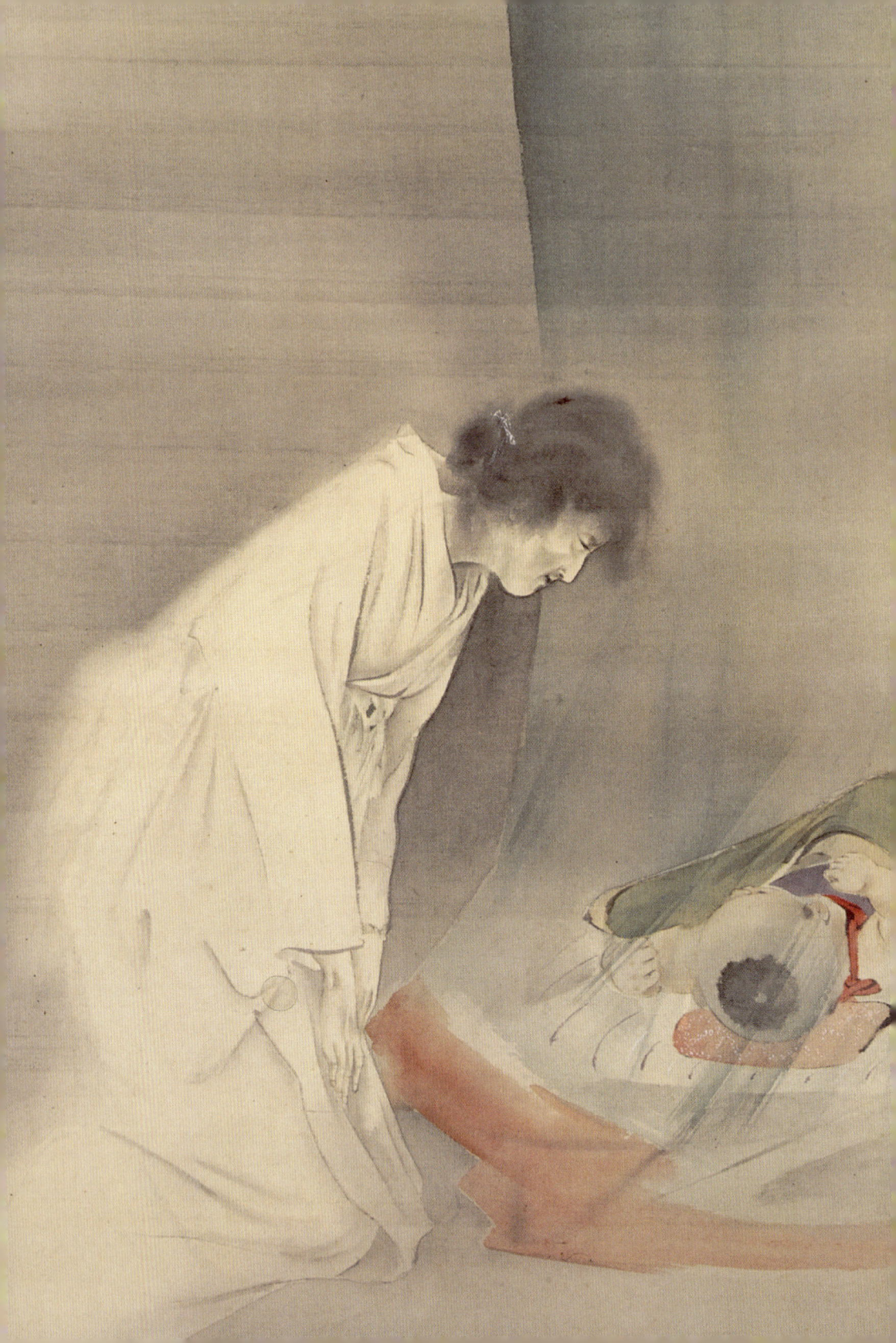

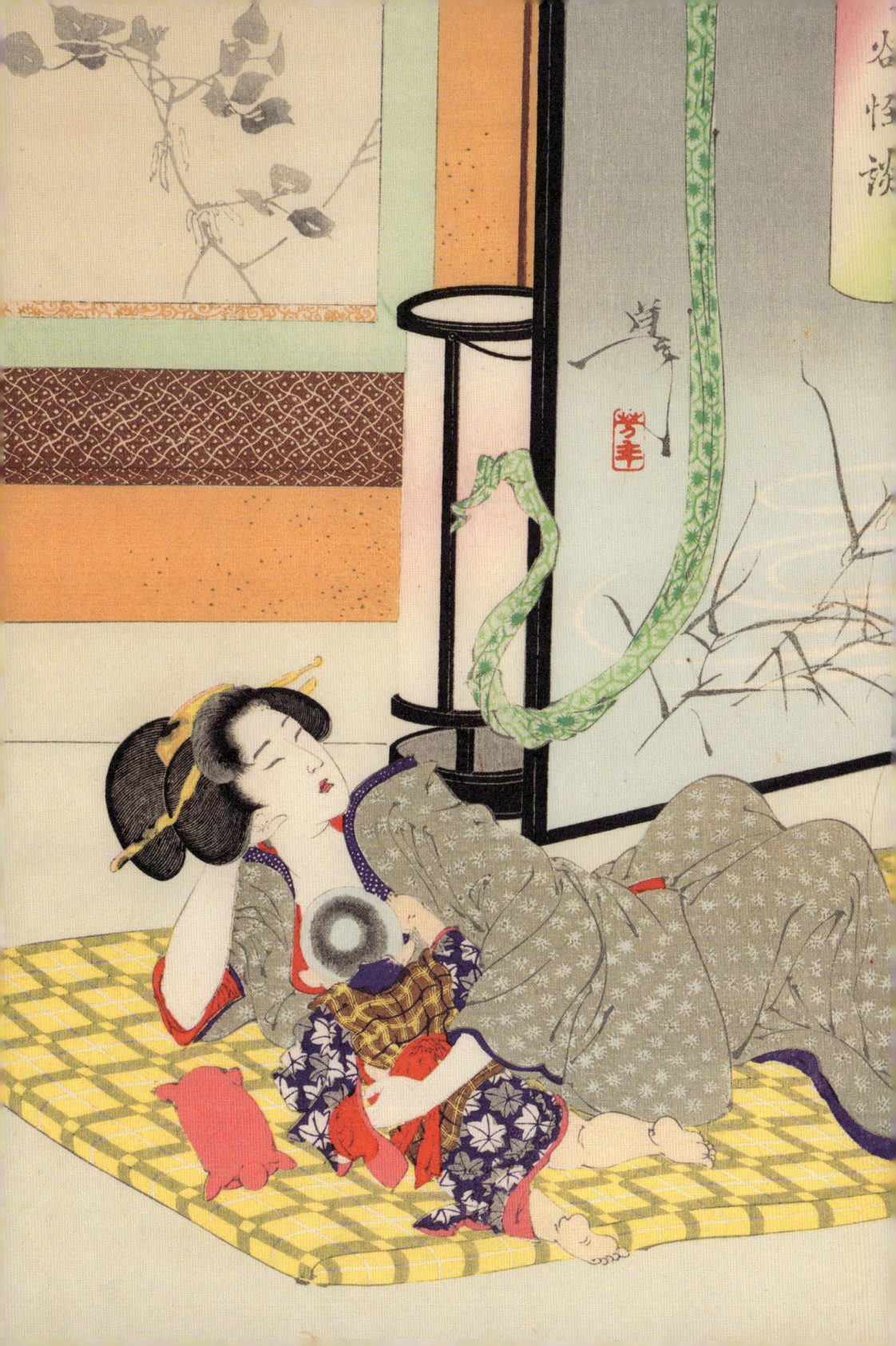

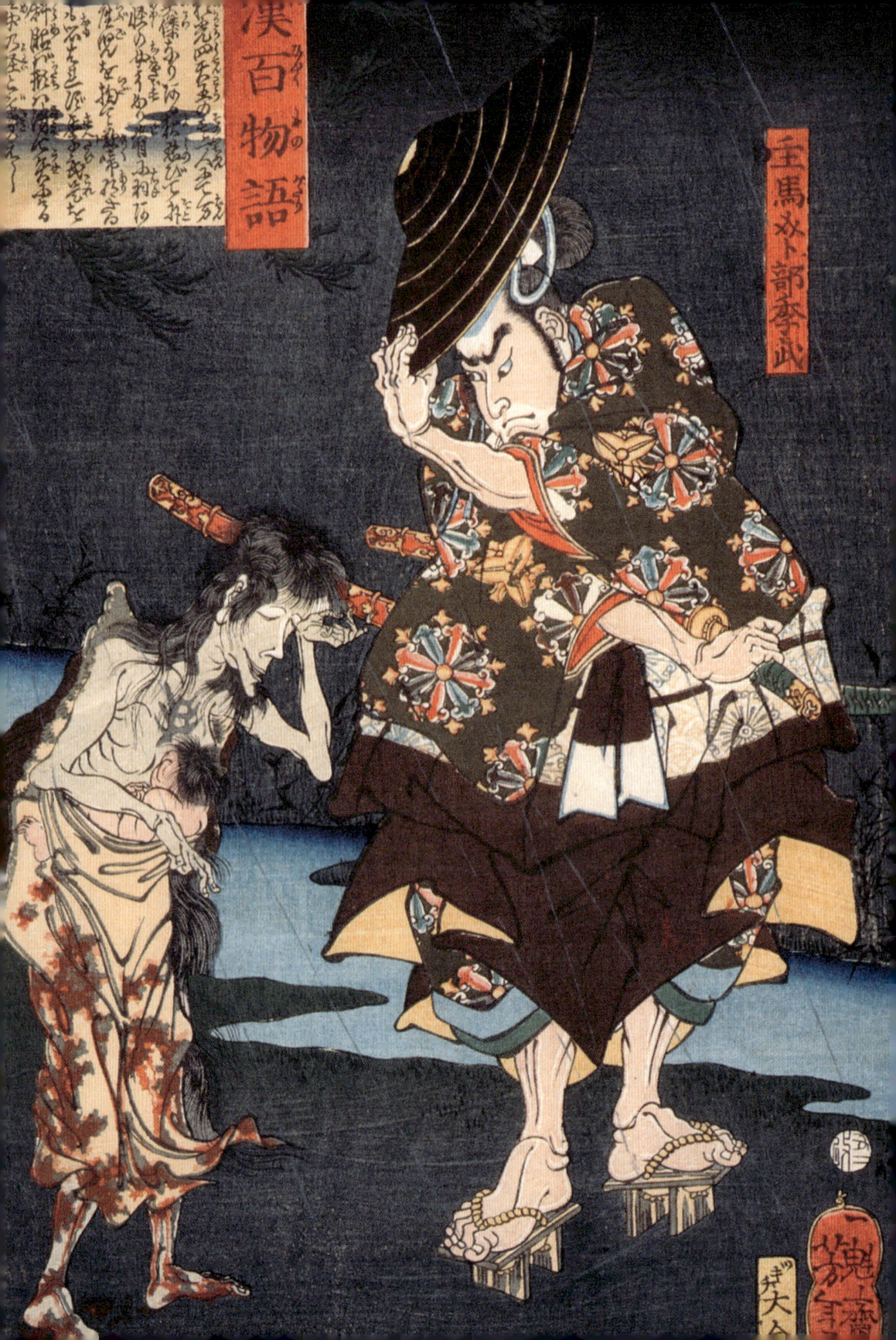

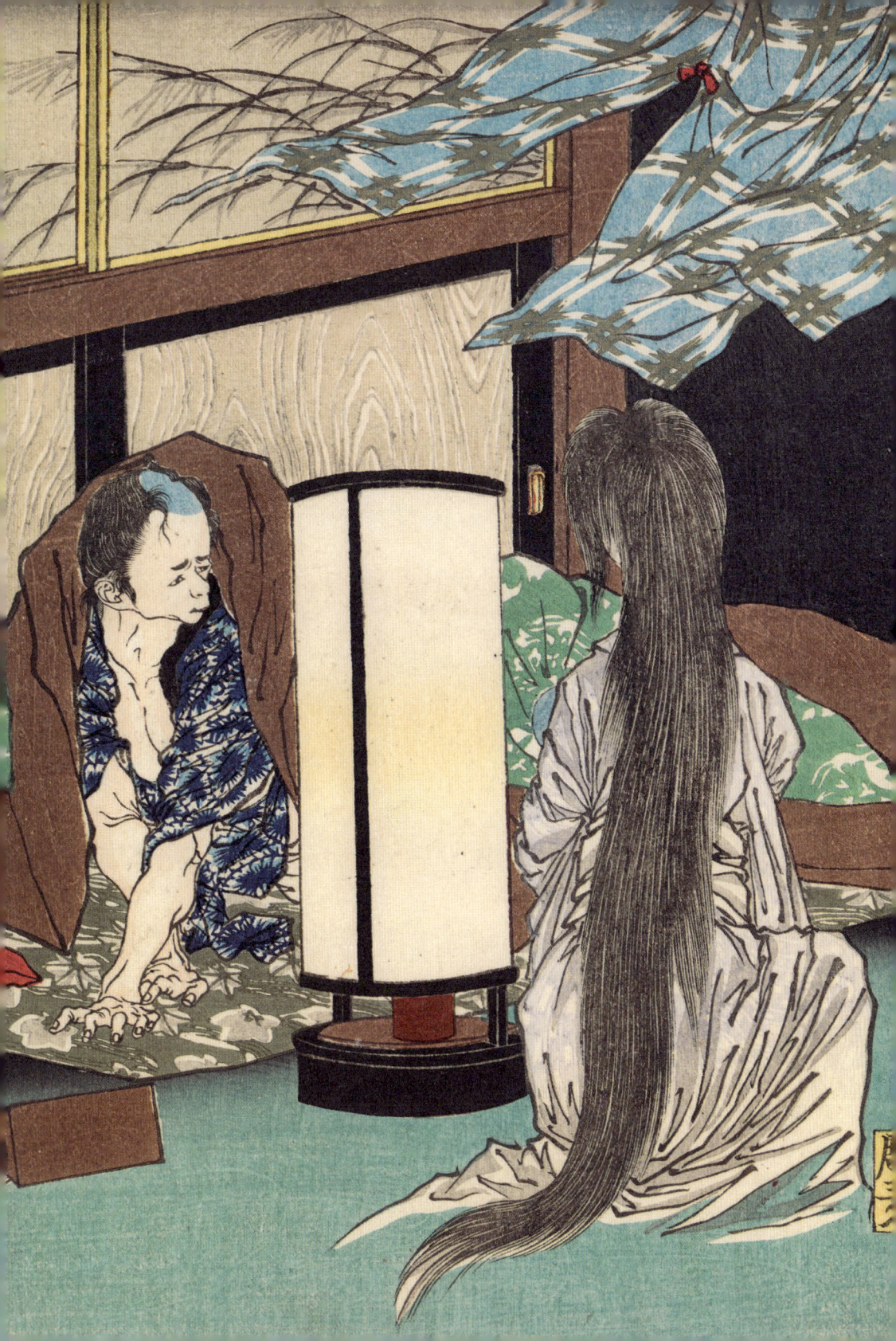

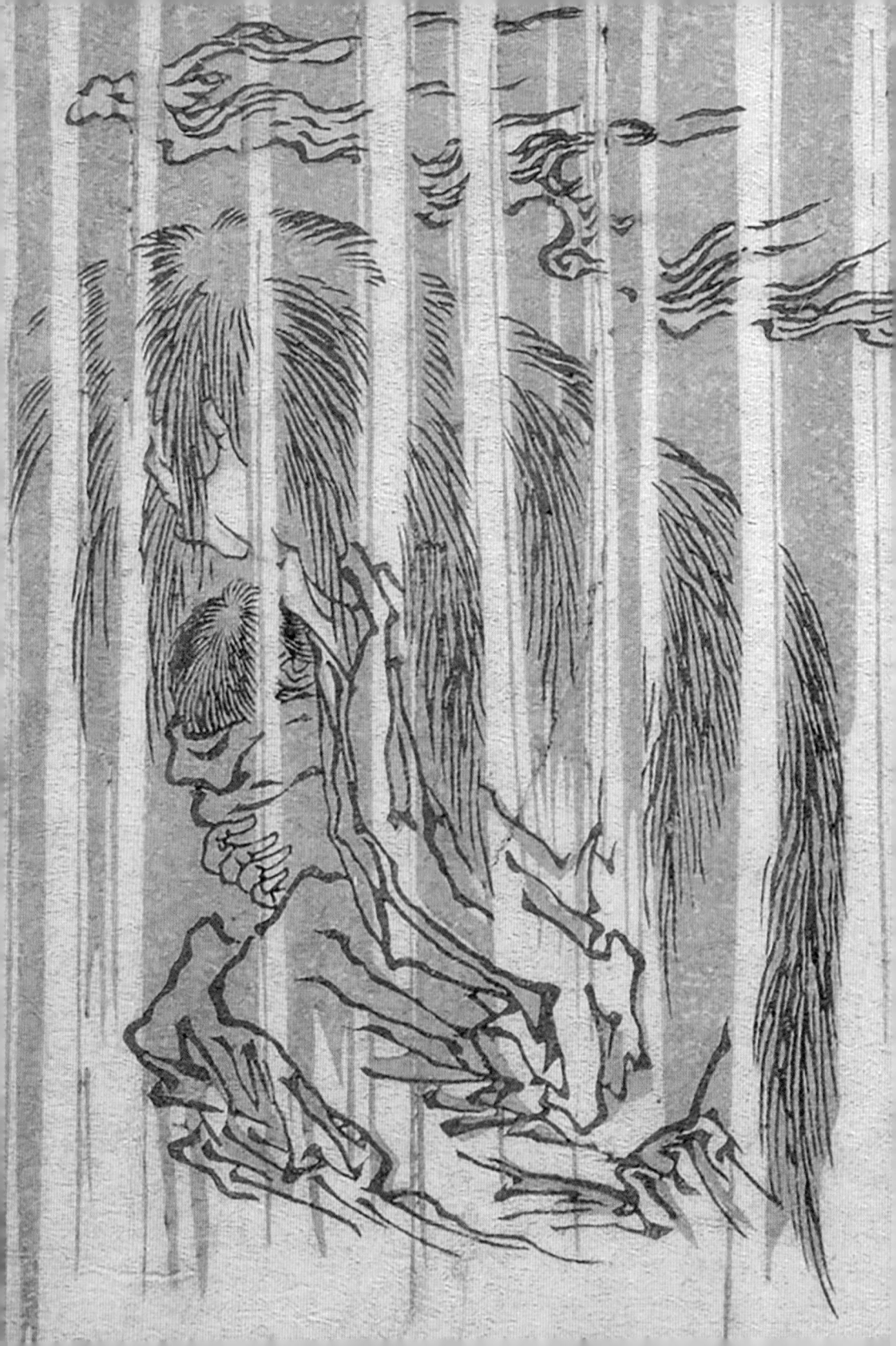

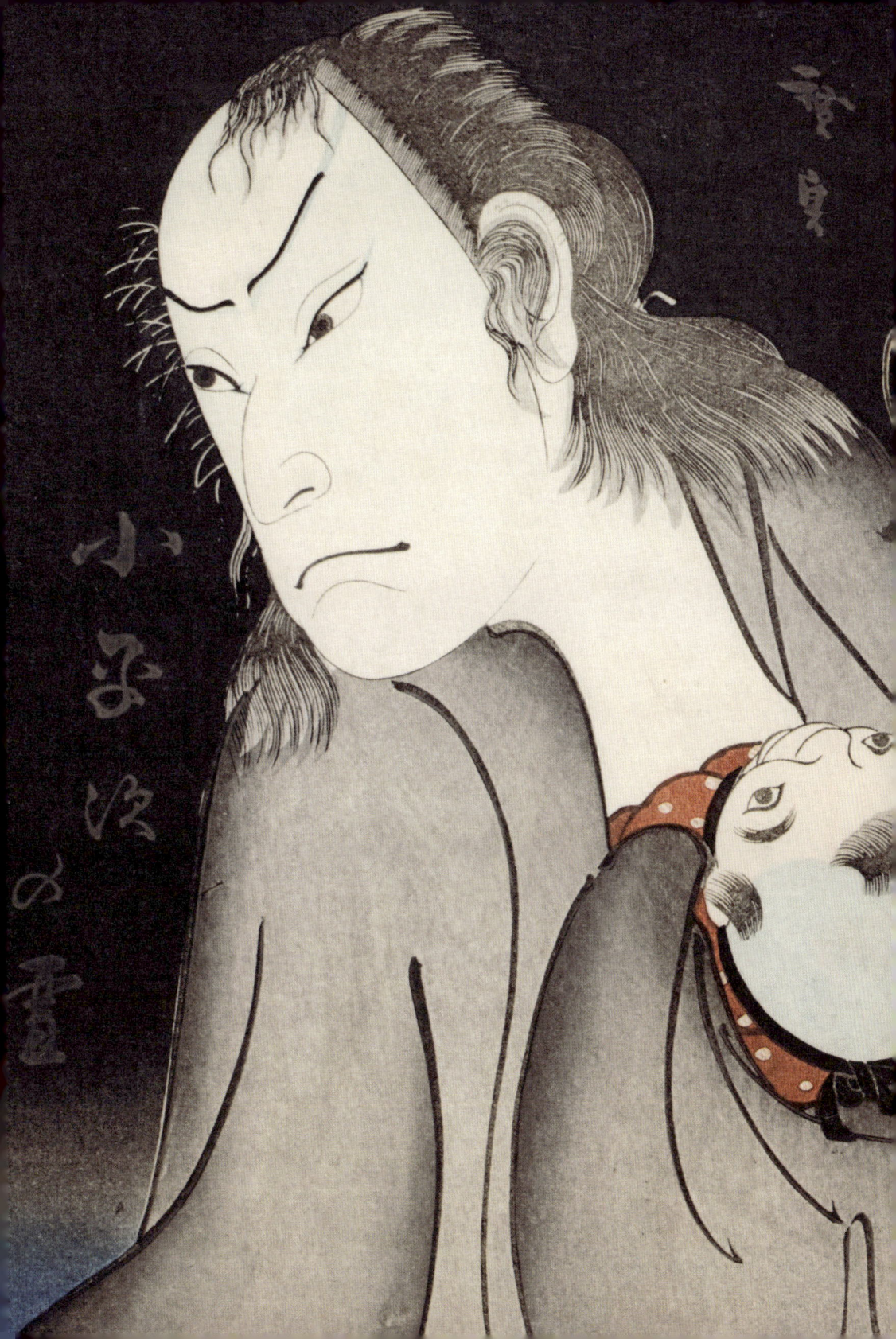

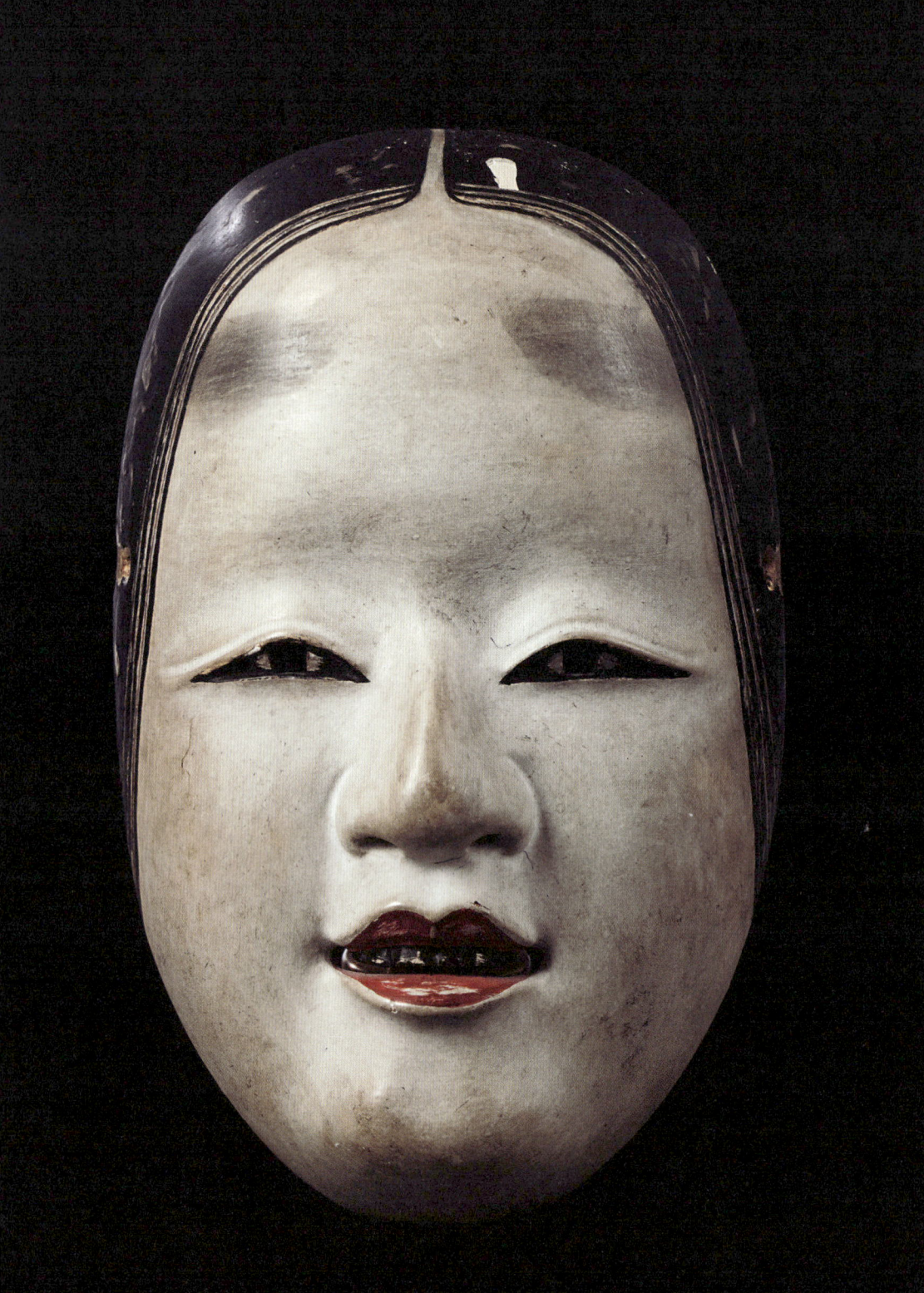

NOH

•

Noh, a mystic and esoteric form of Japanese theatre, offers perhaps the best opportunity to inter-
pret *yūrei* art and become better acquainted with
its mysterious and stirring power. As we have
seen, *yūrei-ga* pictures are two-dimensional artis-
tic figurations of ghosts and fantastical creatures
that refuse to die fully until they have dispensed
justice from the grave. The images are so moving
that they themselves are thought to be 'haunted'.
In Noh performances, by contrast, spectral beings
are embodied with the help of ancient costumes,
stereotyped masks, distinctly eerie voices and
exaggerated body language. The actors seem
almost 'possessed' by the spirits they portray.

Several twentieth-century dramas were
penned by the controversial Japanese writer Yukio
Mishima. His *Five Modern Noh Plays* were aimed
at contemporary tastes but retained the essential
themes of the classical plays: an ill-fated seduction
that ends with a lover frozen to death; anguish at
the prospect of the world ending; misunderstood
or unrequited love, provoking resentment and
frustration; the infernal, morbid spiral of jealousy;
and the denial of life's reality, leading to suicide.
Mishima's works illuminate this vision of frequent
contact between the living and the dead.

At the very end of 'Sotoba Komachi', the first
of the five Noh plays, a young man is led to declare
his ardour and unconditional love to a *yūrei*.
While the whole world apparently sees nothing in
this spectre but a hideous and repulsive being, he
beholds its incredibly beautiful form. For that is
one of the characteristics of these ghosts, and the
same applies to 'fox-spirits', the *yūrei*'s counter-
parts in traditional China: their appearance varies
depending on the person looking at them. To the
one who covets them, to the one whom they seek
to exploit for vengeance or pleasure, they will
have no hideous features. Quite the opposite.

In Mishima's play, the last scene depicts an encounter between an old woman and a poet. The man sees nothing of the reality of this near-centenarian's body; he does not see her wrinkles and ragged clothes, her lice and her long nails, and he does not smell the foul odour of her body. For all that she lets him touch her sagging breasts, he is in ecstasy over her physical beauty. There is no actual metamorphosis, here; rather, a kind of targeted possession of the mind accomplished by the *yūrei*'s tricks and evil spells. After all, is it not said that beauty is in the eye of the beholder, or that love is blind?

The closing dialogue leaves no doubt about the supernatural powers at work here:

POET: It's strange . . . You have the clear eyes of a girl of twenty. Your clothes are exquisitely perfumed . . . How strange you are! You are young again!

OLD WOMAN: Don't say that! Have I not warned you about what will happen if you say that I am beautiful?

POET: If something seems true to me, I must express it, even if I die for it.

OLD WOMAN: What a madman! Enough, I implore you. The moment you spoke of is nothing.

POET: I am going to tell you something . . .

OLD WOMAN: No! No! I prefer not to hear!

POET: The moment has come. The moment we have been waiting for, for ninety-nine nights, ninety-nine years . . .

OLD WOMAN: Stop! Your eyes are gleaming! Stop, I beg you!

POET: I am going to tell you, Komachi. You are beautiful. You are the most beautiful woman in the world. And you will not stop being beautiful, even after ten thousand years.

OLD WOMAN: You will regret saying that.

POET: Never.

OLD WOMAN: Fool! I already see the mark of death on your forehead.

POET: I do not want to die.

OLD WOMAN: I tried to silence you.

POET: My feet, my hands are growing cold. I will meet you, I'm sure of it, in a hundred years, in the same place!

The poet then collapses on the ground, stops breathing and dies.

Associating with ghosts is perilous in itself: the miasma that hangs above any such encounter impairs the health. Declaring eternal love to them, though, is tantamount to signing one's death warrant. It is condemning oneself to follow the spectre into the other world.

What Mishima's magnificent writing also demonstrates is the continuity of these stories of love and death: not uniting in one life leaves the possibility of meeting in another. It is as though lives were interlinked, as though fates were decided from one life to the next, continuously. Is that so terrible? No. Rather, it is a hope, a waiting for the right moment, for the 'right life', to experience at last a love that is full and entire: total, blossoming, and divine.

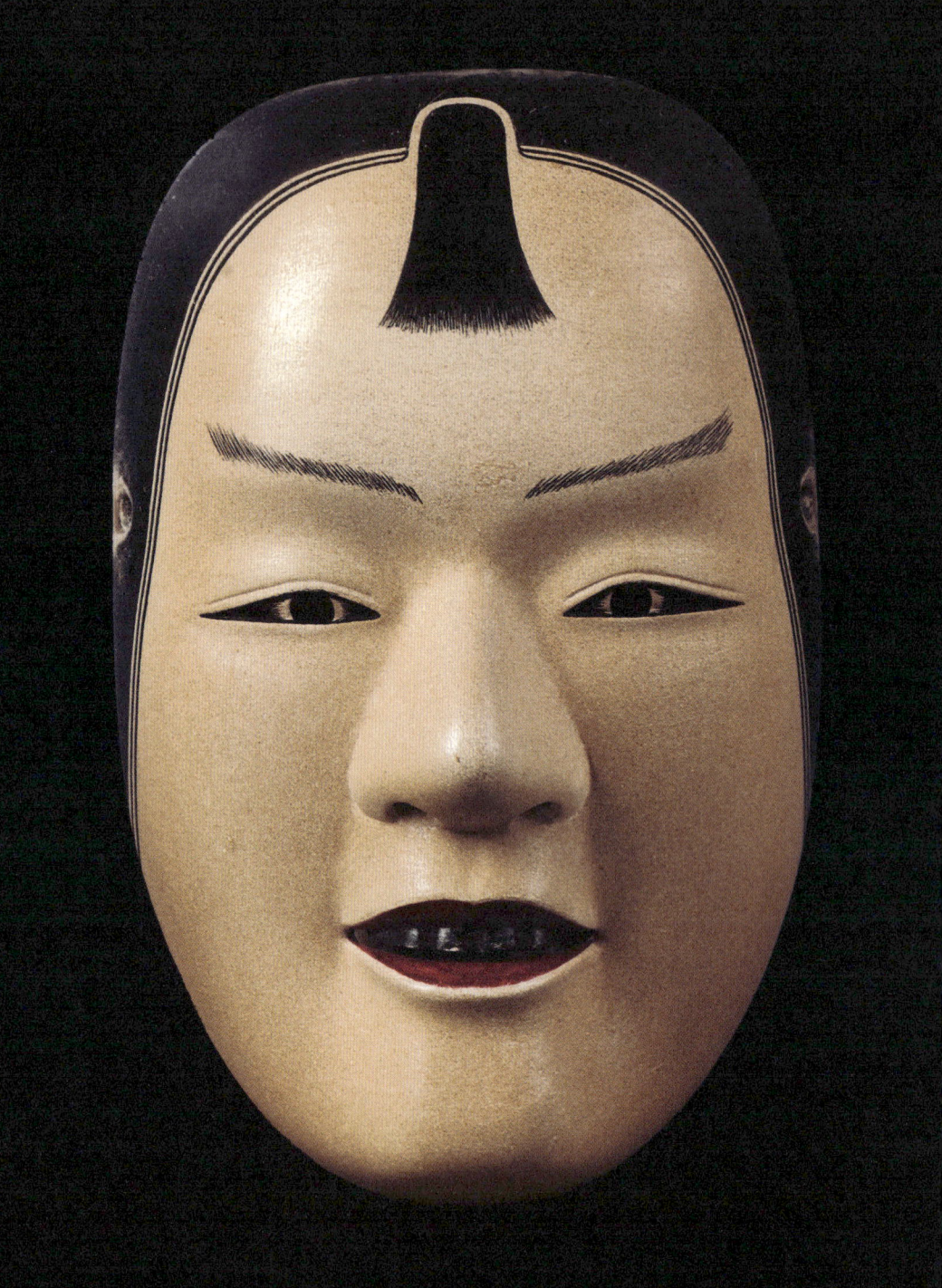

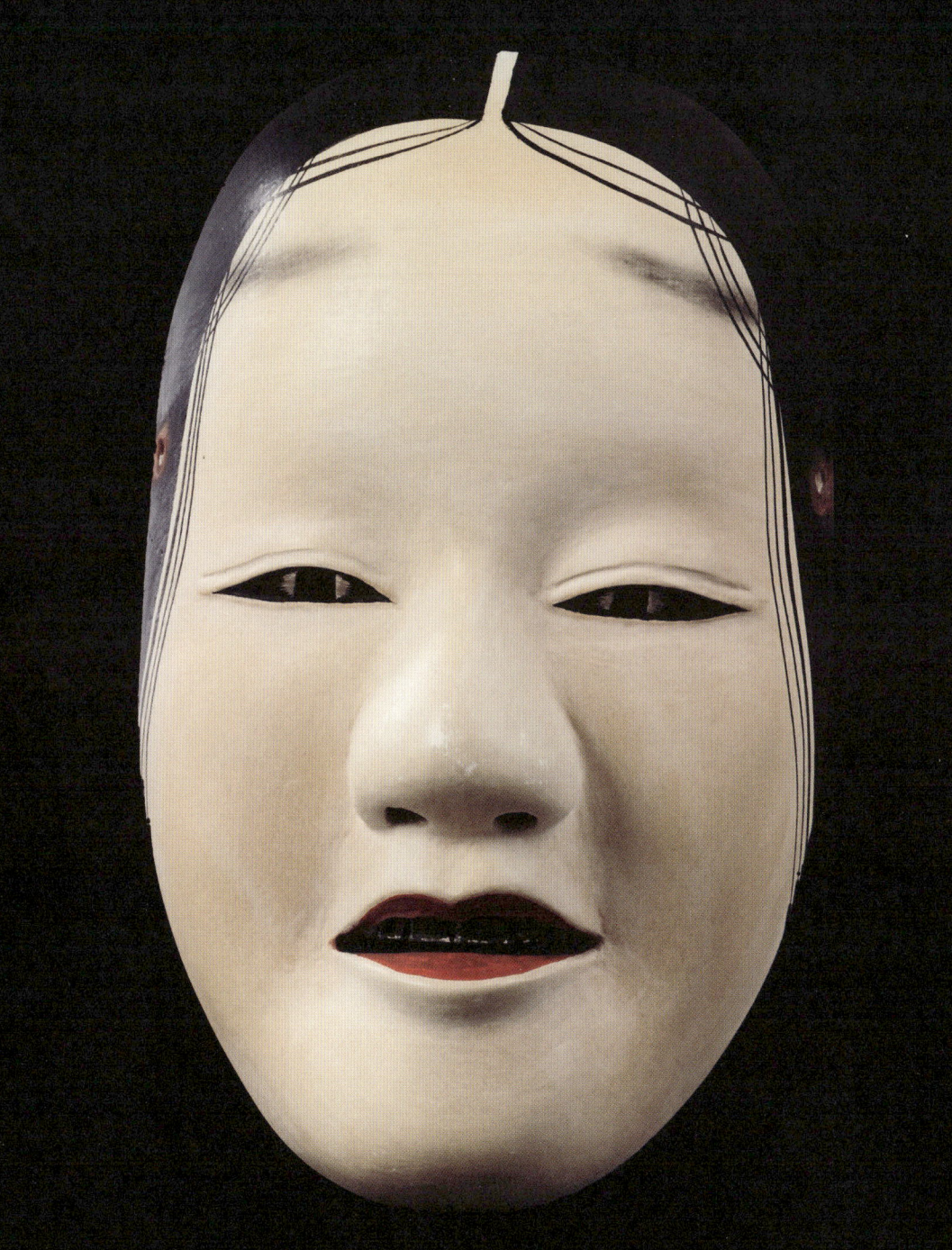

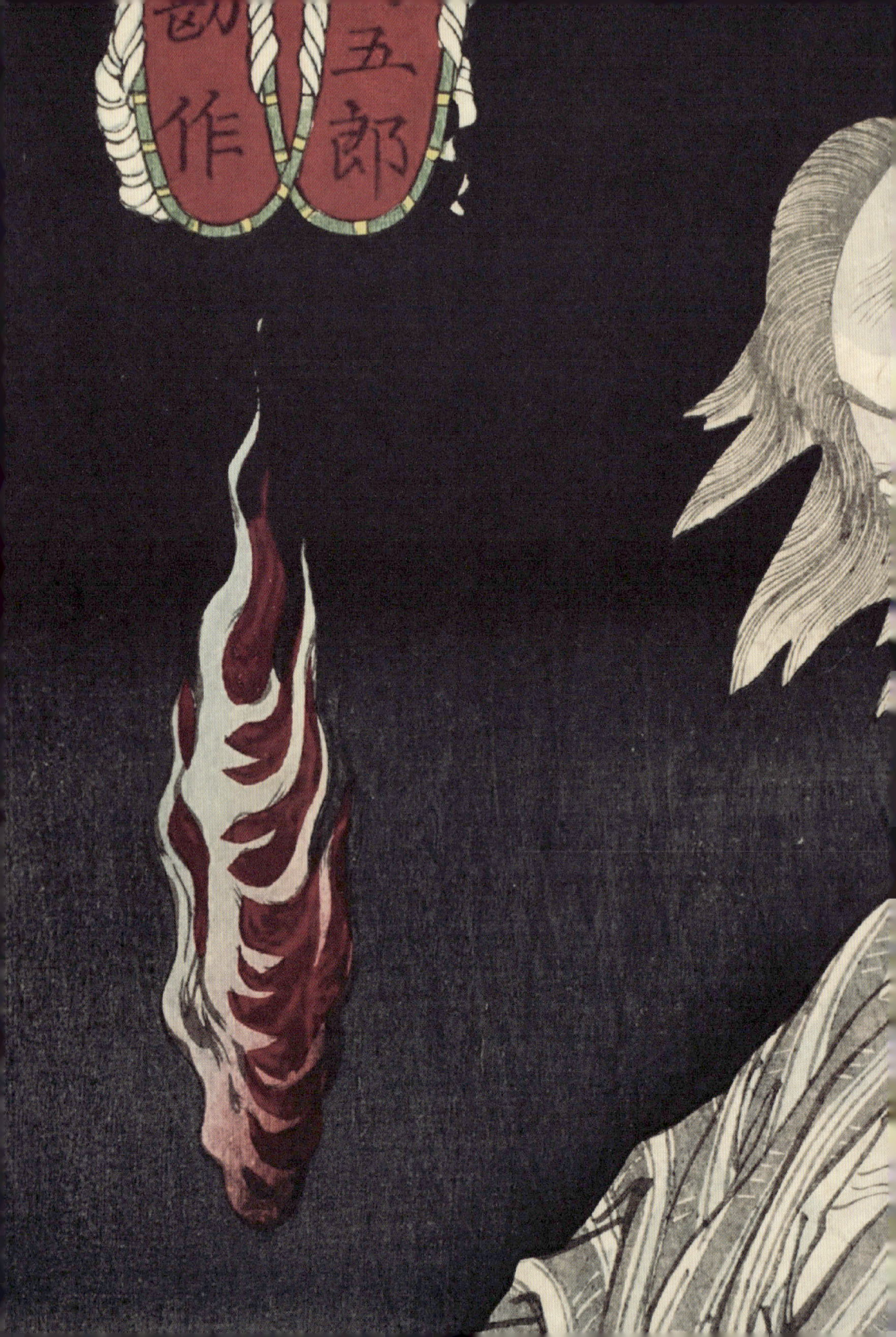

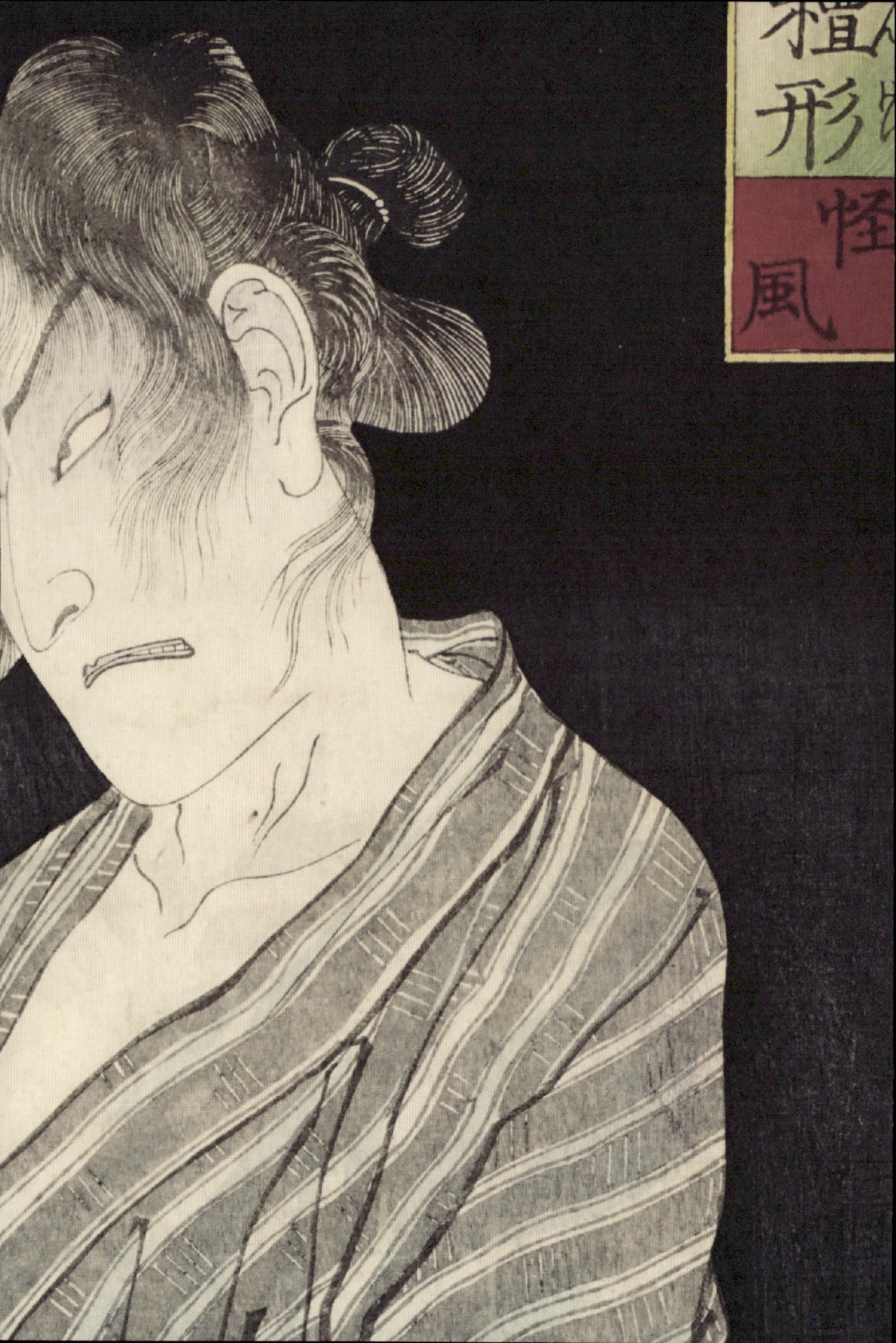

檀人
形
怪風

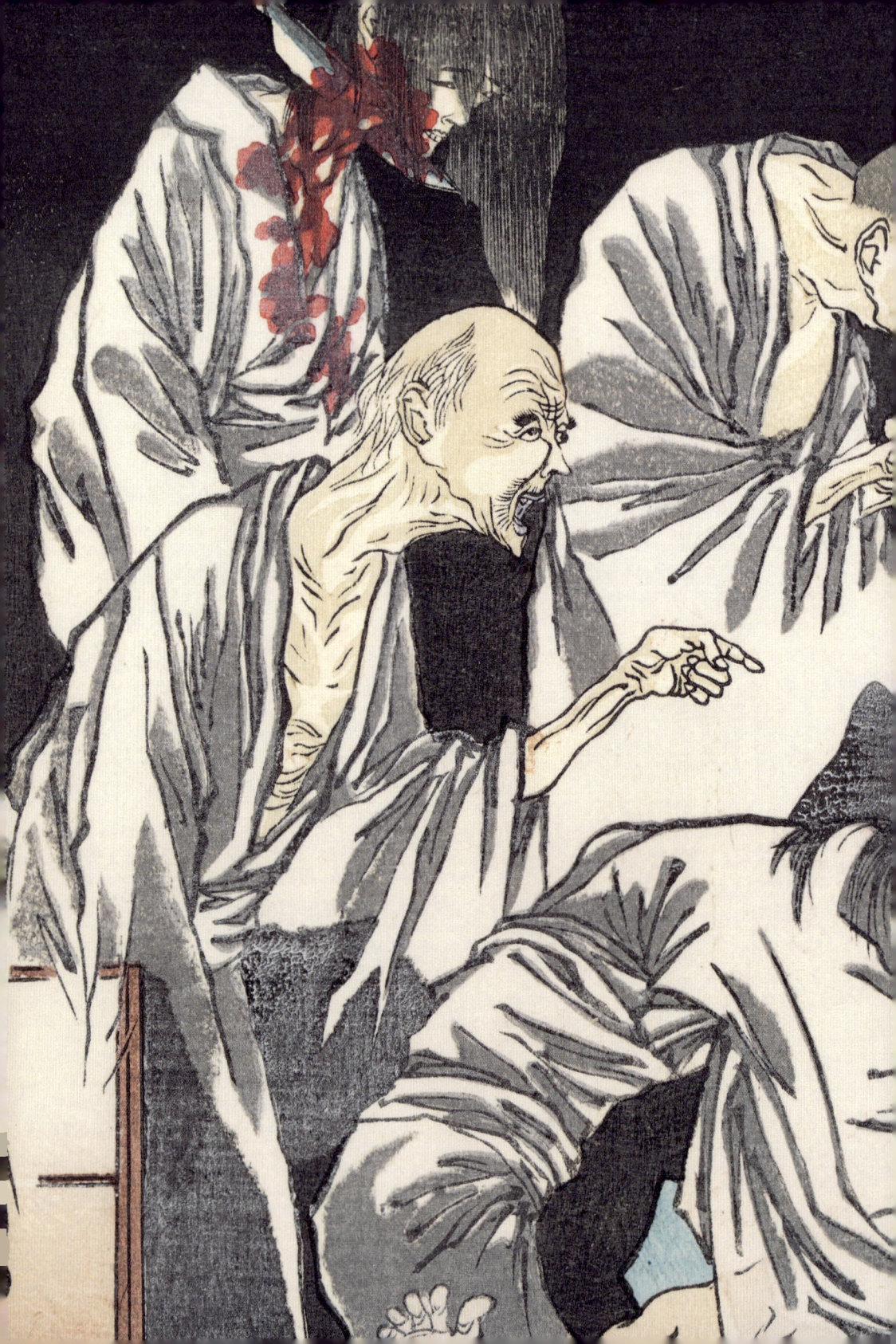

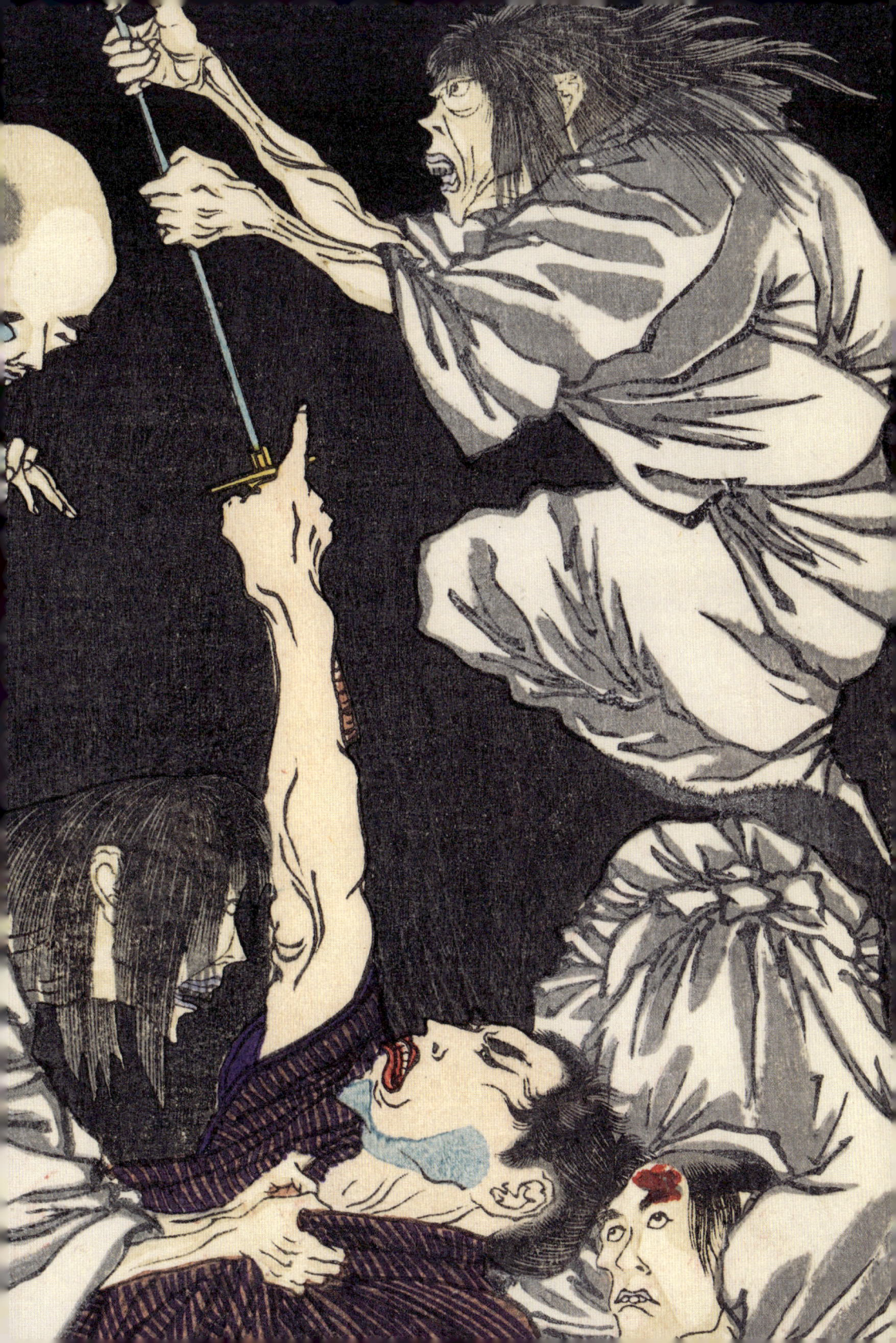

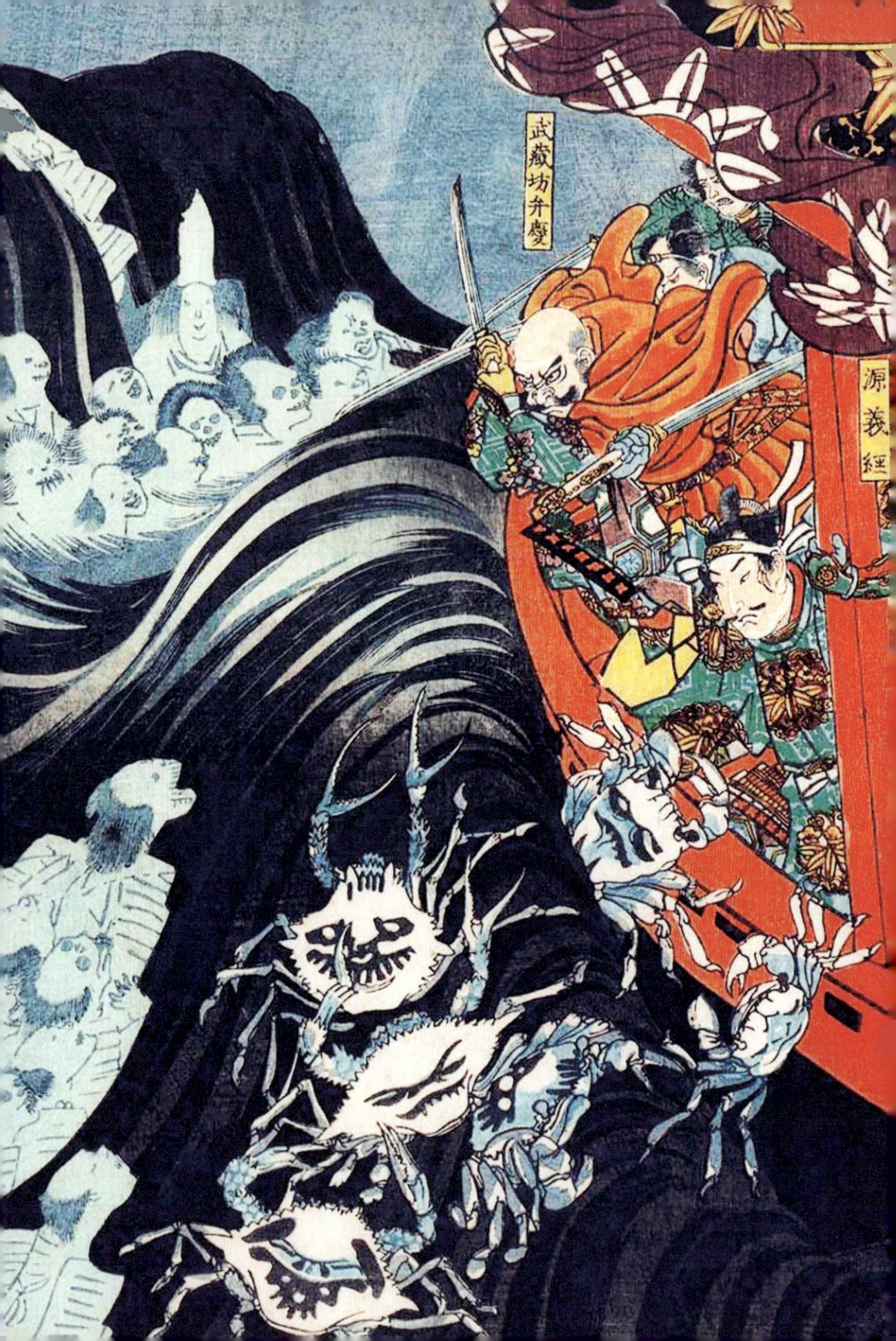

武蔵坊弁慶

源義経

FUNAYŪREI

•

The sea is fully a part of Japanese culture. But with it come shipwrecks and bodies lost forever in the waters, be they fishermen, sailors on commercial boats or soldiers killed in naval combat (the Taira clan, for example, on the occasion of the Battle of Dan-no-ura, off the southern point of Honshū, in 1185).

How can funerary rites be observed in the absence of a corpse? How can the soul's eternal rest be ensured and the cycle of reincarnation continued without a full funeral ceremony? In the absence of these rituals, the spirits of those swallowed by the tides become 'boat ghosts' (*funayūrei*), haunting the seas, harbours, ports and reefs. Equipped with a giant ladle, their features misshapen by putrefaction or by hybridisation with sea creatures, they constantly harass sailors, capsizing their vessels and causing them to drown. These spirits are often conflated with sea monsters (*yōkai*), phantom boats and other creatures that are half demon and half wrathful divinity.

Certain conditions favour their appearance, which is always at night: full moon, storm, fog, and so on. Now ship-wreckers from beyond the grave, they are capable of casting spells to lure in vessels and then destroy them or prevent them from sailing onward; they make men fall into the sea or cause fishermen to fall into their own nets.

Countless rituals have been developed by sailors in order to forearm themselves against these *yūrei*. Tattoos are a first line of defence; they are seen as protective divinities literally 'under the skin', capable of banishing all evil spirits, including *funayūrei*. Votive offerings are situated between superstition and magico-religious practice and are designed to win over the benevolence and leniency of angry spirits. They are placed on the front of the boat, on the sides of the hull, at the bottom of the hold or dropped in the sea foam on

leaving port. They include flowers, incense, ashes, adzuki beans, and so on. Other sailors believe they can attract or repel the ghosts by smoking or casting large stones instead of an anchor.

Fear of these creatures has led to sailing being taboo on certain days, especially the last day of the year and during the August celebration of Obon, a festival commemorating the dead. It is best not to tempt the 'devil'.

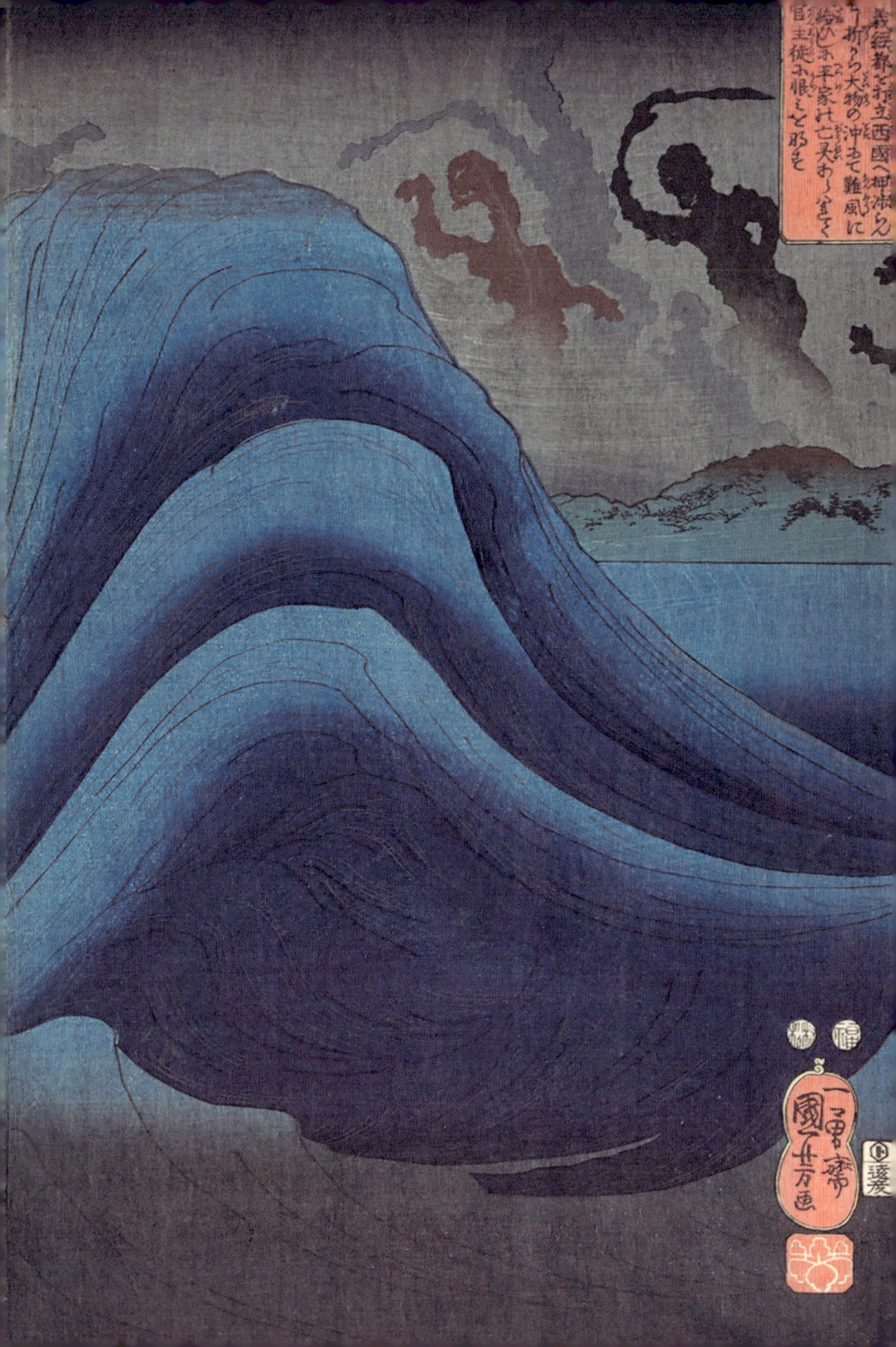

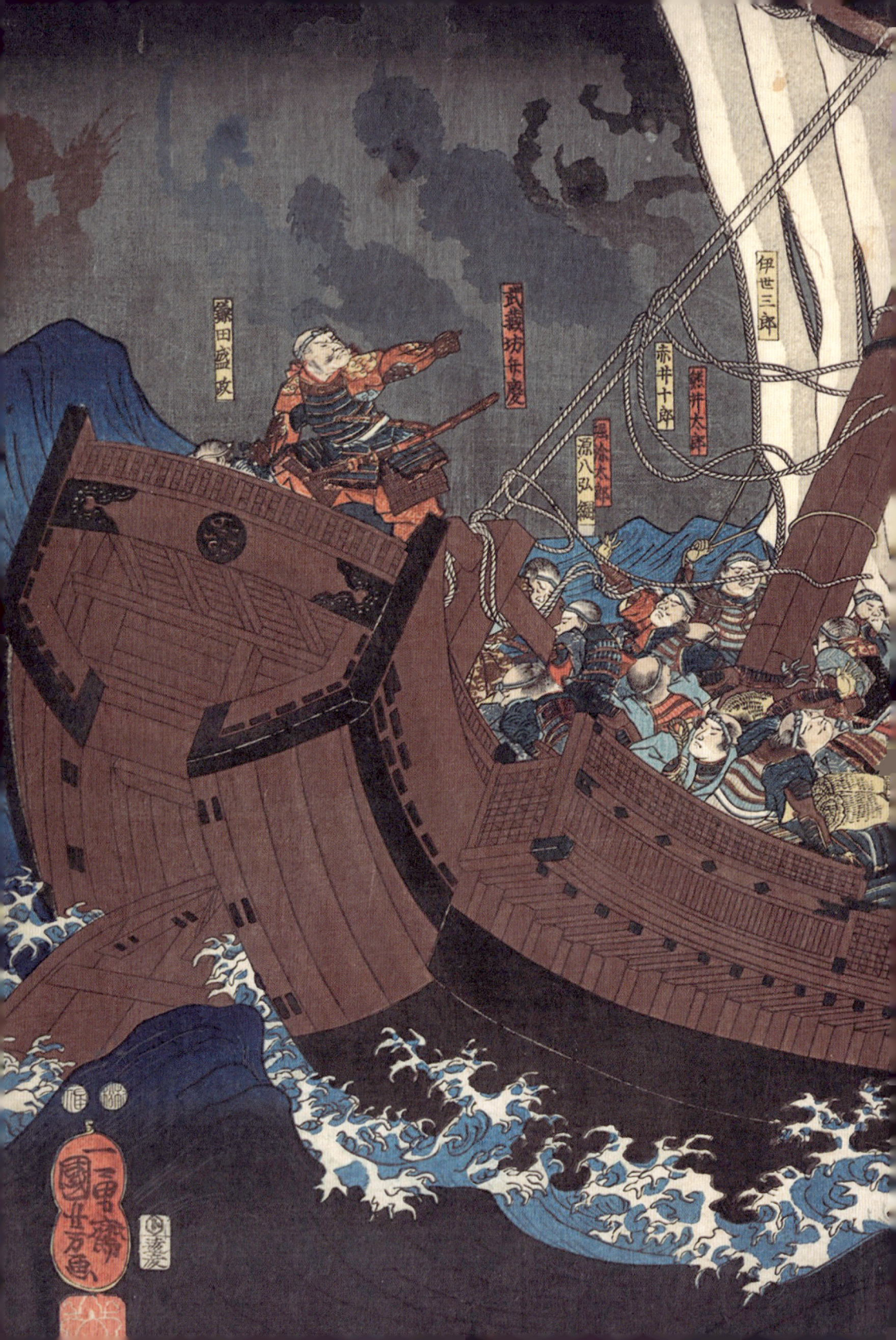

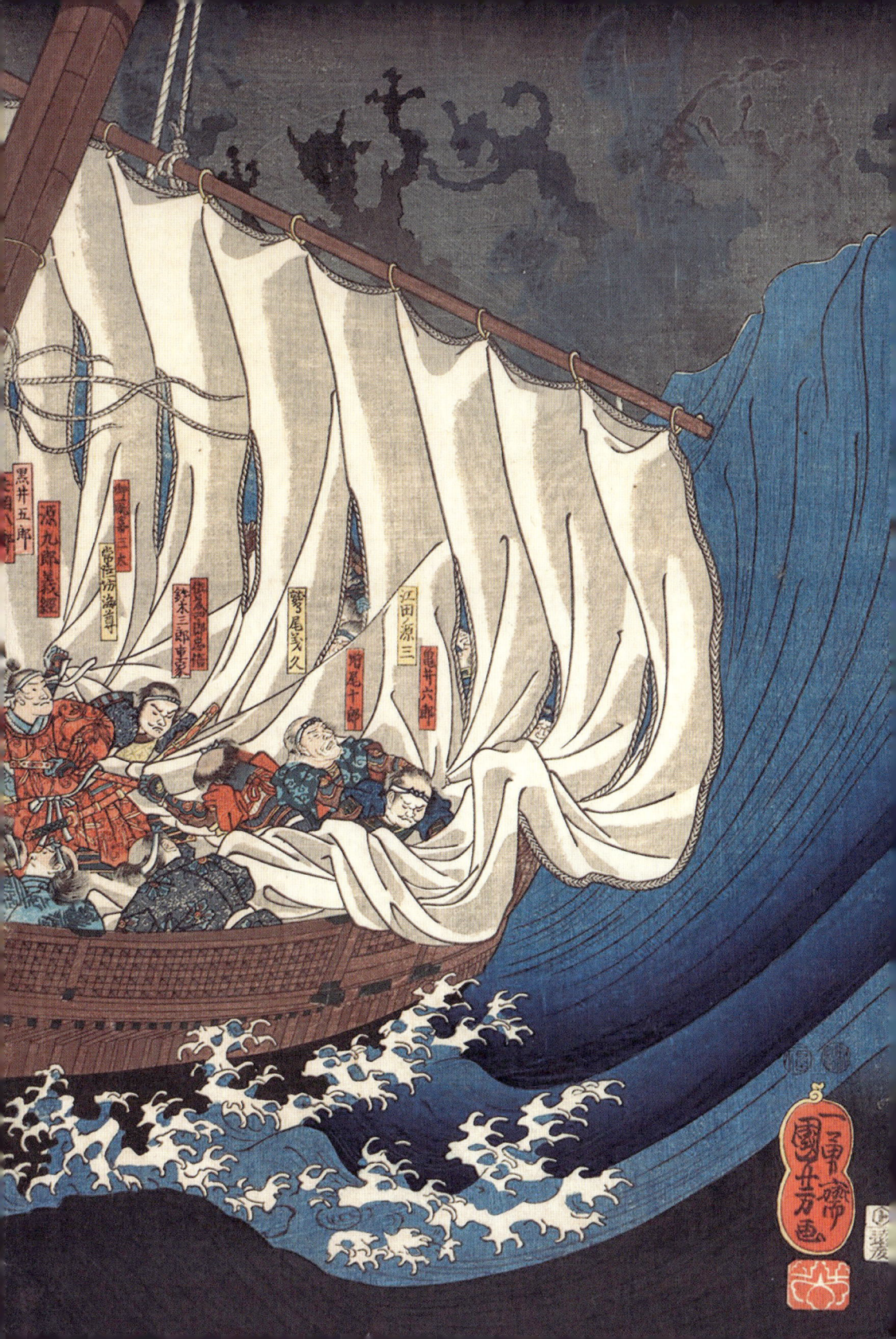

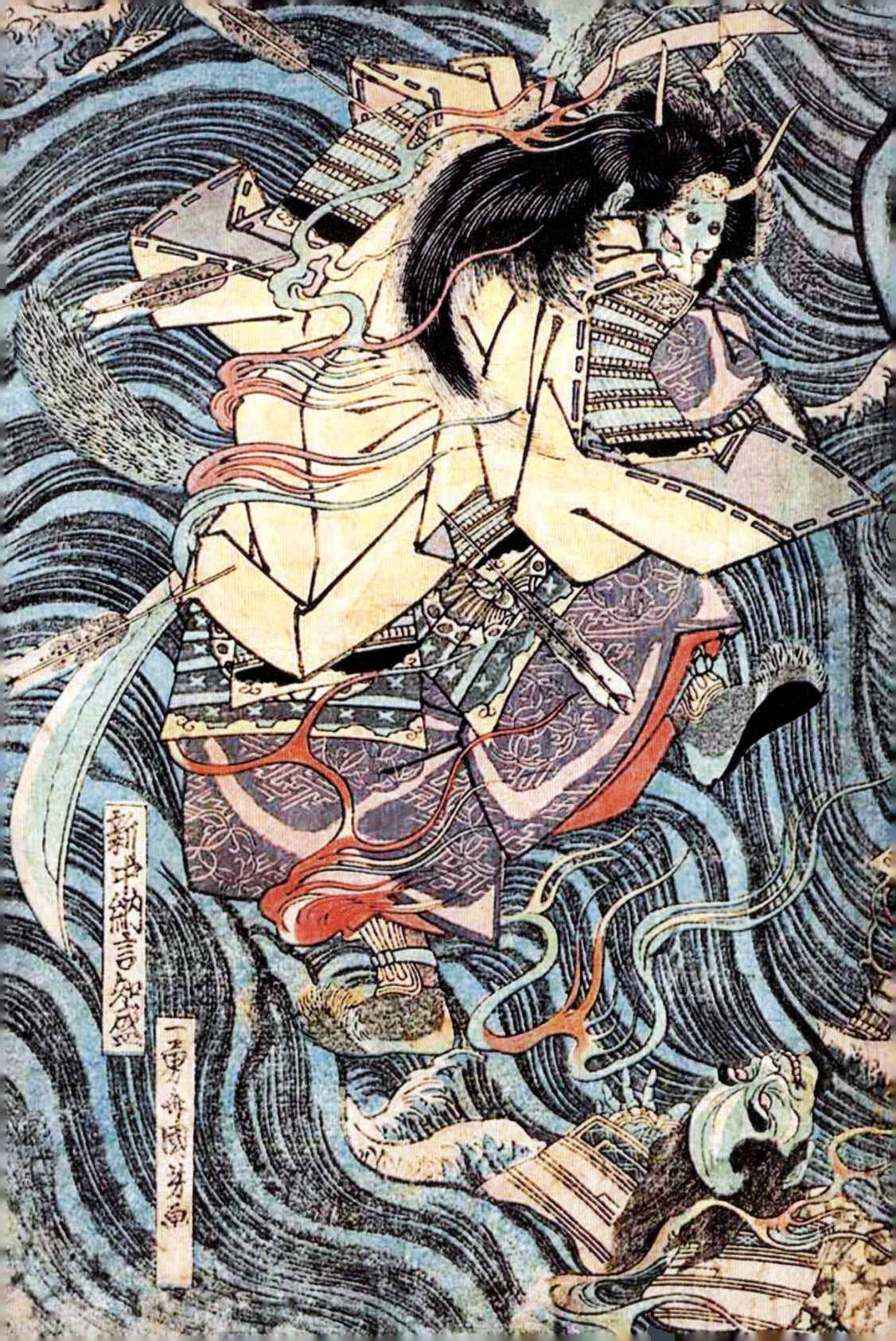

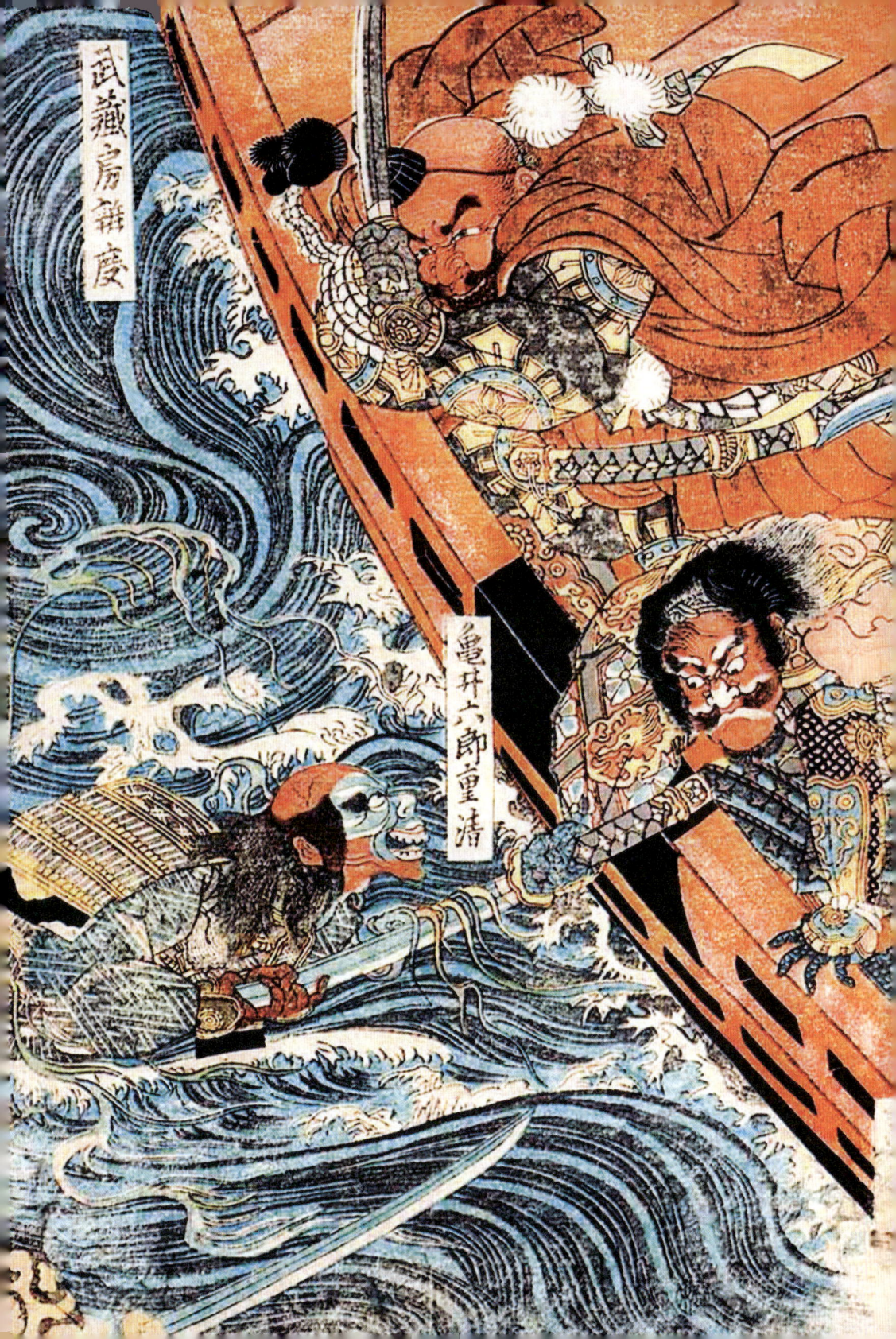

武藏房辨慶

龜井六郎重清

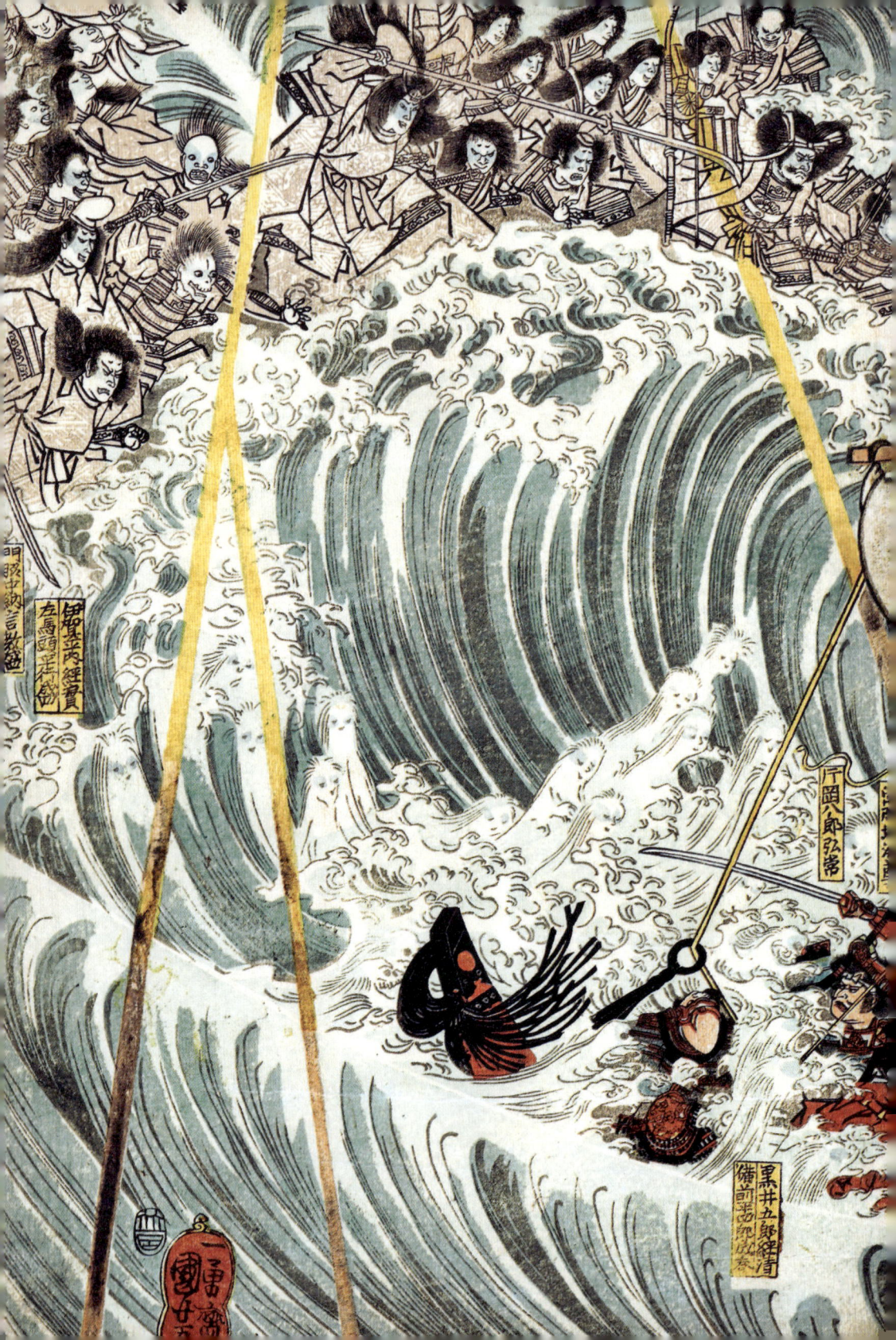

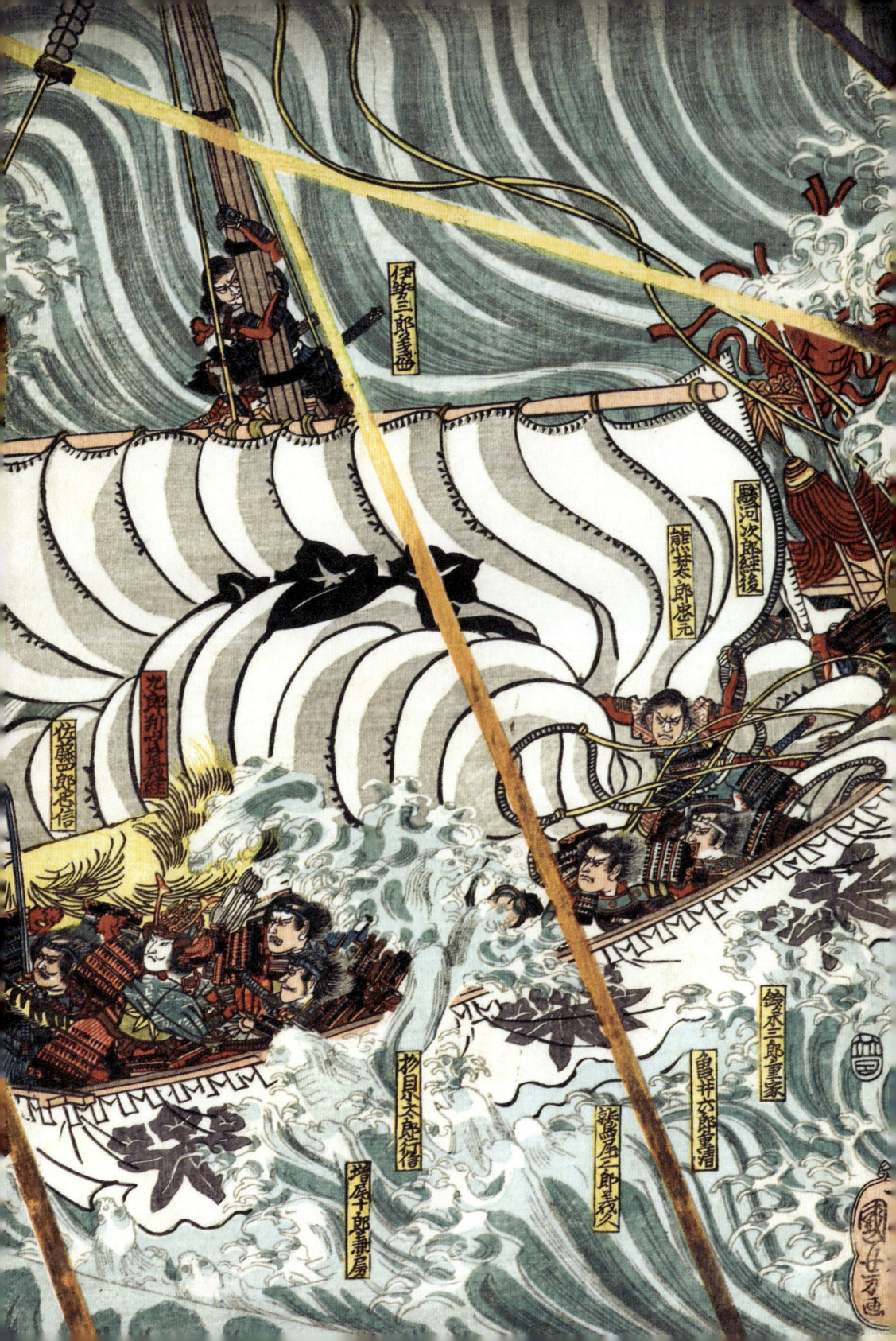

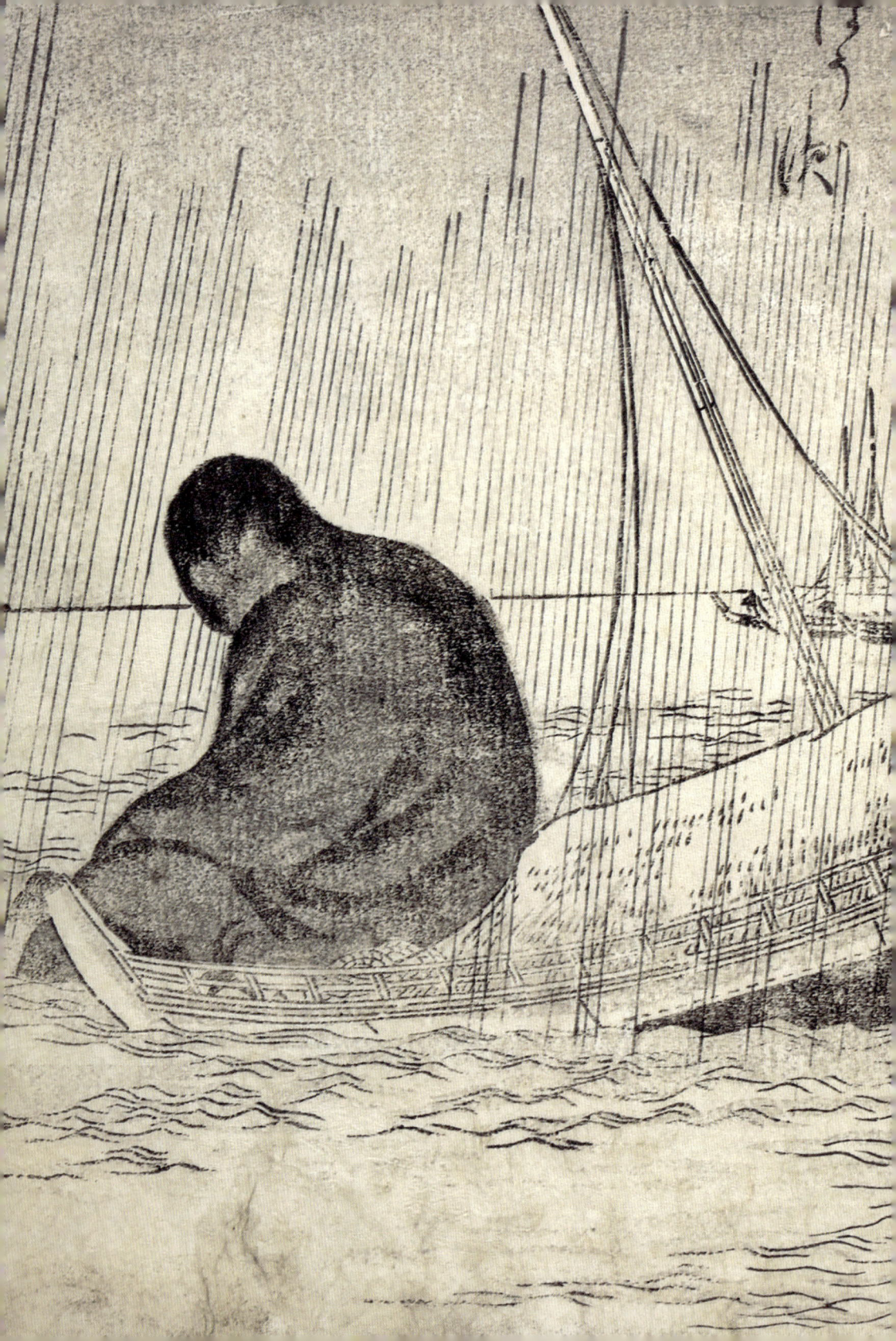

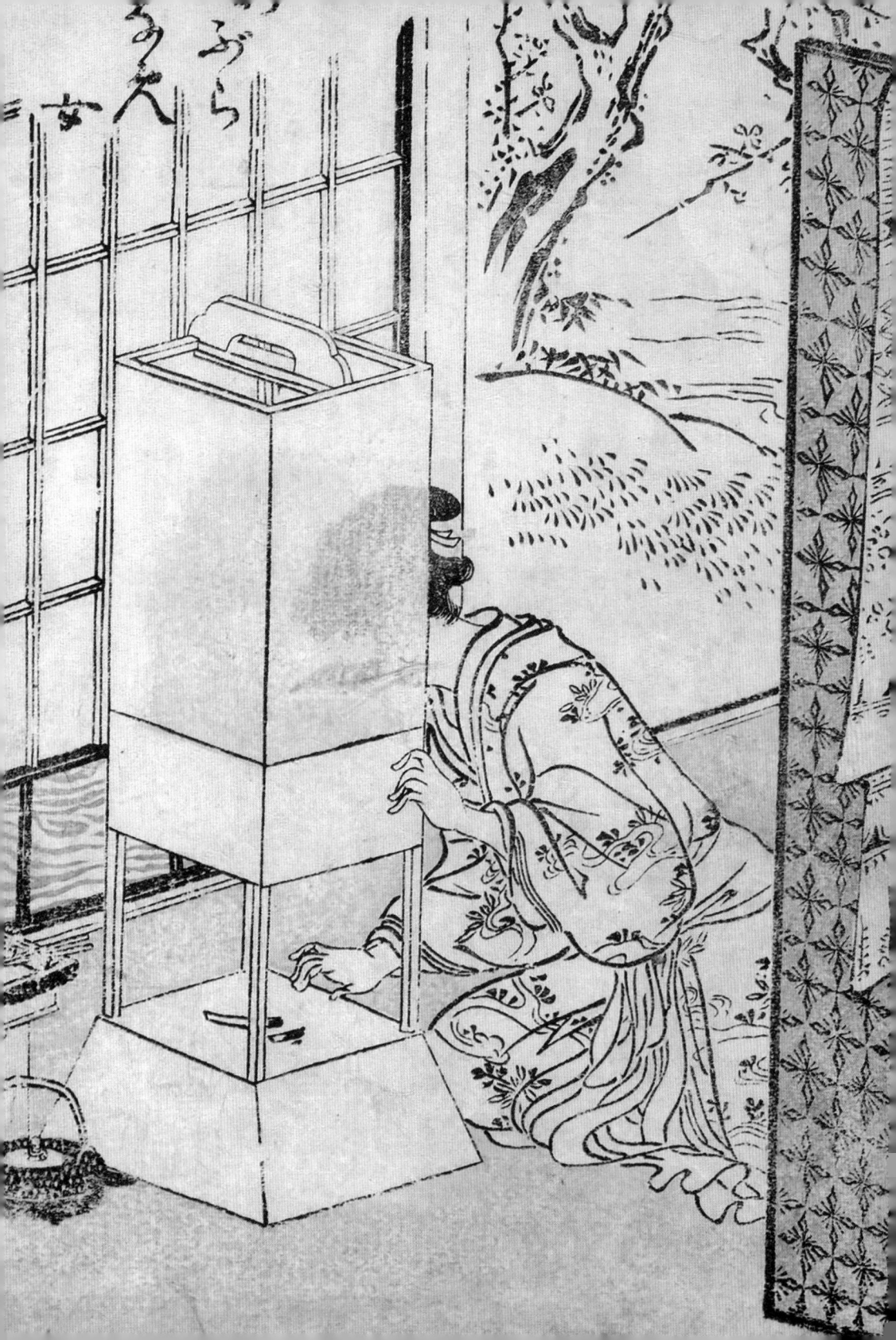

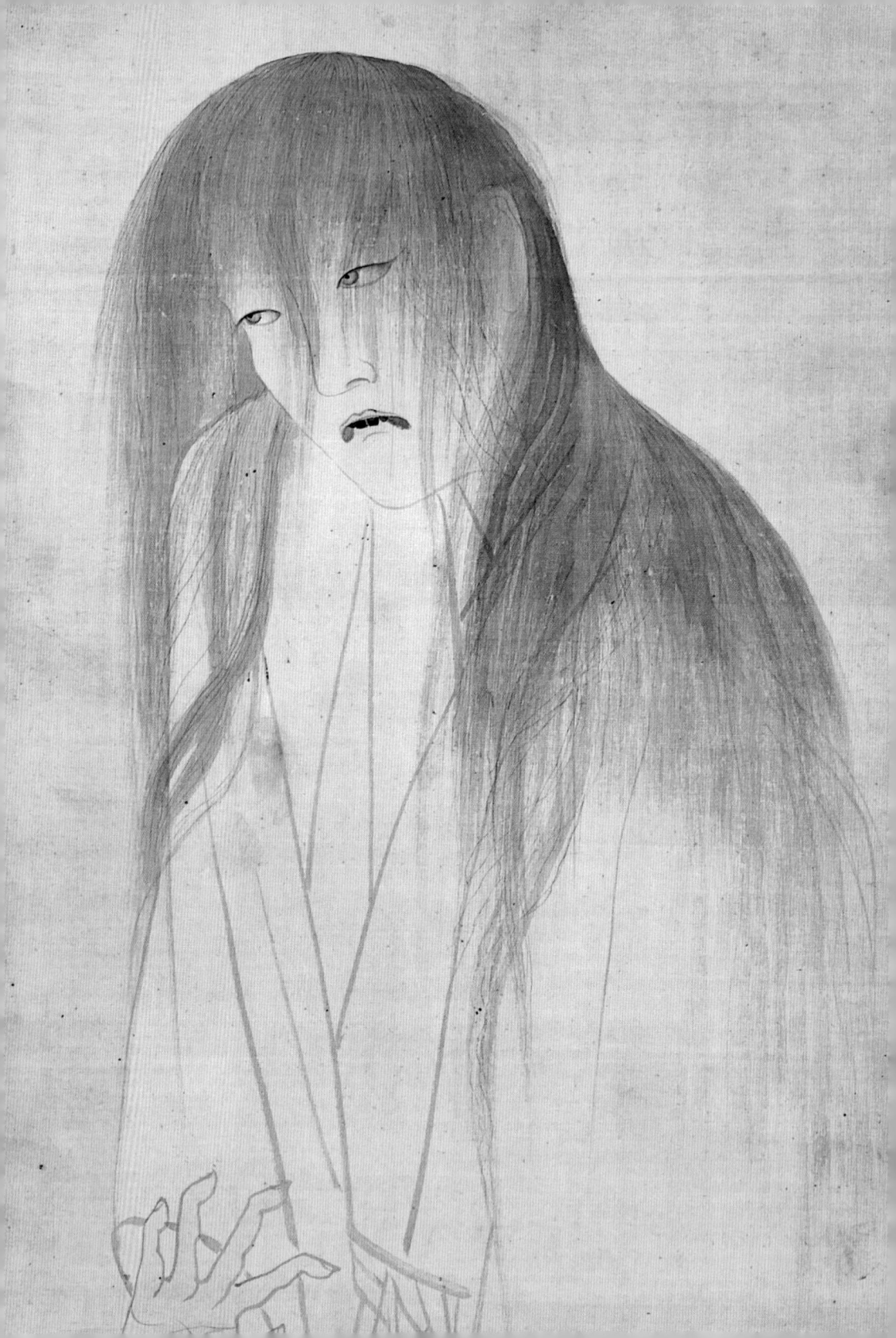

YUKI-ONNA

•

Yuki-onna is a phantom as pale as the snow and as white as death. Several legends surround this fabled creature who transforms into an icy tempest the moment she is touched or melts instantly when she plunges into a hot bath. Her skin is extremely cold and almost transparent. She is sometimes accompanied by a young child demanding cuddles from passers-by. When the child is picked up, it grows bigger and bigger until it ends up smothering the person who holds it, crushing and freezing them at the same time. Yuki-onna is dangerous. She breathes in the vitality (*seiki*) of the living; she tears out children's livers or sucks their energy by kissing them full on the mouth. She leads all who exchange a few words with her to a certain death. Her name and legend are invoked as a warning to young people against playing in the snow or near snowbound forests, for it is there that she prowls, awaiting her prey.

This *yūrei* is often represented carrying a child in her arms. Her lips are turned blue by the cold or she is surrounded by a snowstorm. Again, depending on the region of Japan where her story is told, several versions exist as to her origins. She can be a woman abandoned in a blizzard in the middle of winter, a wife murdered by her husband far from all civilisation, or a mountain spirit. If she crosses the path of the living, she asks them for water, 'no matter whether hot or cold'. Giving her cold water makes her grow (sometimes to a considerable size); giving her hot water makes her disappear in a whitish cloud or a fine rain. Sometimes, when seducing men, she kills them after lovemaking by chilling them to the bone.

Yuki-onna can be magnanimous, though. In one story, when a man has slept with her and is 'meant' to die, she spares his life on account of his great beauty and youth, and makes him promise not to say anything about their relations

99

on pain of seeing the curse come true. He keeps his word for many years until one day he admits to his wife that as a young man he made love with a ghost. His wife then reveals to him who she truly is: Yuki-onna herself! She 'pardons' him again, this time because of the child that they have together. She does not want to see the child become an orphan.

In other variations, Yuki-onna is a divinity who lives on the Moon, a place where she can give free rein to her lust. Eventually growing weary of her life of carnality, she contemplates Earth with curiosity from her sleeping-room windows. One night she travels on the winds of a snowstorm to Earth, where she is stranded. Ever after, at full moon, she appears to lost travellers at night, pointing with slender fingers to her palace above the clouds.

The most beautiful version is perhaps the one that was told in the very early twentieth century by Lafcadio Hearn, a writer who travelled widely and settled down in Japan. One winter evening, two woodcutters – elderly Mosaku and young Minokichi – are cut off in a forest by a snowstorm. At dusk, they take shelter in a cabin they have spotted in the mountains. During the night, Minokichi wakes up and sees a gorgeous woman. She is entirely white and seems to be flying through the air. She approaches his old companion and breathes into his face. A second later, he is dead and frozen. Minokichi, frightened and half-asleep, then sees the 'White Woman' turn towards him and draw another breath to kill him, too. But she changes her mind and murmurs in his ear: 'I intended to treat you like the other man. But I cannot help feeling some pity for you, – because you are so young. . . . You are a pretty boy, Minokichi; and I will not hurt you now. But, if you ever tell anybody – even your own mother – about what you have seen this night, I shall know it; and then I will kill you. . . . Remember what I say!' Minokichi promises and survives.

Years later, he meets a woman with very light skin who is called Oyuki ('the snow-woman'). They get married and have many children. Theirs is a loving home, but Minokichi is puzzled by

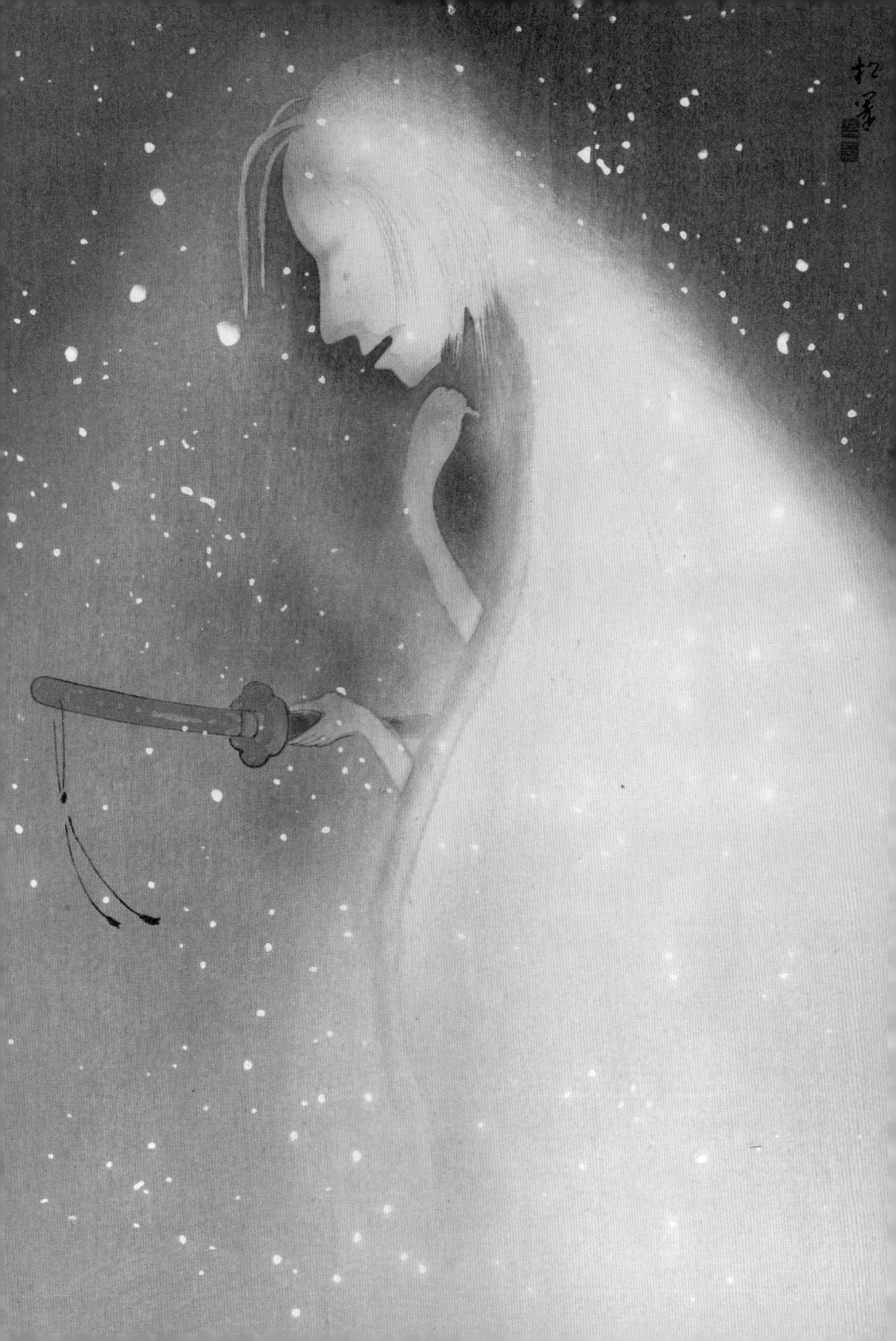

something: his wife is not aging. One evening, when he is tired or has had too much to drink, he begins to confess the events of his past and recalls the 'White Woman' who spared his life. He barely finishes speaking before Oyuki reveals to him her true identity: she is Yuki-onna, a fantastical bringer of death and disaster, but also a compassionate creature. Because she has borne his children, and because she loves him, she spares him a second time but disappears for ever in a cloud of icy mist.

How many legends, variations, details we have here! Sometimes the tales clash, and they vary according to their region of origin. A rich folkloric magico-religious tradition informs each of these *yūrei* figures. This diversity is a testament to the vividness of people's belief in the mysterious *yūrei* and *yōkai*, which are often overlayered and conflated.

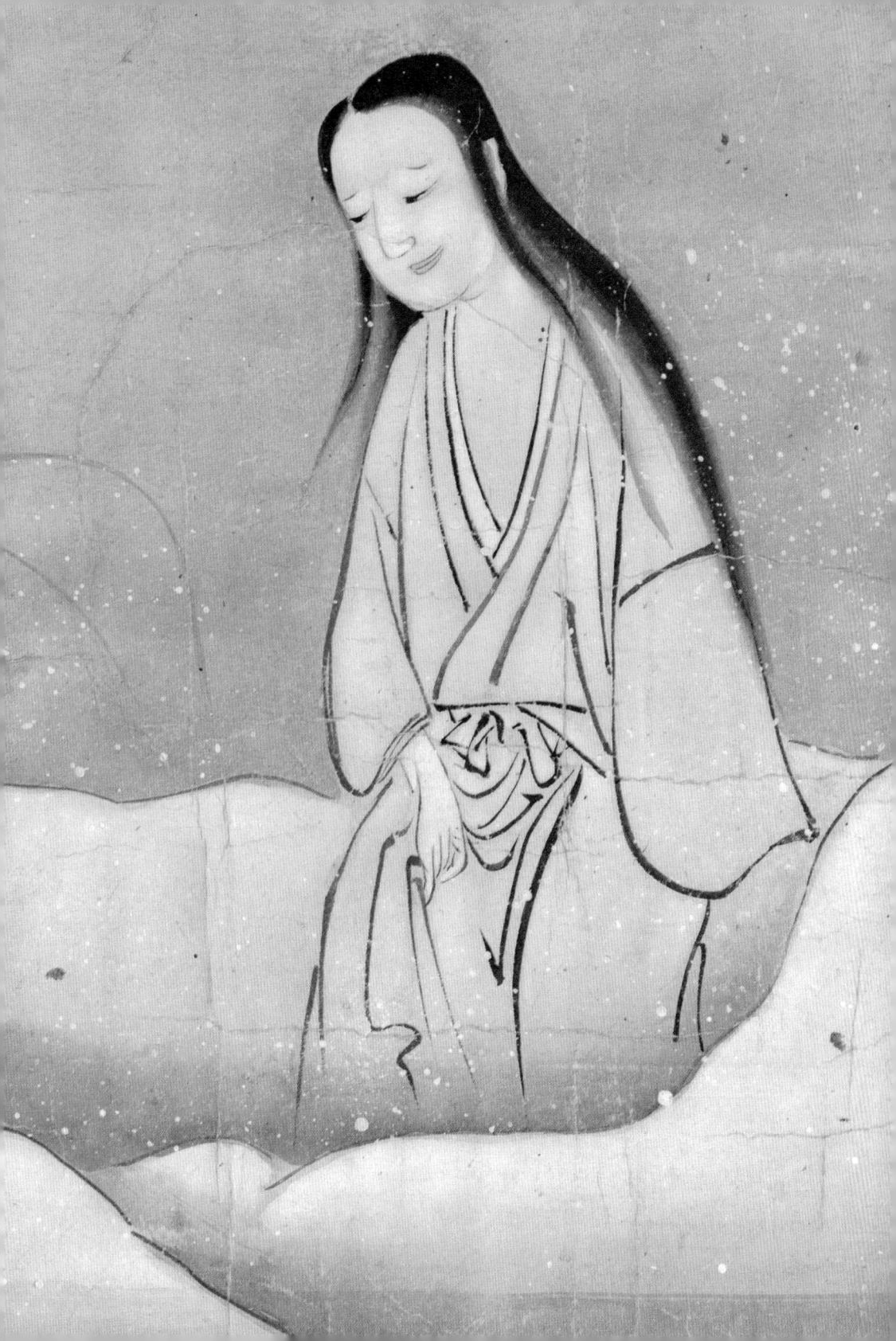

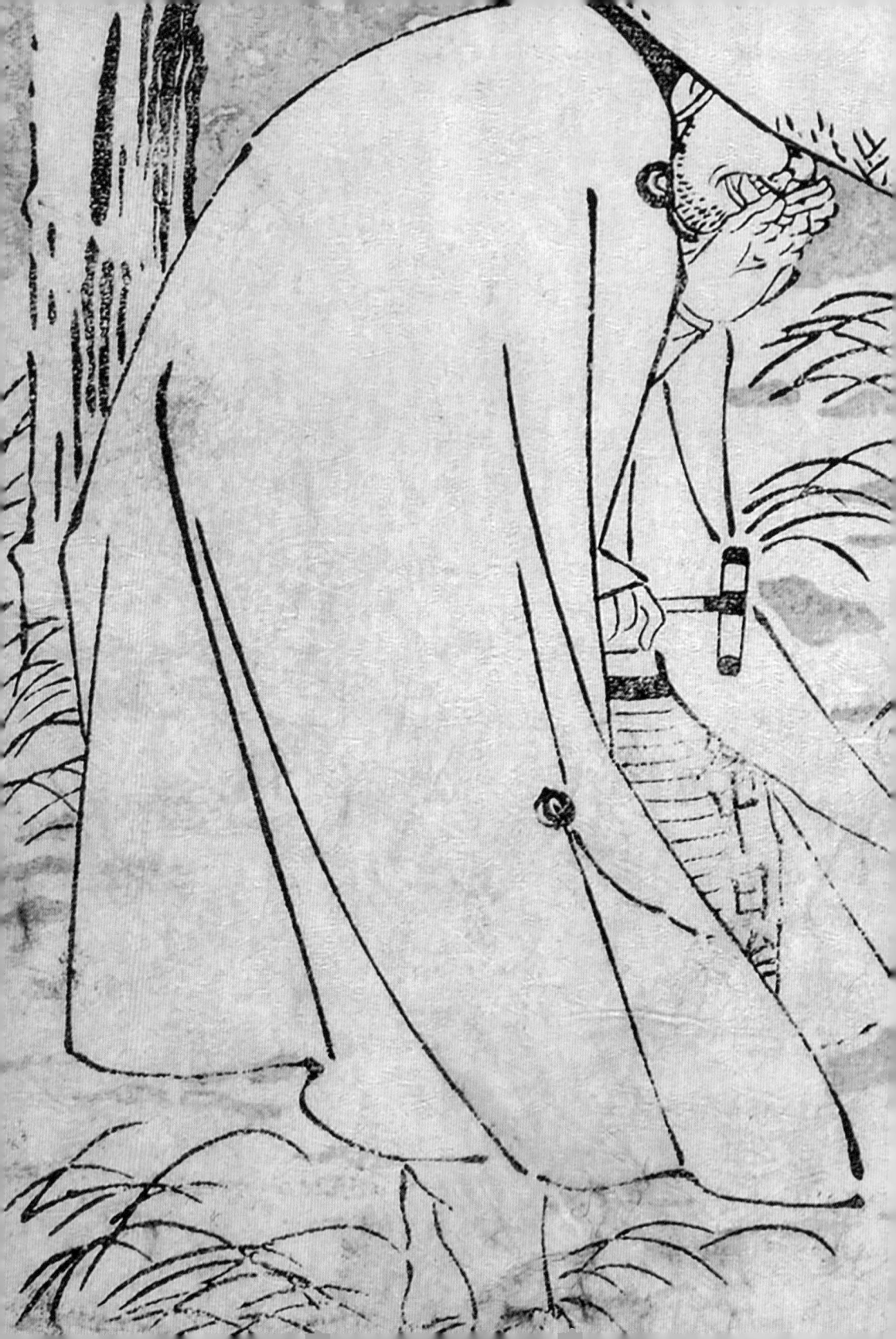

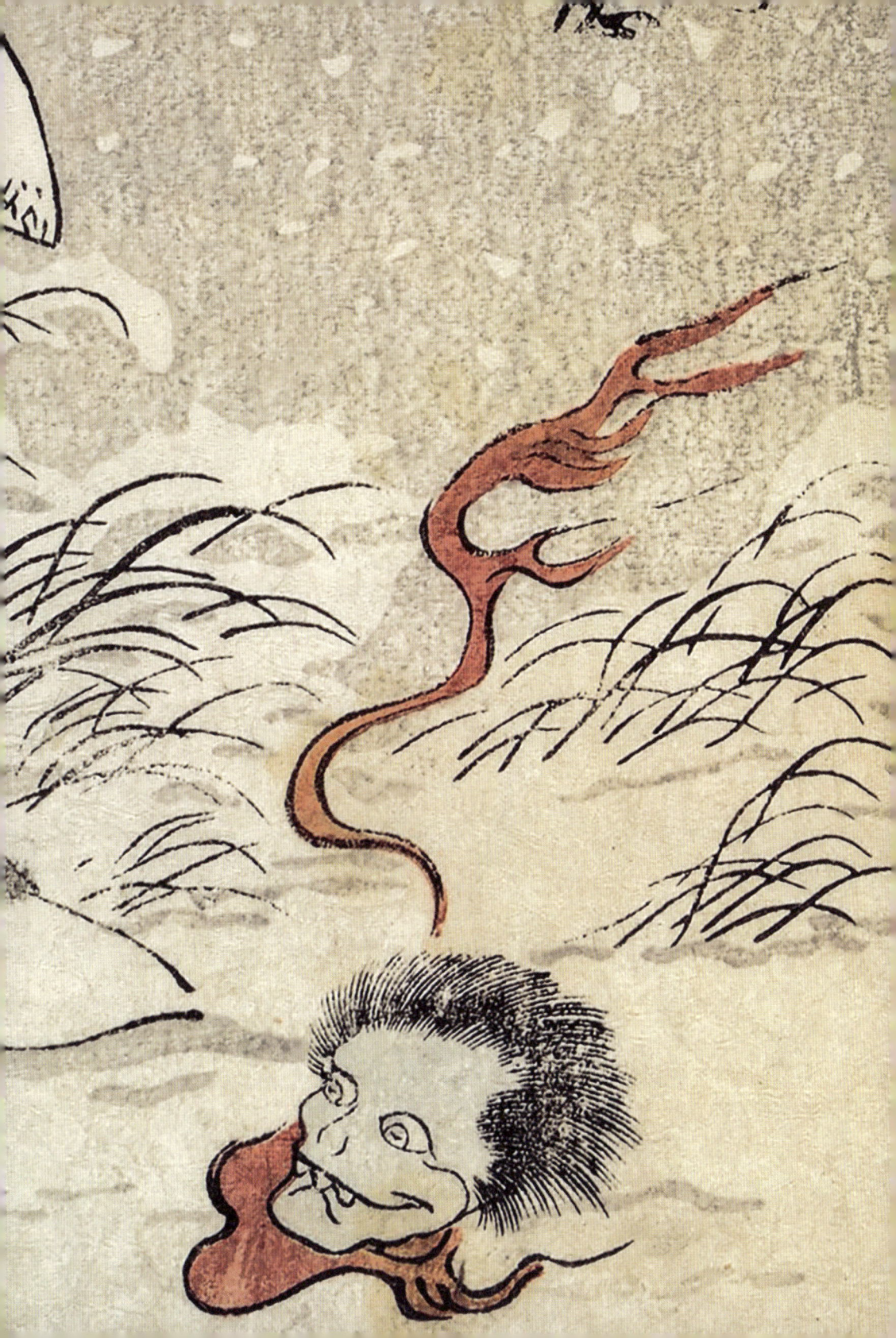

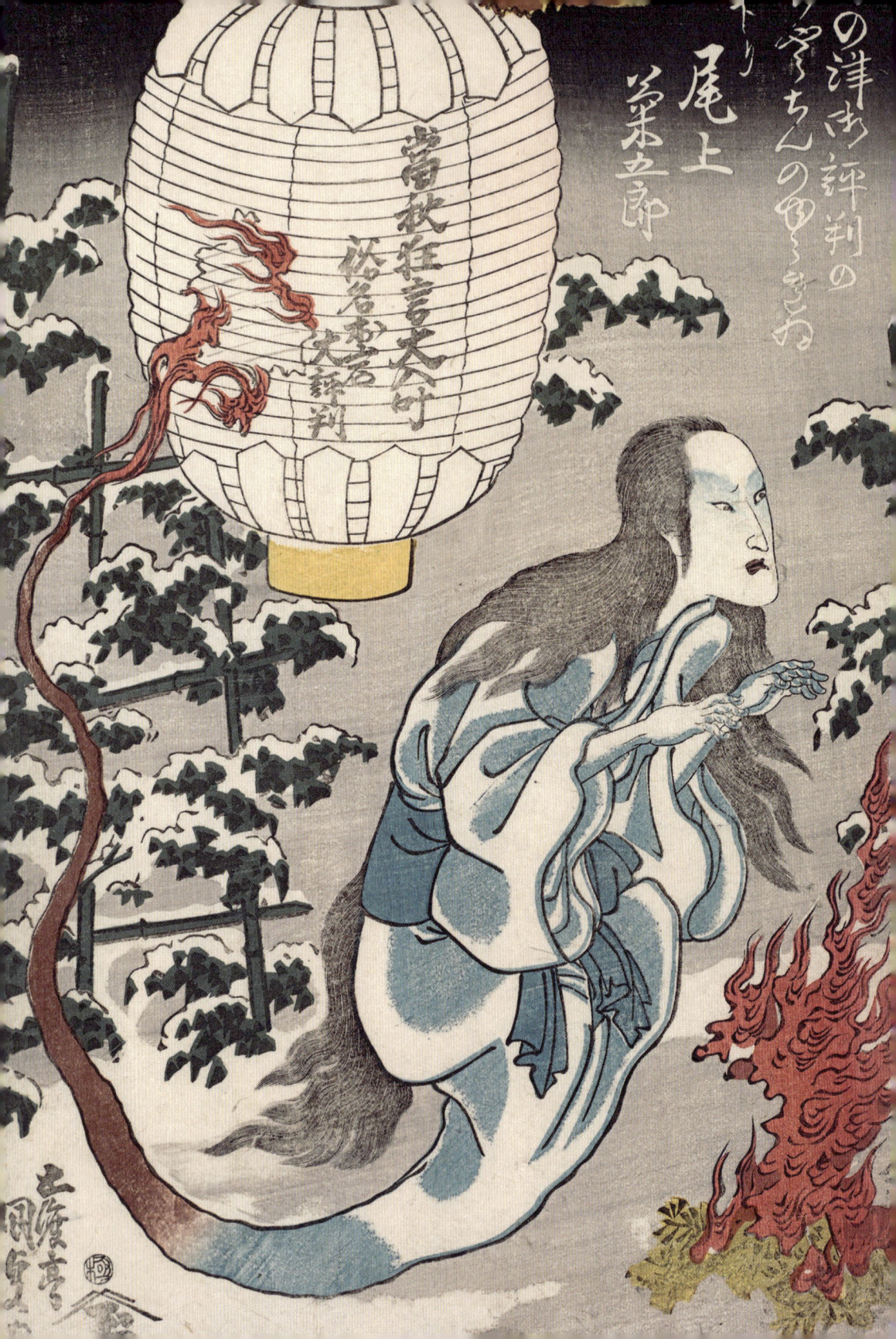

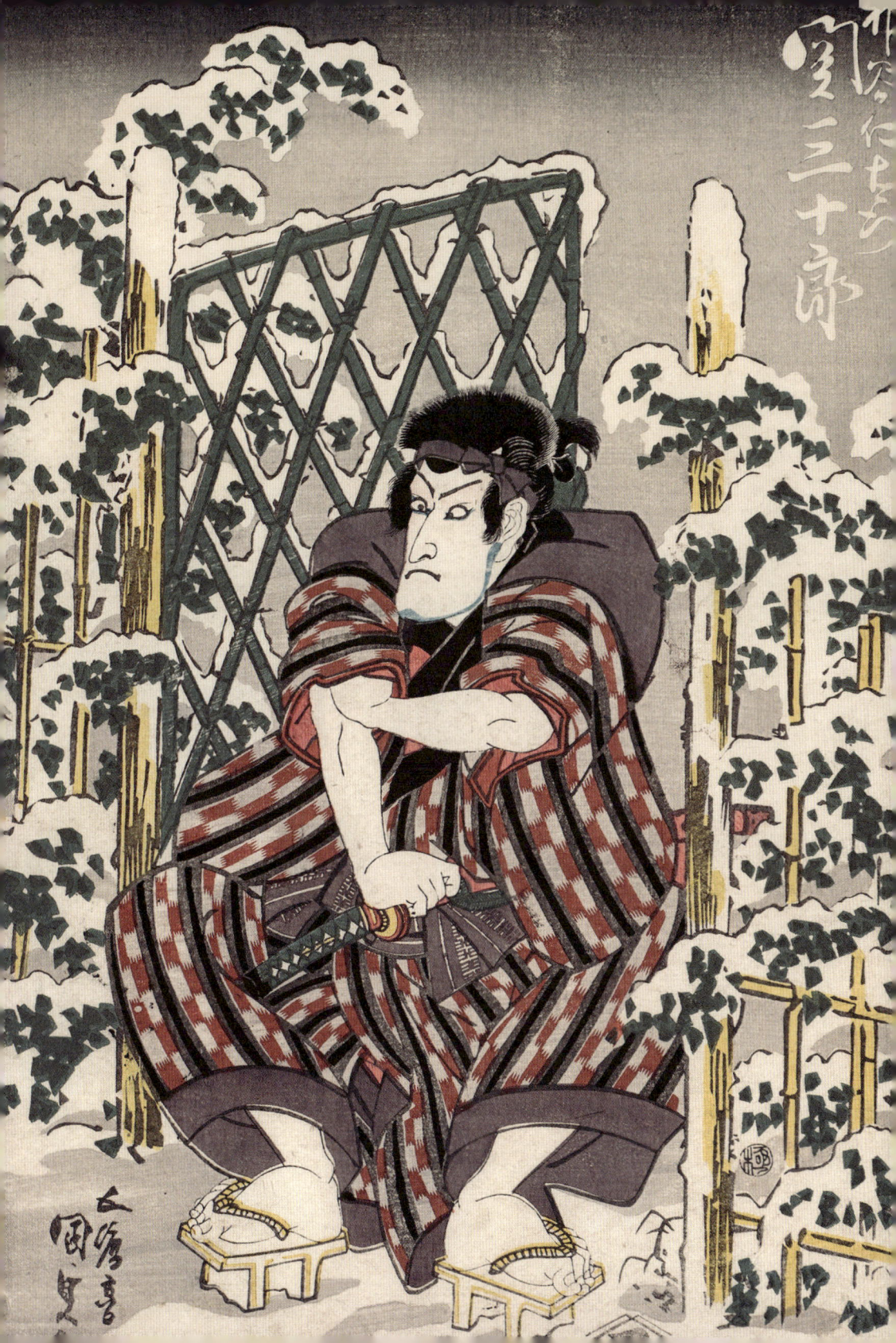

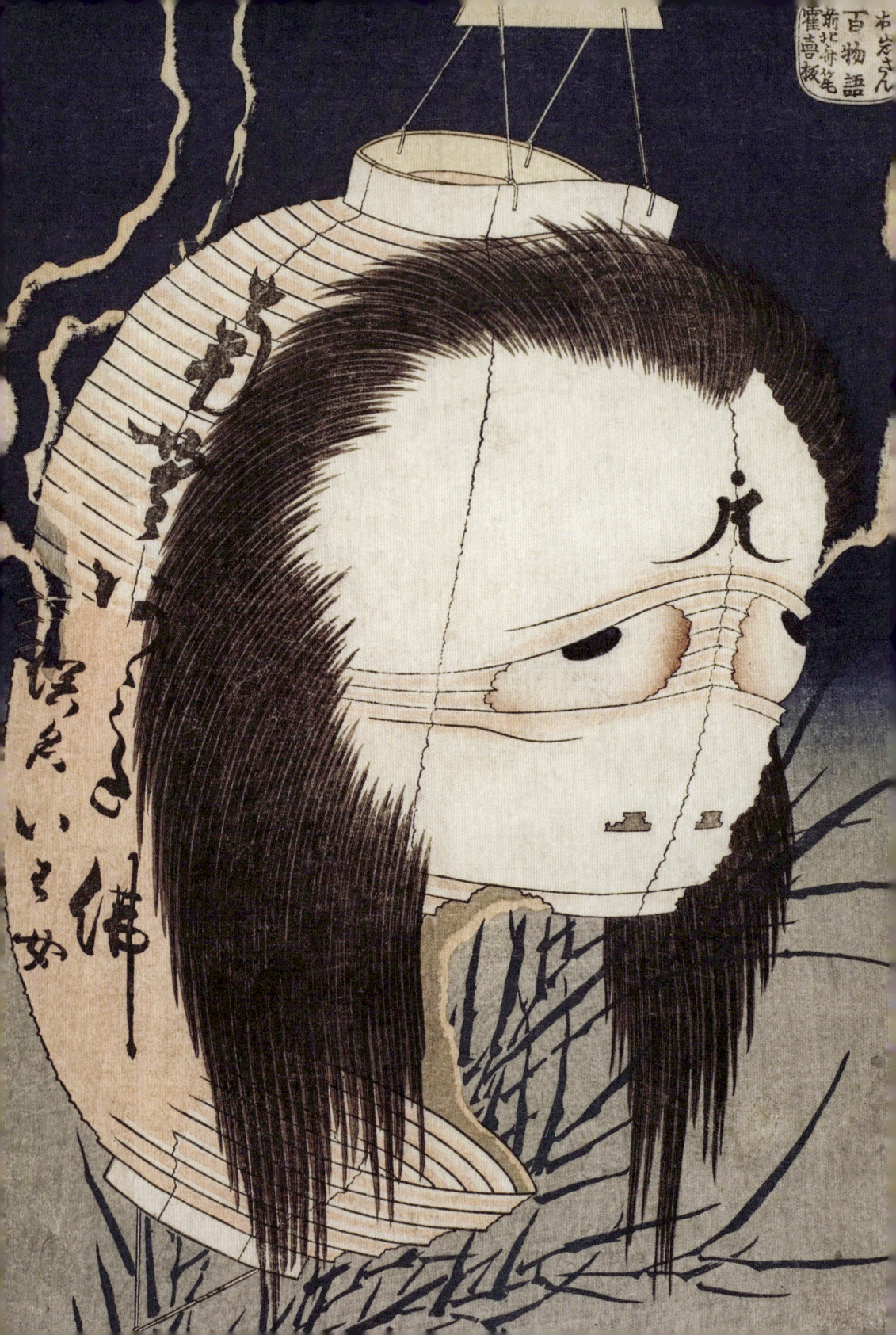

OIWA, THE FACE OF DEATH

•

It was in July 1825, in a long Kabuki play named *Yotsuya kaidan*, that the figure of Oiwa, probably Japan's most famous *yūrei*, first appeared. Her image has featured in all art forms since. The story is one of abandonment, betrayal, death and vengeance. It takes place in the seventeenth century, if the record of her death in Myogyo-ji temple, near Tokyo, on 22 February 1636, is to be believed. Tamiya Iemon, a mercenary (*ronin*), wants to separate from his wife Oiwa so he can be with his lover Oume. Jealous of Oiwa's beauty, Oume sends her poisoned face cream. When Oiwa uses it, she feels a searing pain; her skin burns terribly and her flesh begins to putrefy, taking on a blue-green colour. Slowly, she starts to die, but the process is not quick enough for her husband, who sends one of his men, Takuetsu, to rape her – a dishonour that would give him grounds for rejecting her. However, her face is so hideously disfigured that Takuetsu cannot bear to touch her; to finish her off, he contents himself instead with holding up a mirror to her. Mad with rage, she grabs a sword and begins to run wildly, threatening all who come near her. Takuetsu tries to calm her but in her attempt to escape from him, she accidentally slits her throat. She dies in a pool of blood on the floor of her own house, but not before casting a final curse upon her husband Iemon. From that point on, she appears to him over and over, haunting and harrying him to death. In Katsushika Hokusai's print, we see the ronin Iemon desperately drawing his sword in front of his wife's spectre as it emerges from a gigantic lantern.

In the centuries that followed, Oiwa came to embody the wife betrayed by her husband, the vengeful ghost that attacks bad men and restores justice to all abandoned women. To recognise her among the many *yūrei*, we need only note her left eye, melted or deformed by the poison, the bluish or greenish colour of her decomposed face and the patches of bare skin on her head where the poison caused her hair to fall out. In the Kabuki play, we see Oiwa shortly after she applies the fatal cream. In dramatic contrast to intensely erotic scenes of a courtesan smoothing her long hair, she is later shown alone before a mirror, pitifully pulling out clumps with her comb until an immense pile builds up on the stage.

This is a dangerous role to play, and actors are advised, given the risk of accident or sudden death, to first ask the *yūrei*'s permission by going to bow before Oiwa's grave in Myogyo-ji temple.

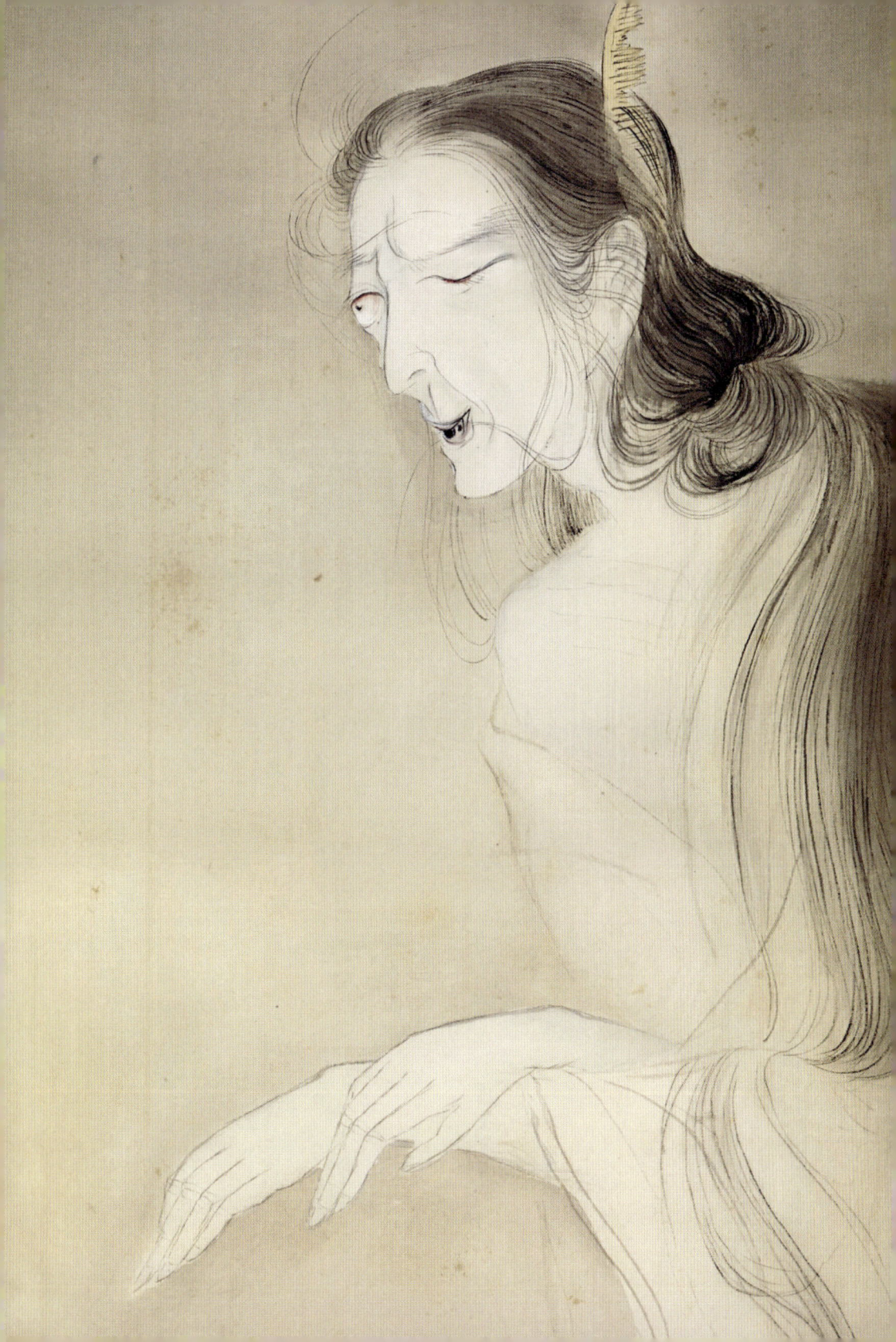

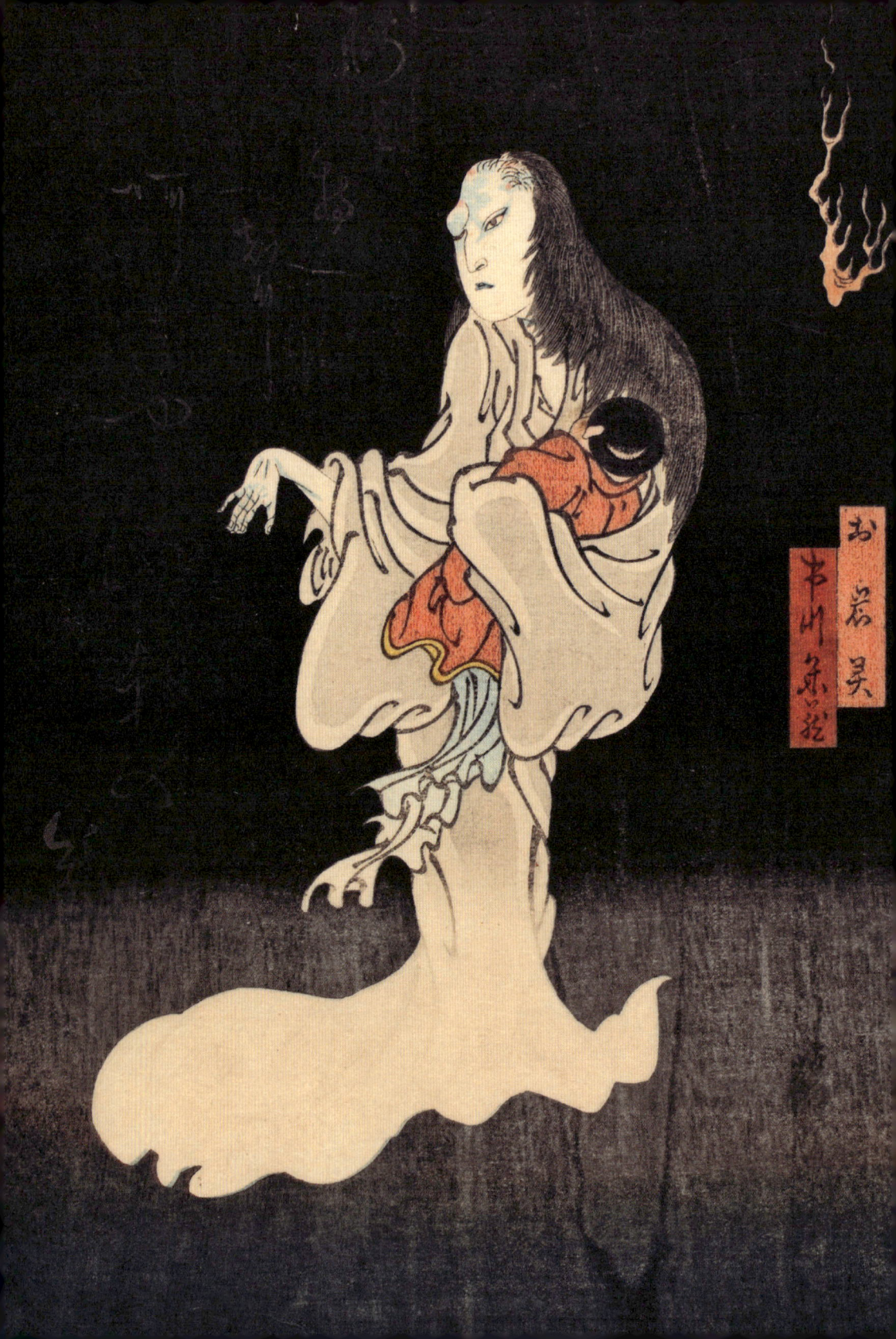

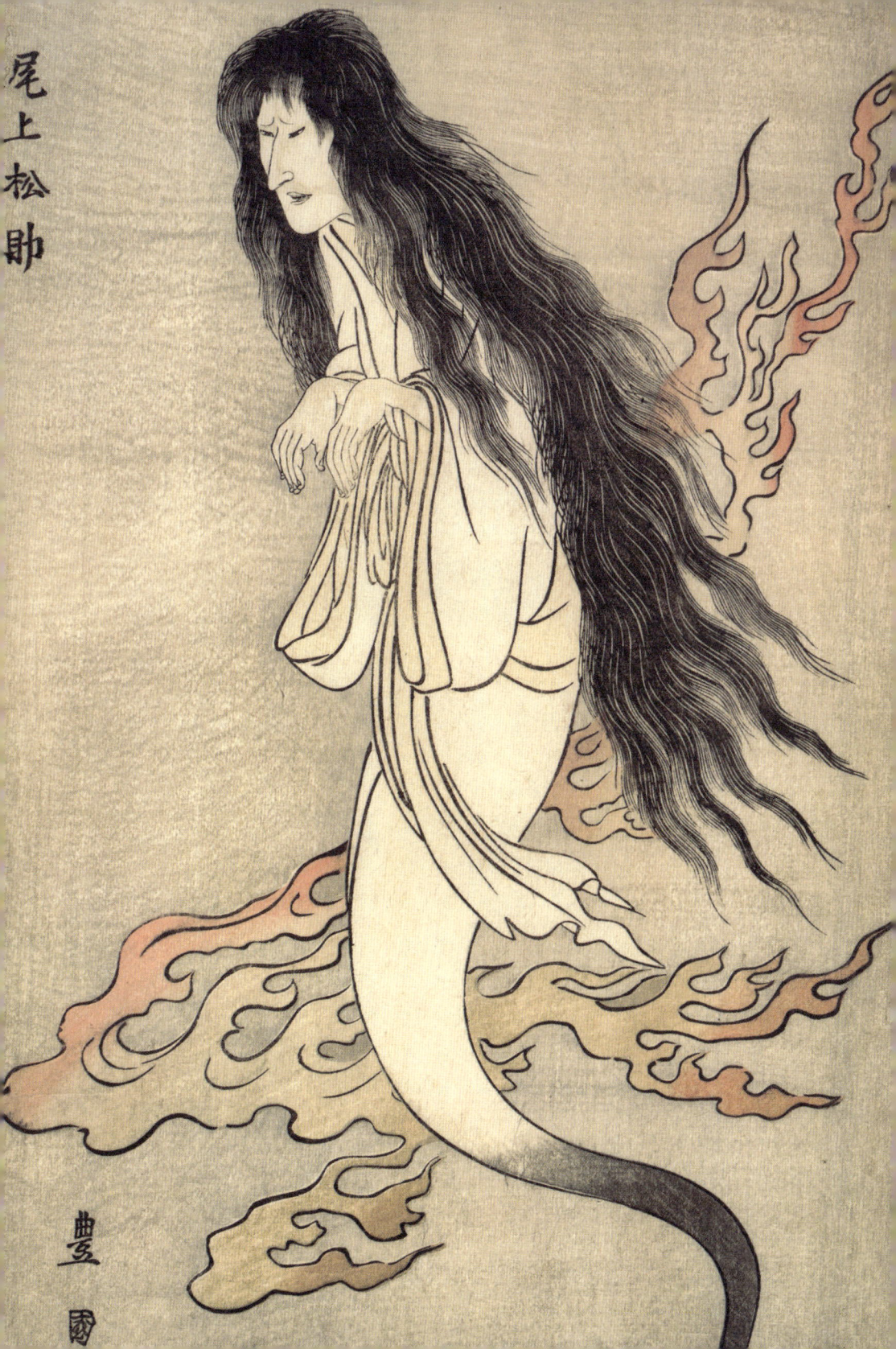

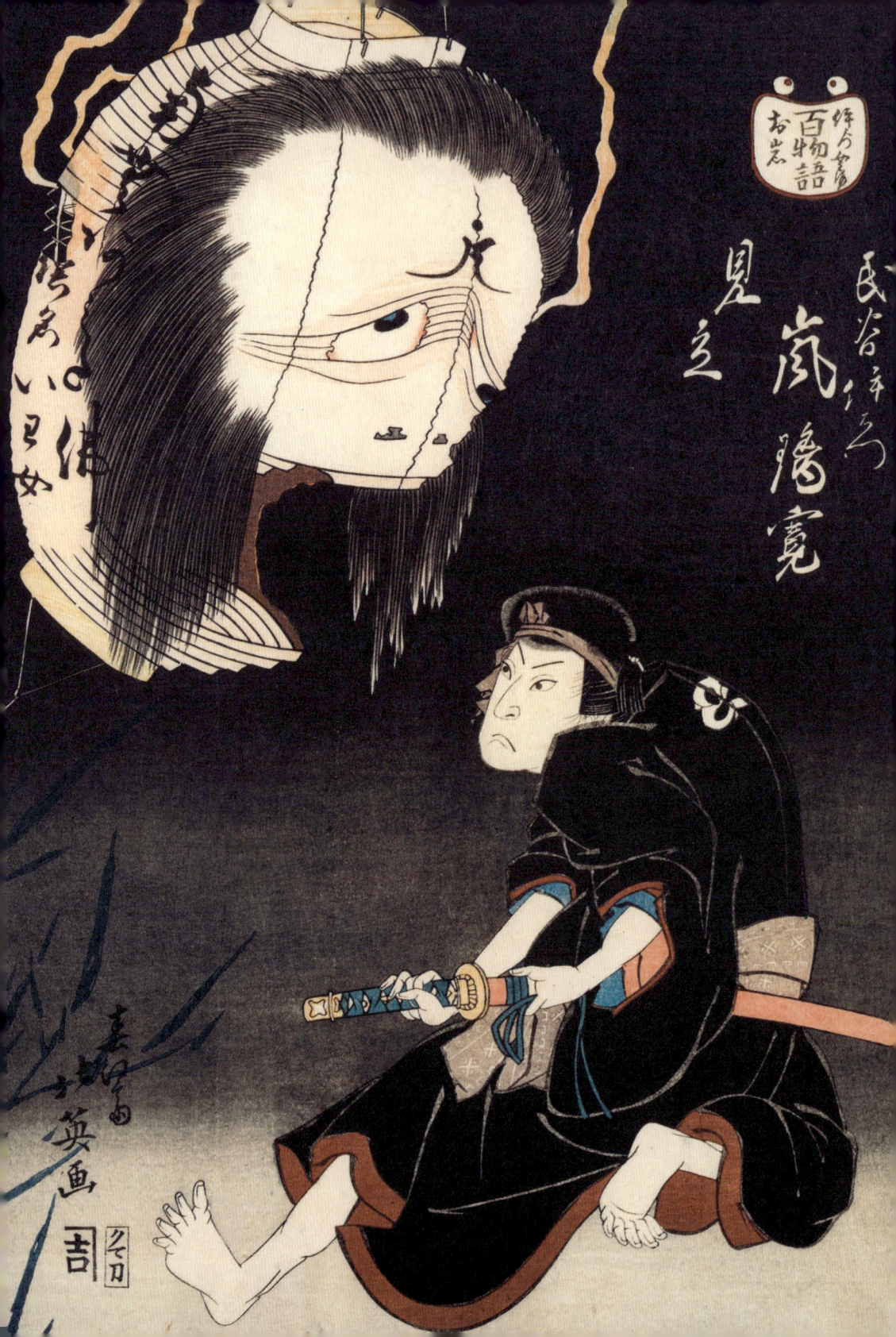

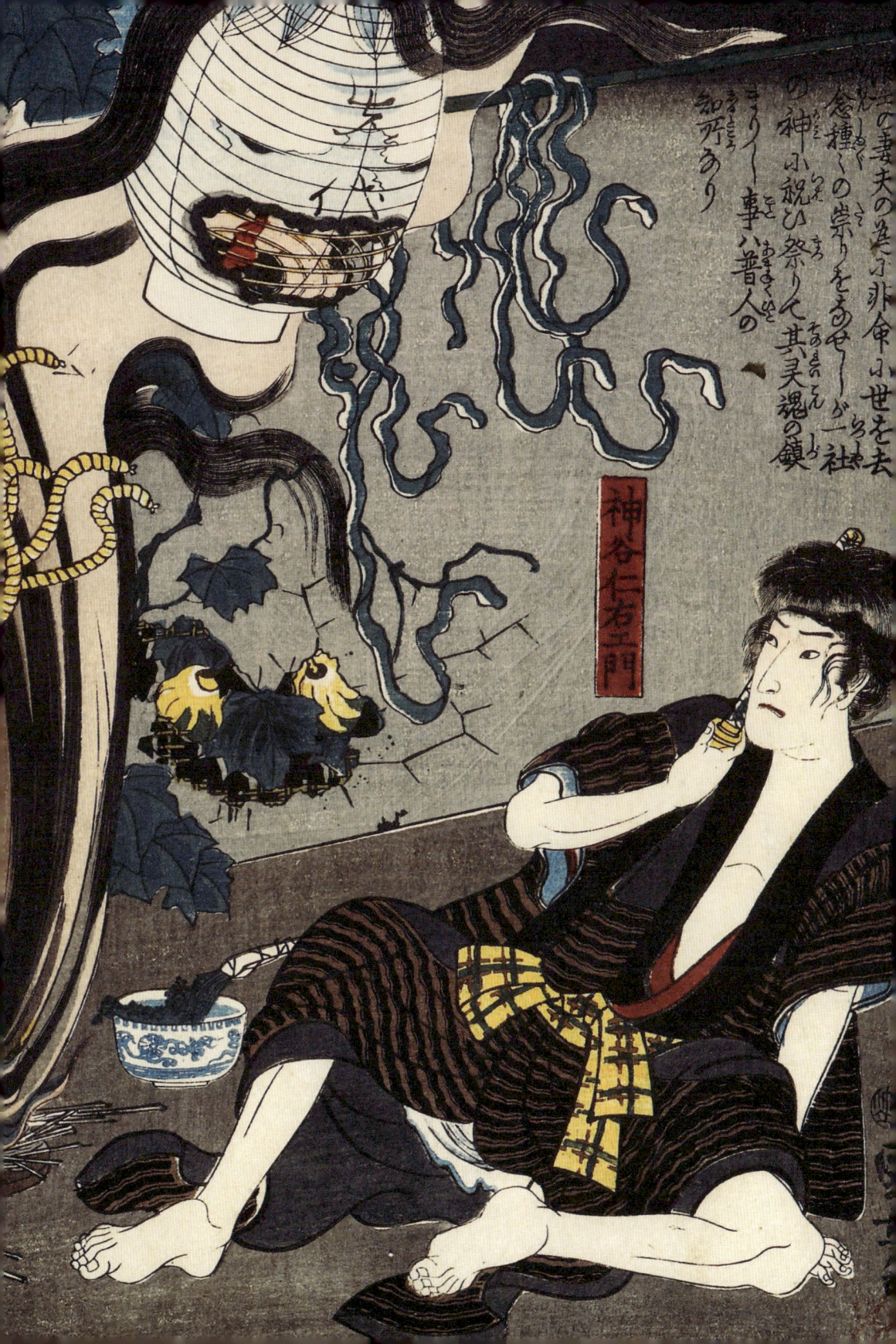

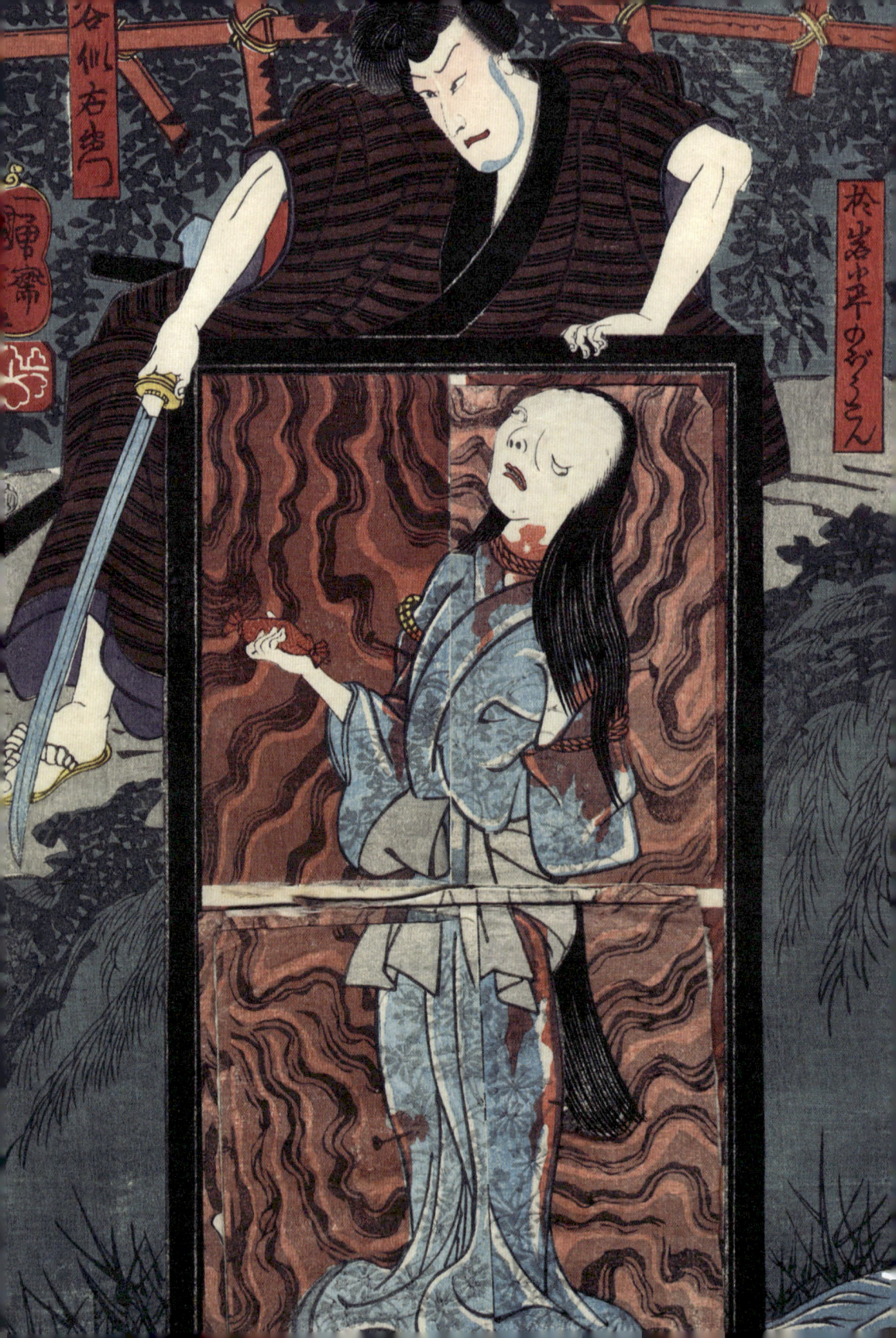

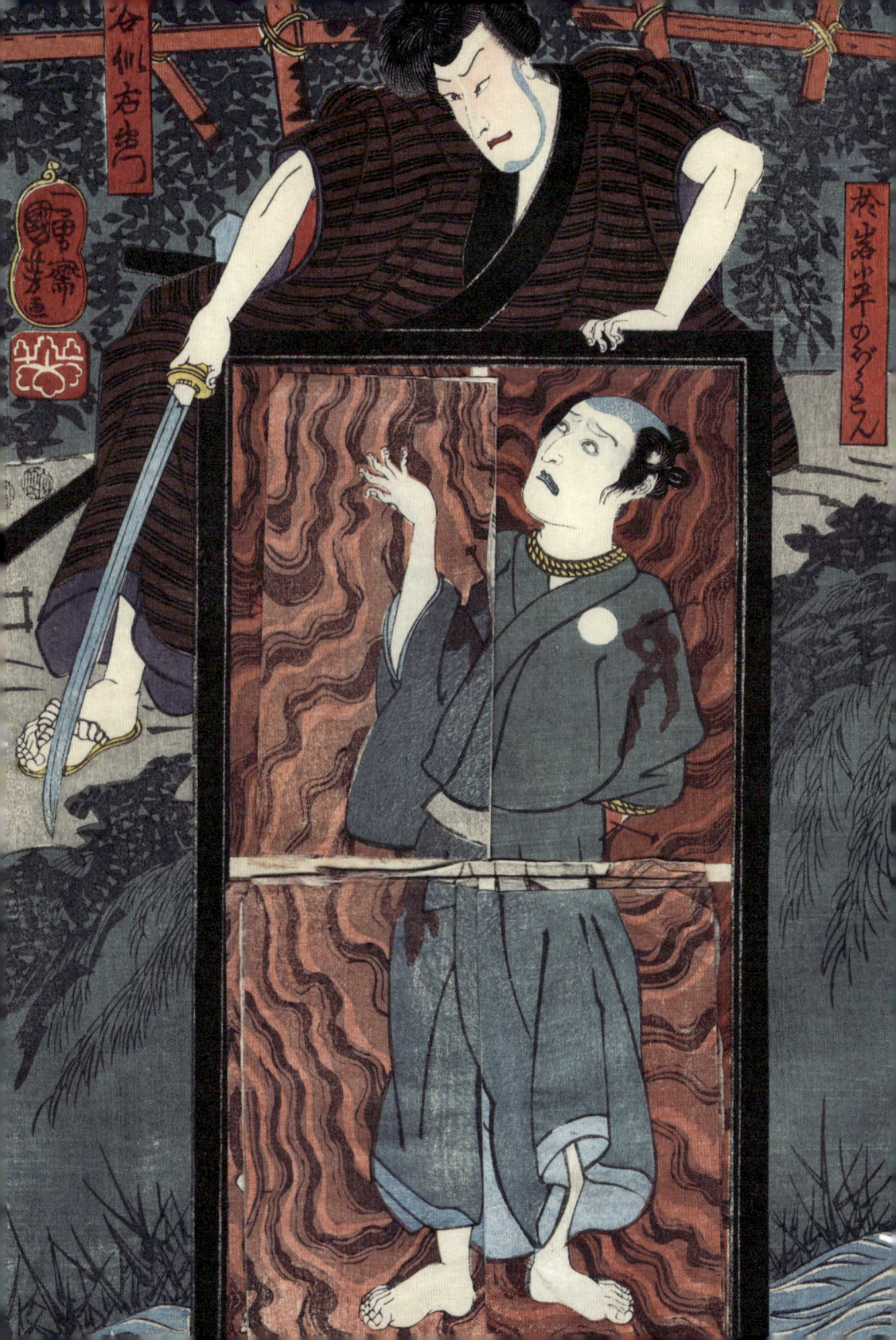

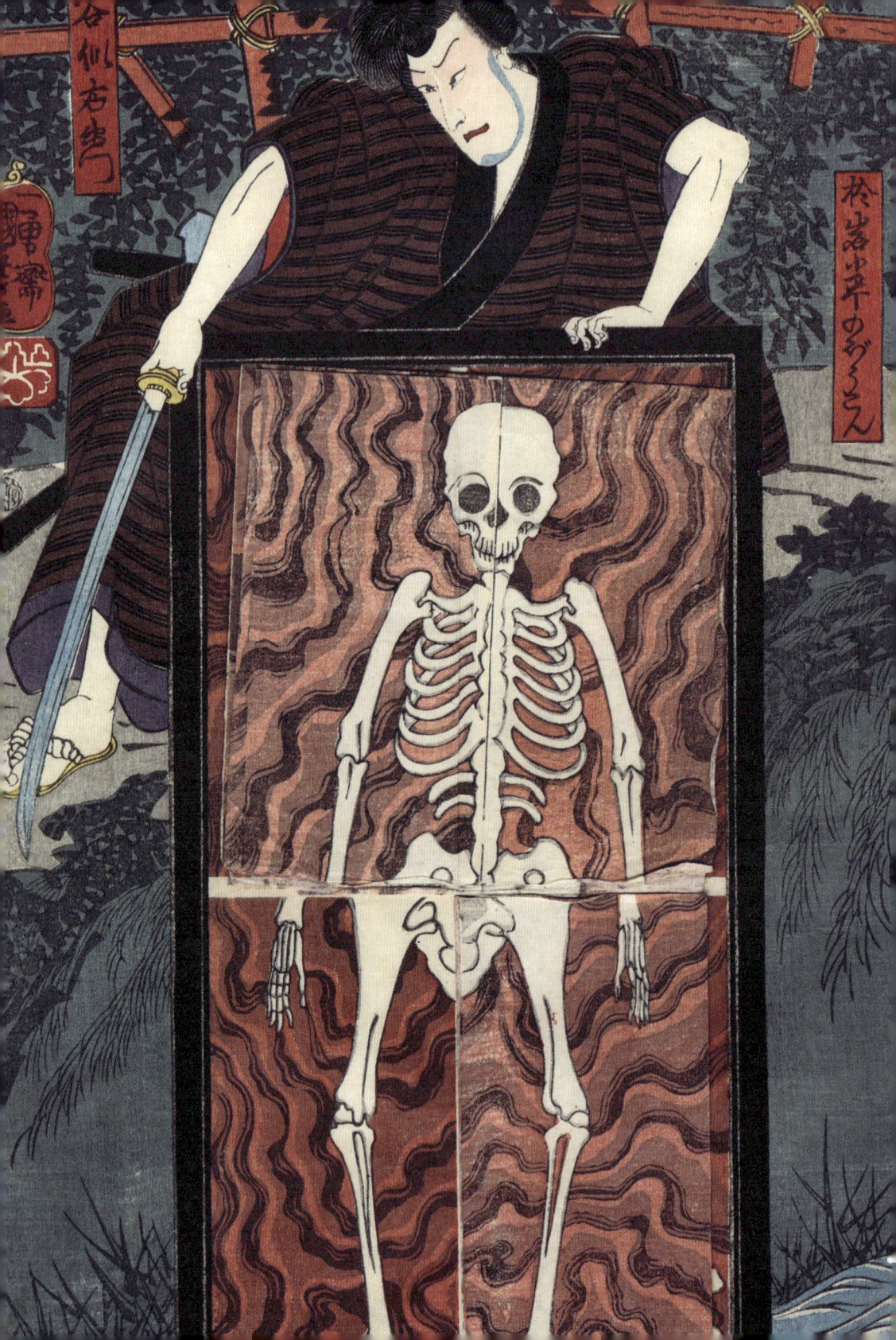

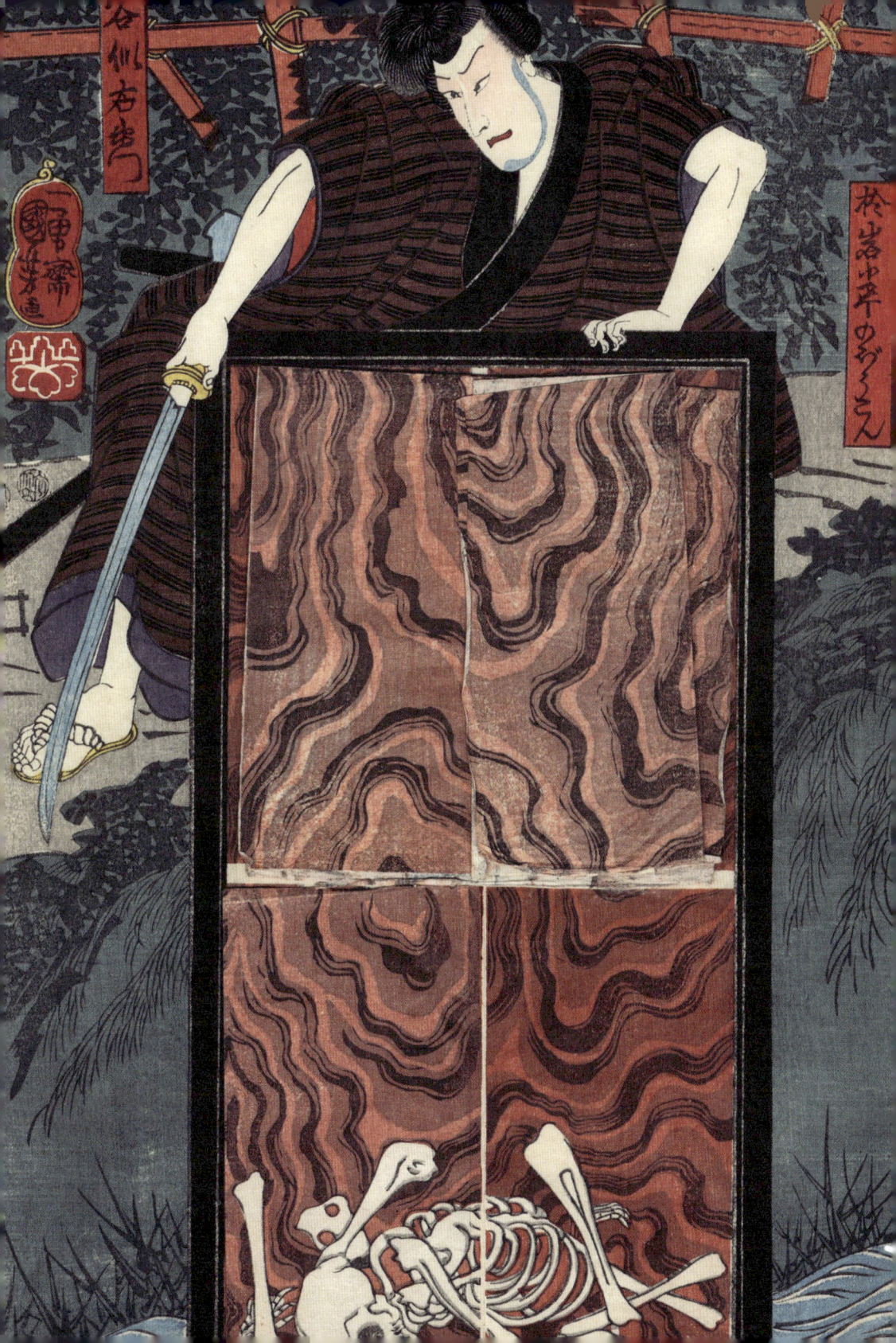

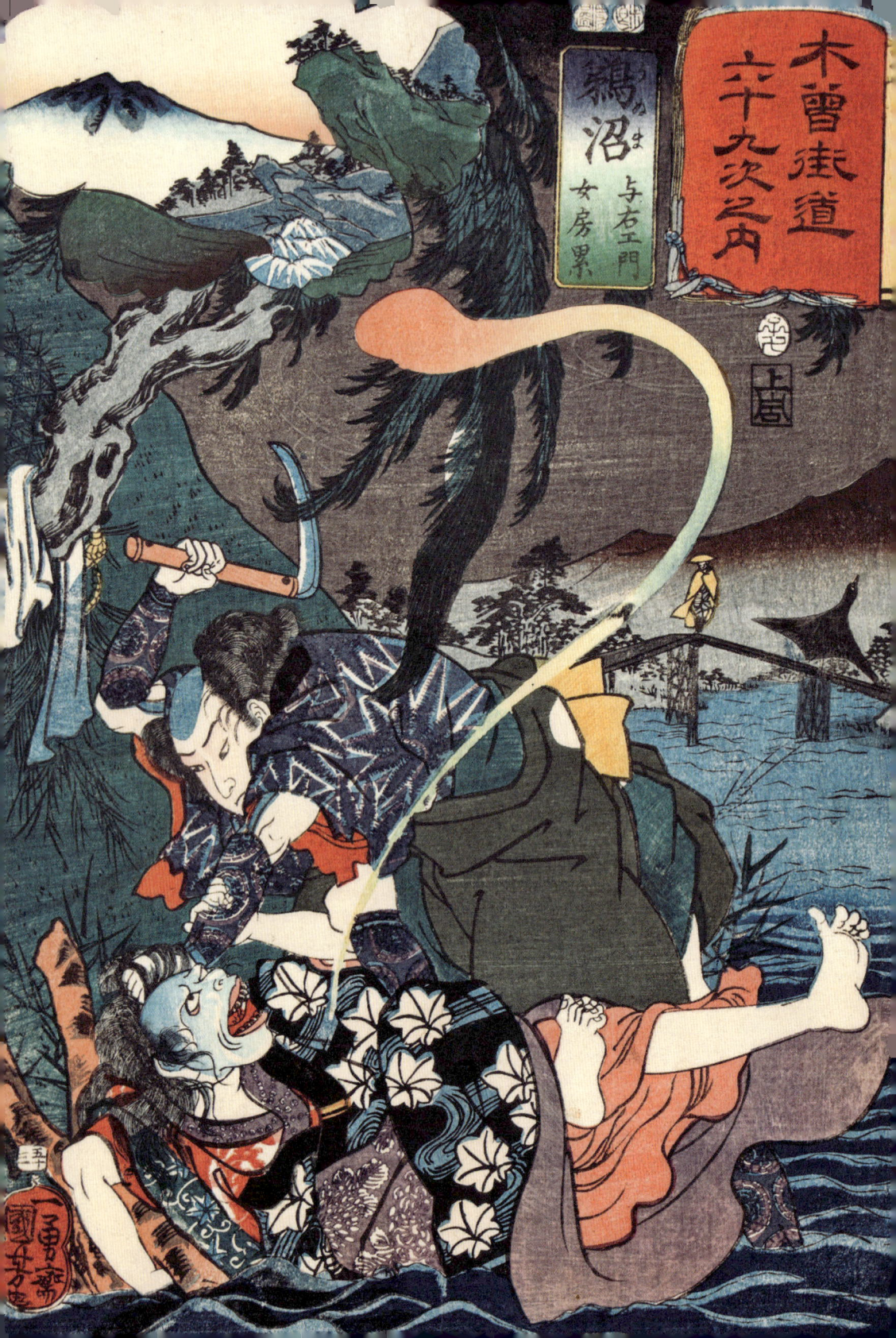

木曾街道六十九次之内

鵜沼　与右ェ門　女房累

KASANE

•

Misfortune follows the cursed from generation to generation, as though a single life is not enough. Such is the story of Kasane. This tale starts with a farmer who drowns his son-in-law, blaming him for his daughter Orui's deformities (she is lame and her face is disfigured). Later, Orui takes care of a traveller named Yoeman and marries him, but Yoeman rejects her after a few years and slits her throat with a sickle on a riverbank. At that moment, Orui is transformed into 'Kasane', an alternative reading of the kanji character for her name, which means 'repetition' in reference to the way past acts continue to affect new existences. Kasane, now, is not a human but a *yūrei*. She wreaks vengeance on Yoeman through his wives, one after the other, afflicting them with neurological or respiratory illnesses, driving them mad, or killing them.

The story of Kasane appears in *Tale of the Salvation of a Vengeful Spirit*, written in about 1690 by the monk Zanju, and it became very popular within Kabuki theatre. One episode, especially, was played out very often: that of the monk Yūten who, in 1672, performed an exorcism on a fourteen-year-old girl who was gasping for breath and suffering repeated, terrible convulsions – the work of Kasane's ghost, who had possessed her.

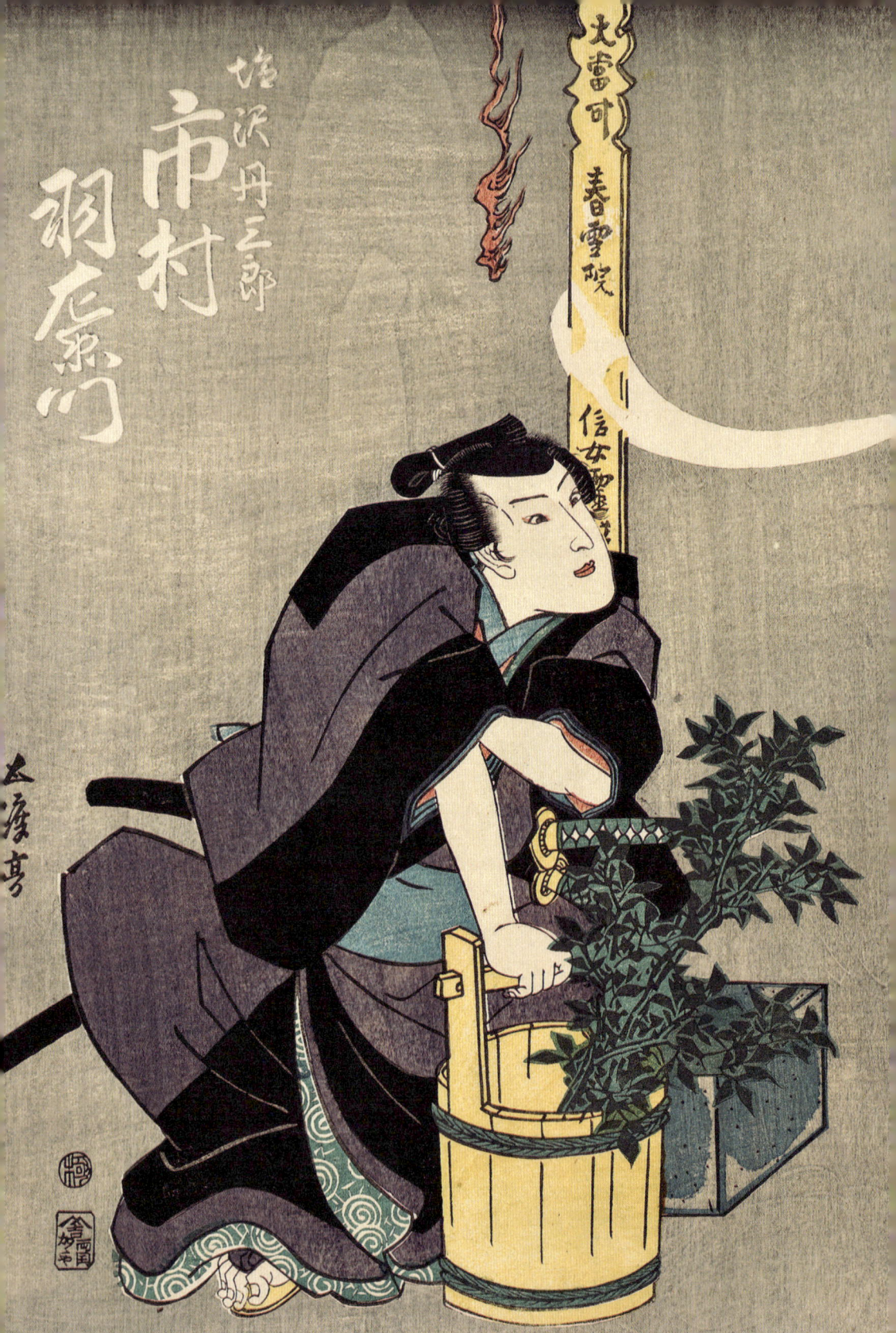

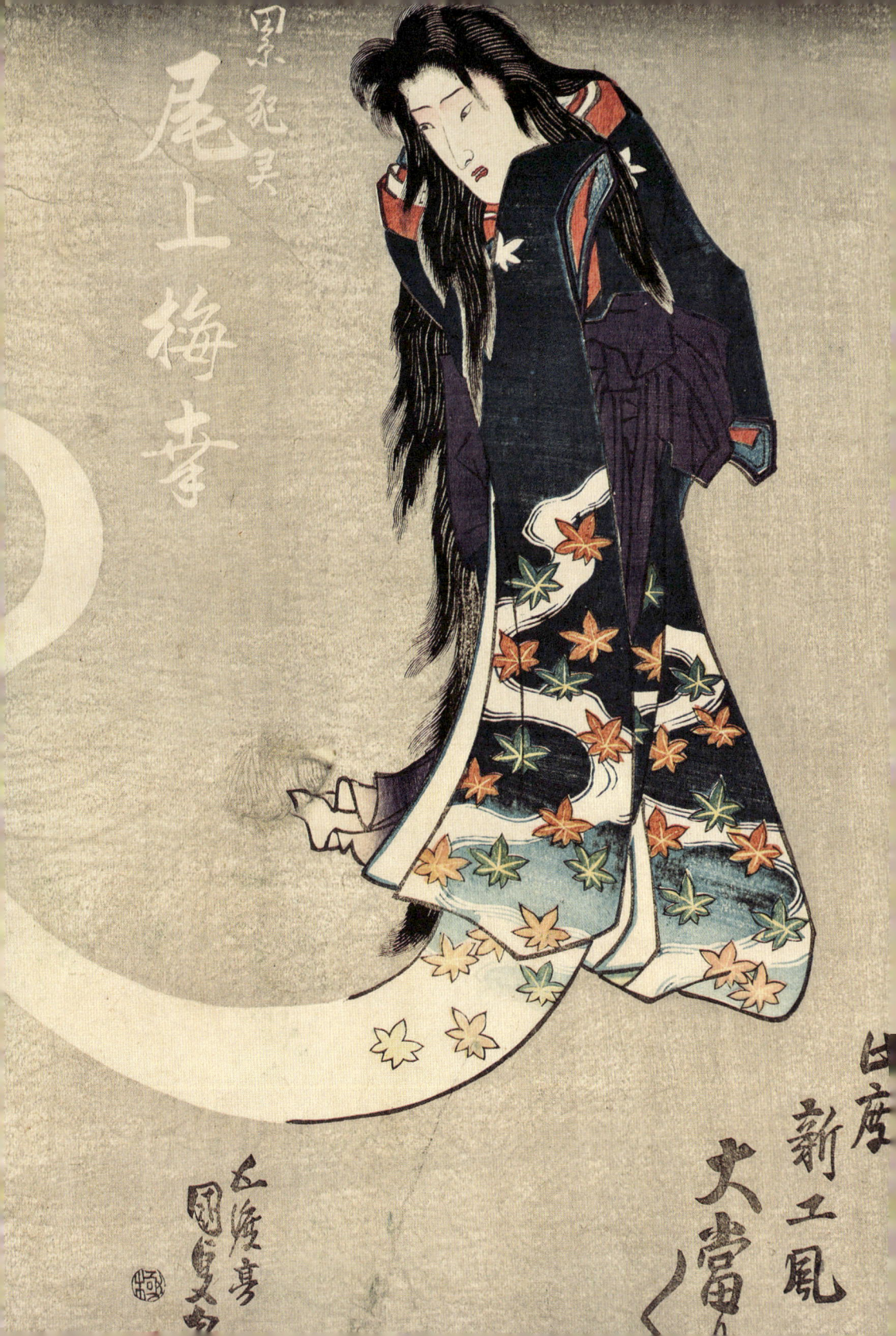

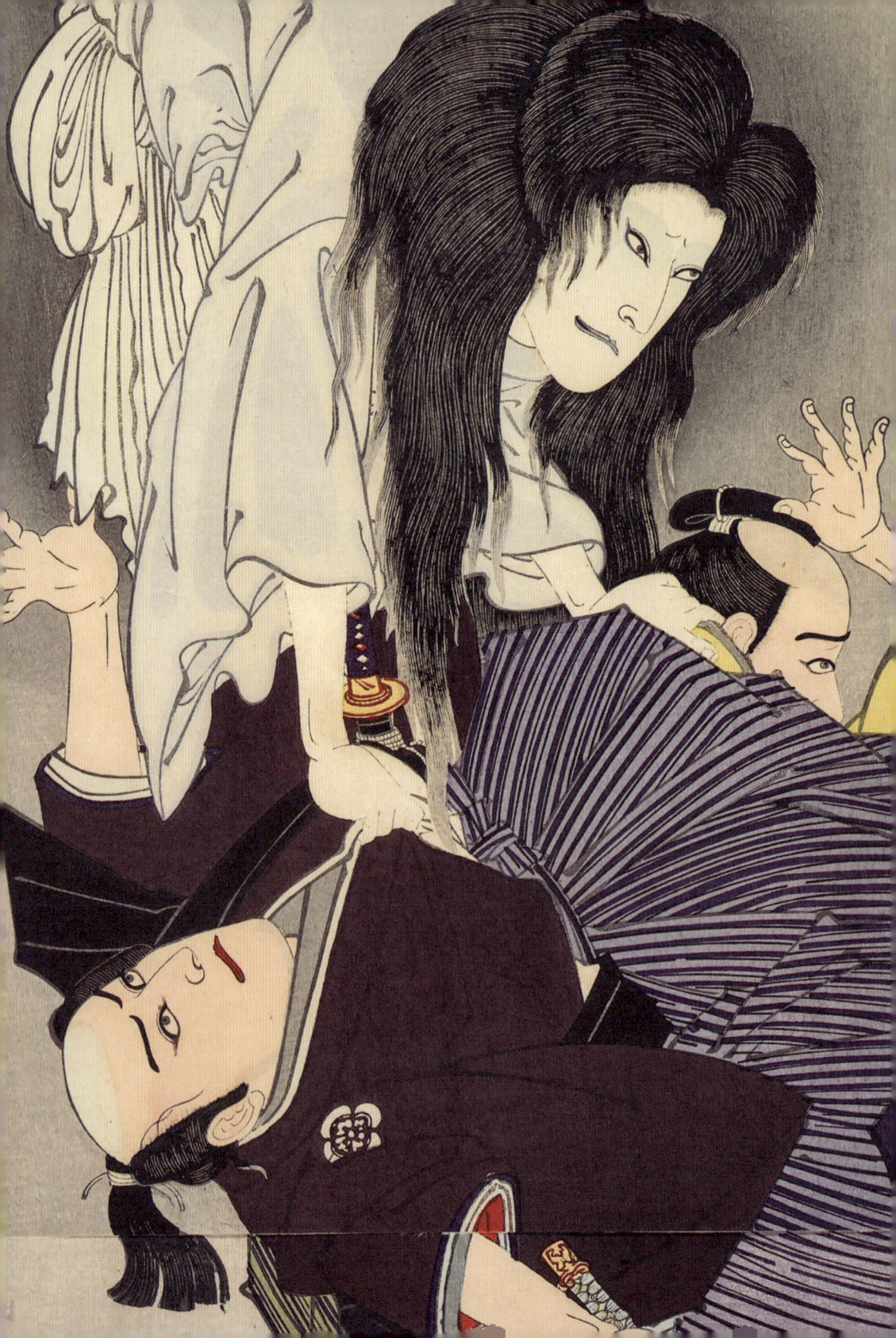

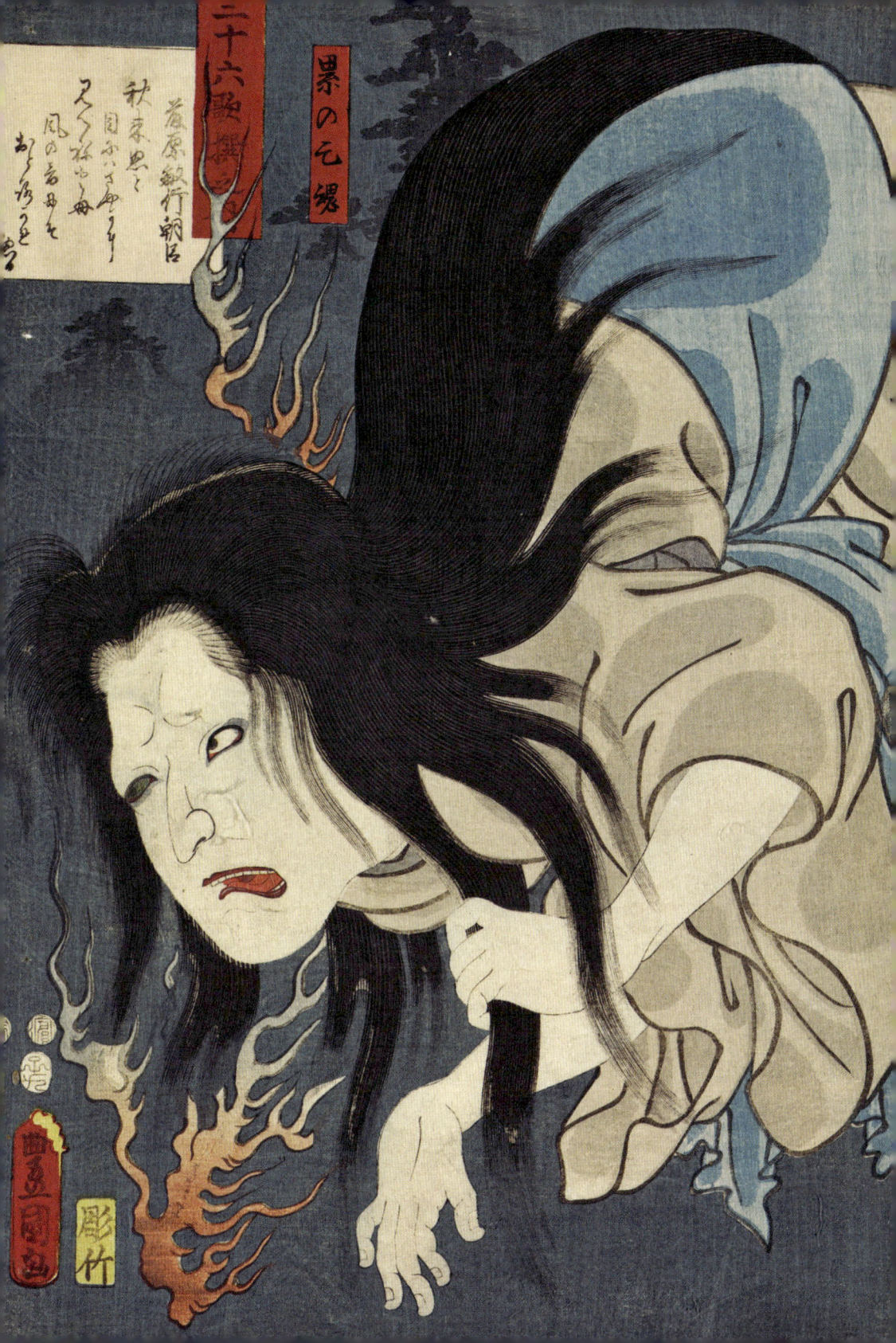

HEADS
THAT FLY

•

It is hard to say whether *rokurokubi* and *nukekubi* are ghosts (*yūrei*) or monsters (*yōkai*). They are, at any rate, fantastical creatures whose heads can detach from their bodies and fly or whose necks can stretch so far that their head seems independent. It is almost as if the mind were freeing itself of the body, or as though the spiritual were distancing itself from the temporal. Some say that their image, often depicted in *yūrei-ga*, is the figuration of dreams or of sleepwalking. It is also said that some women bear a physical sign of their ability to extend their neck during the night or detach their head completely. Hold their hair back, and you can make out a faint ring-shaped bruise at the base of their neck.

A tale recorded by the writer Jippensha Ikku in the early nineteenth century depicts one of these apparitions. It is the story of a monk named Kaishin who one day runs away with his lover Oyutsu. But Oyutsu falls ill, delaying their journey onward, and very soon the couple find themselves short of food and money. One evening, Kaishin kills Oyutsu and hides her body. Returning to secular life, he very soon forgets his former love in the arms of a young girl he meets in an inn. But during the night, the young girl's neck begins to stretch ominously and her face suddenly exhibits the features of Oyutsu. At dawn, distraught and plagued by remorse, Kaishin confides in the girl's father, who confesses to being a murderer too. His evil deed – killing a woman and stealing her money – had enabled him to build his inn, but the bad karma had burdened his daughter with a terrible curse (*rokurokubi*). Kaishin sees that if he is to appease the spirits and re-establish spiritual balance, he has but one

127

choice. In the end, he provides Oyutsu a decent grave, with the story of his betrayal carved into the headstone, and re-joins the monastery he left.

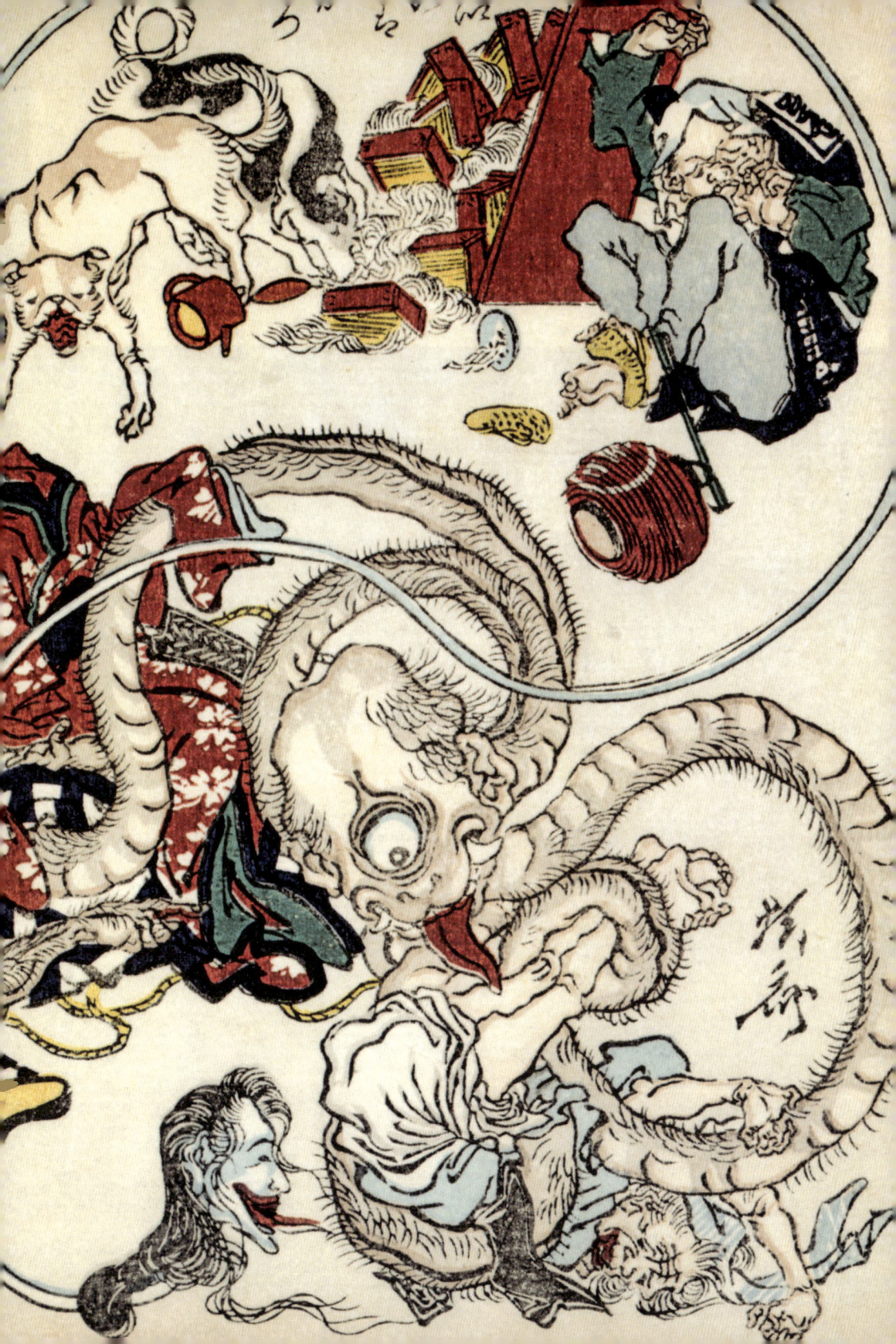

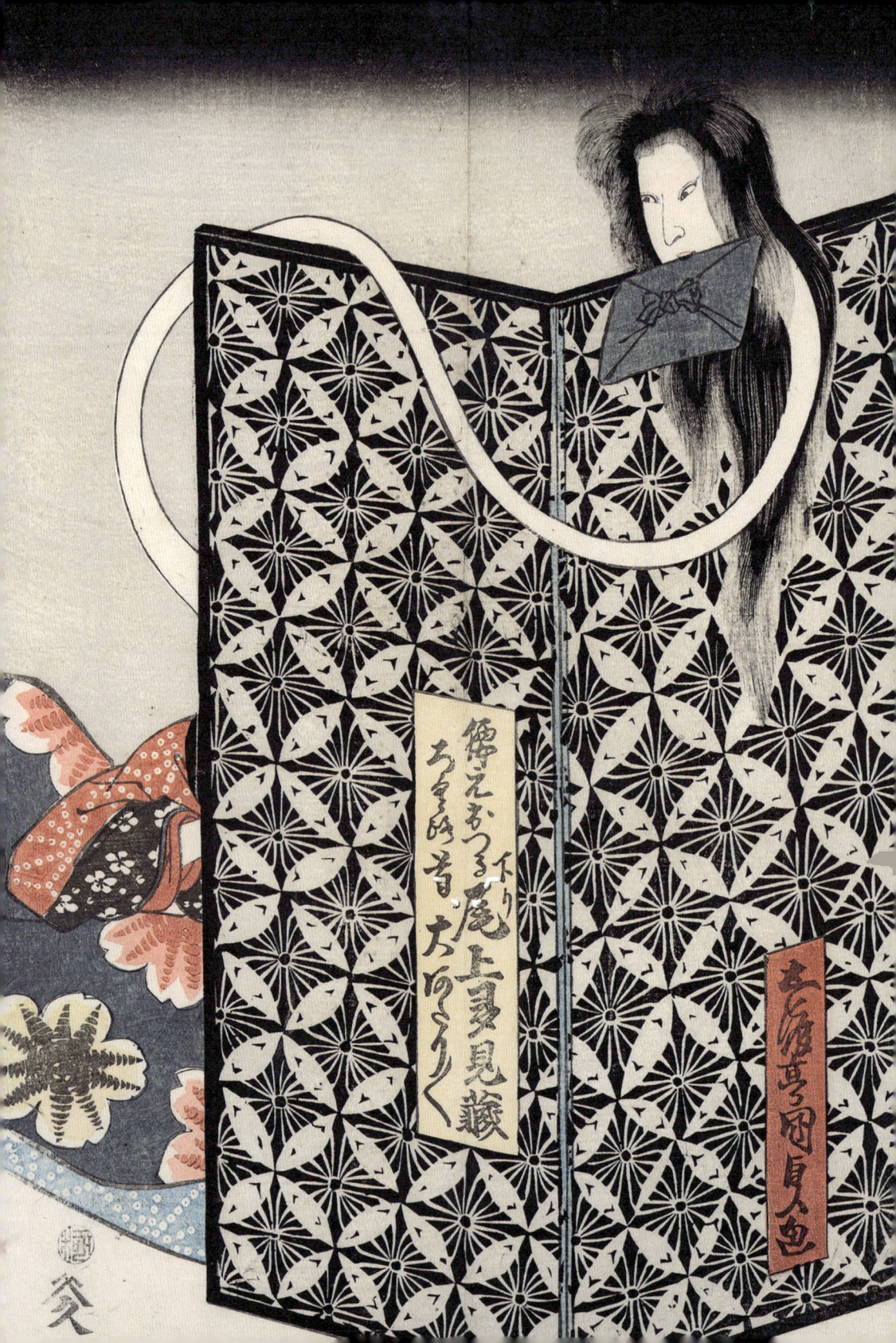

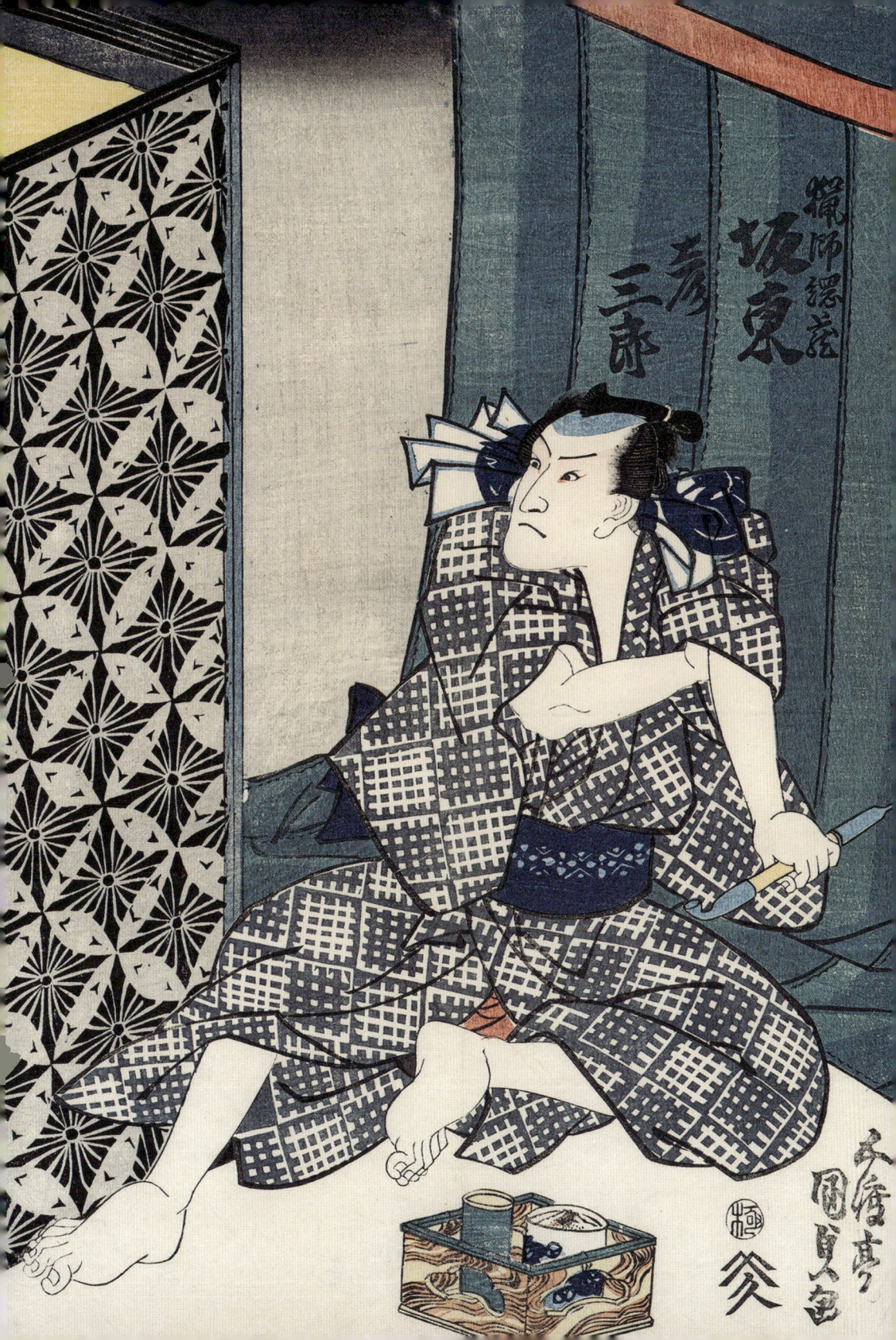

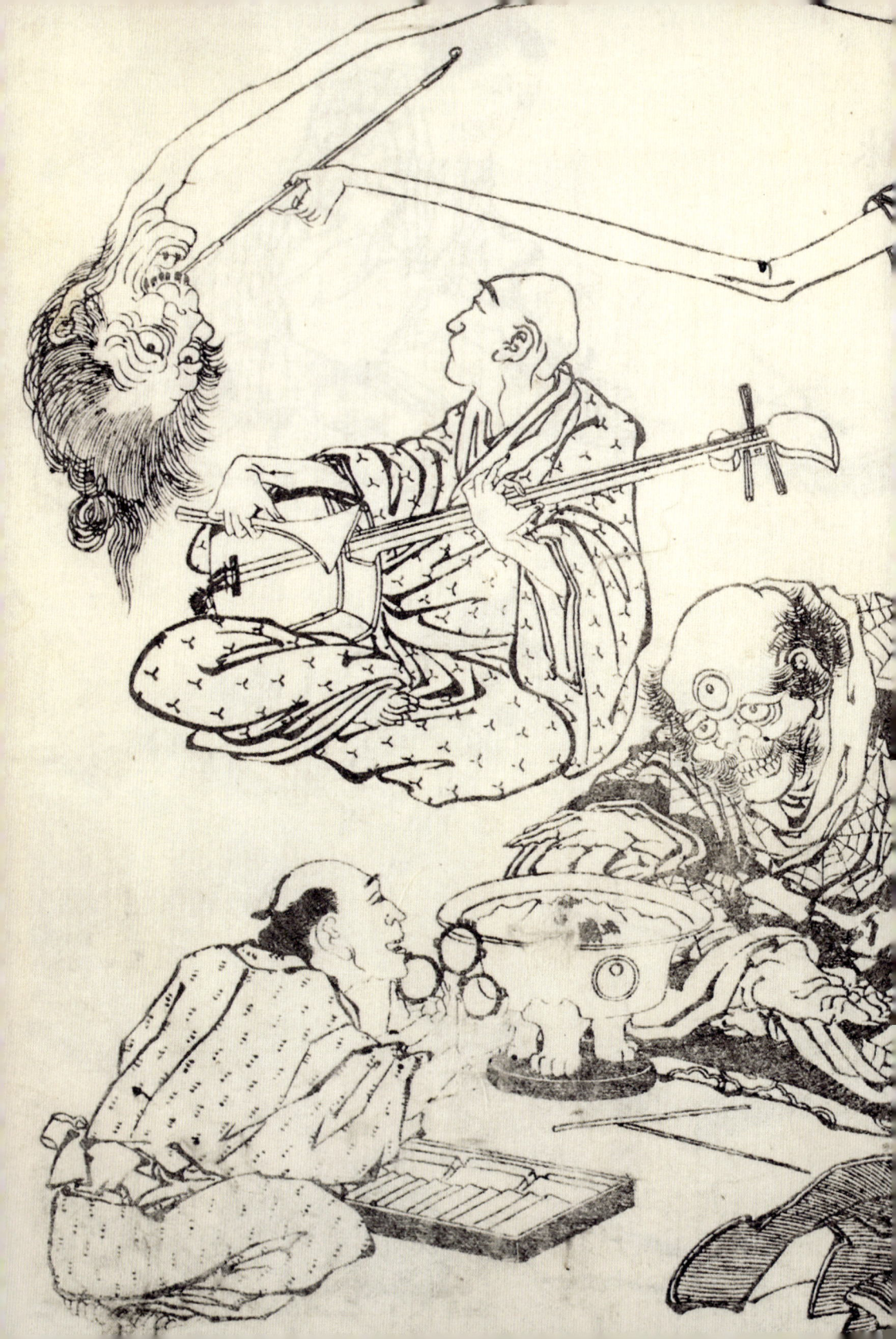

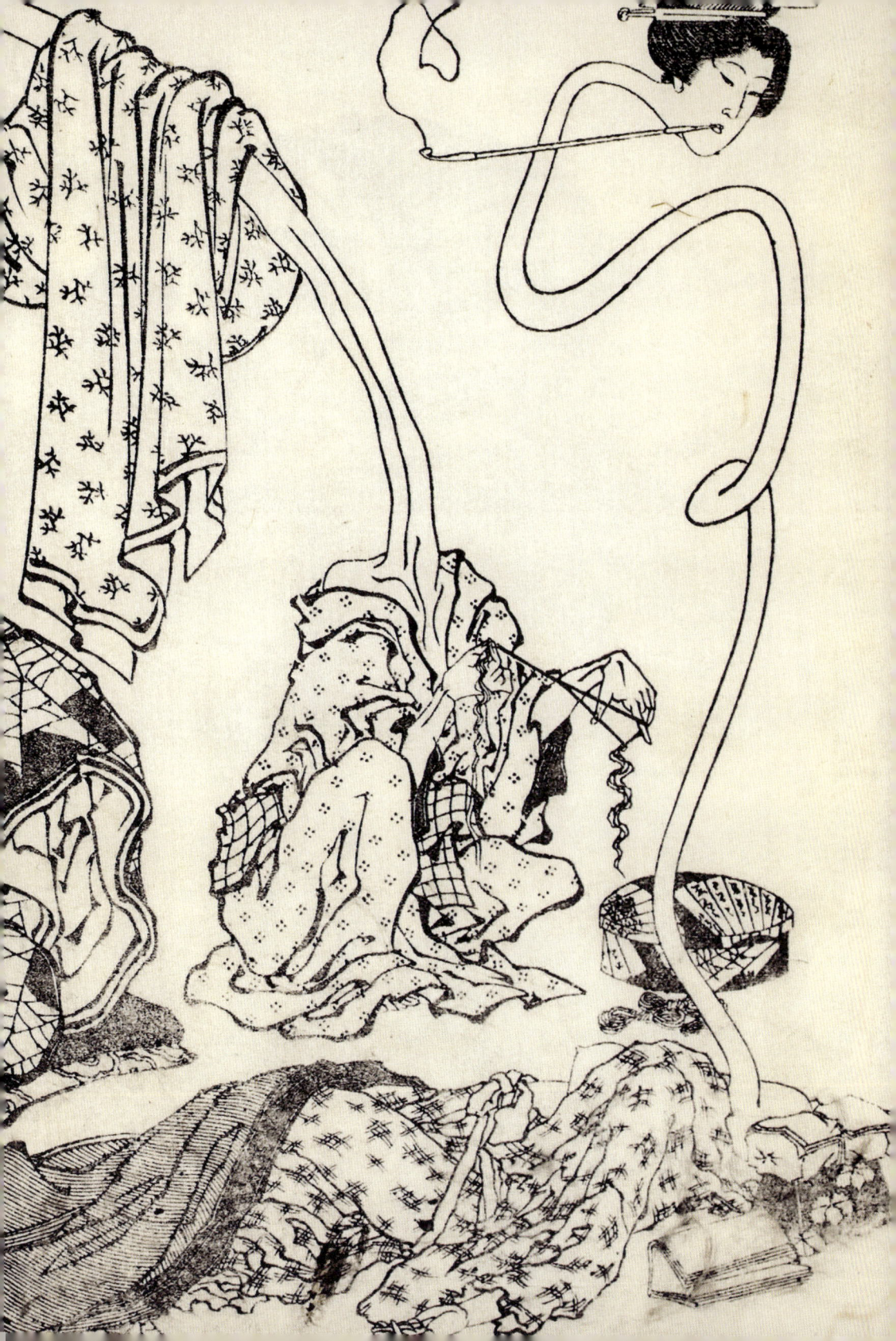

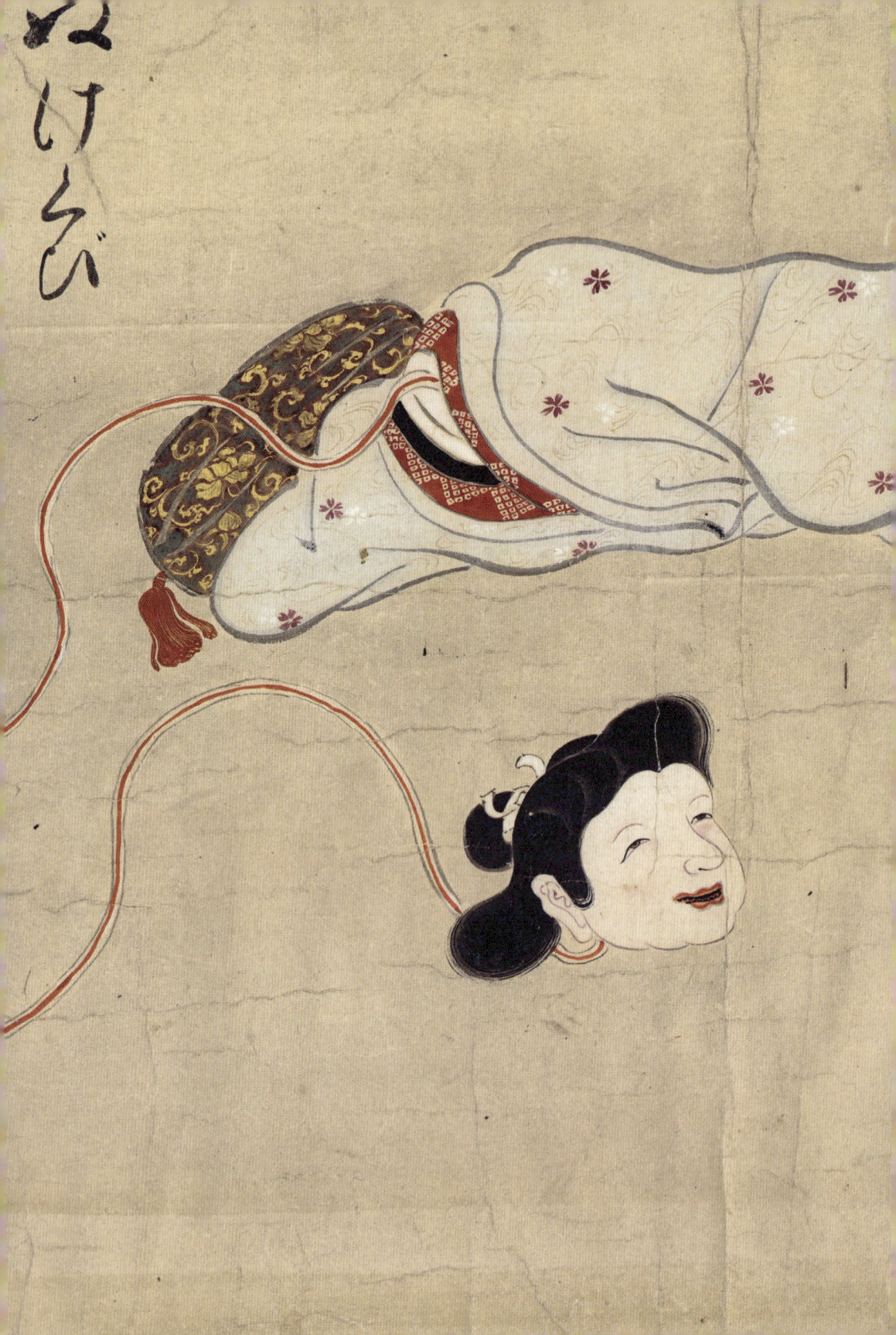

ぬけくび

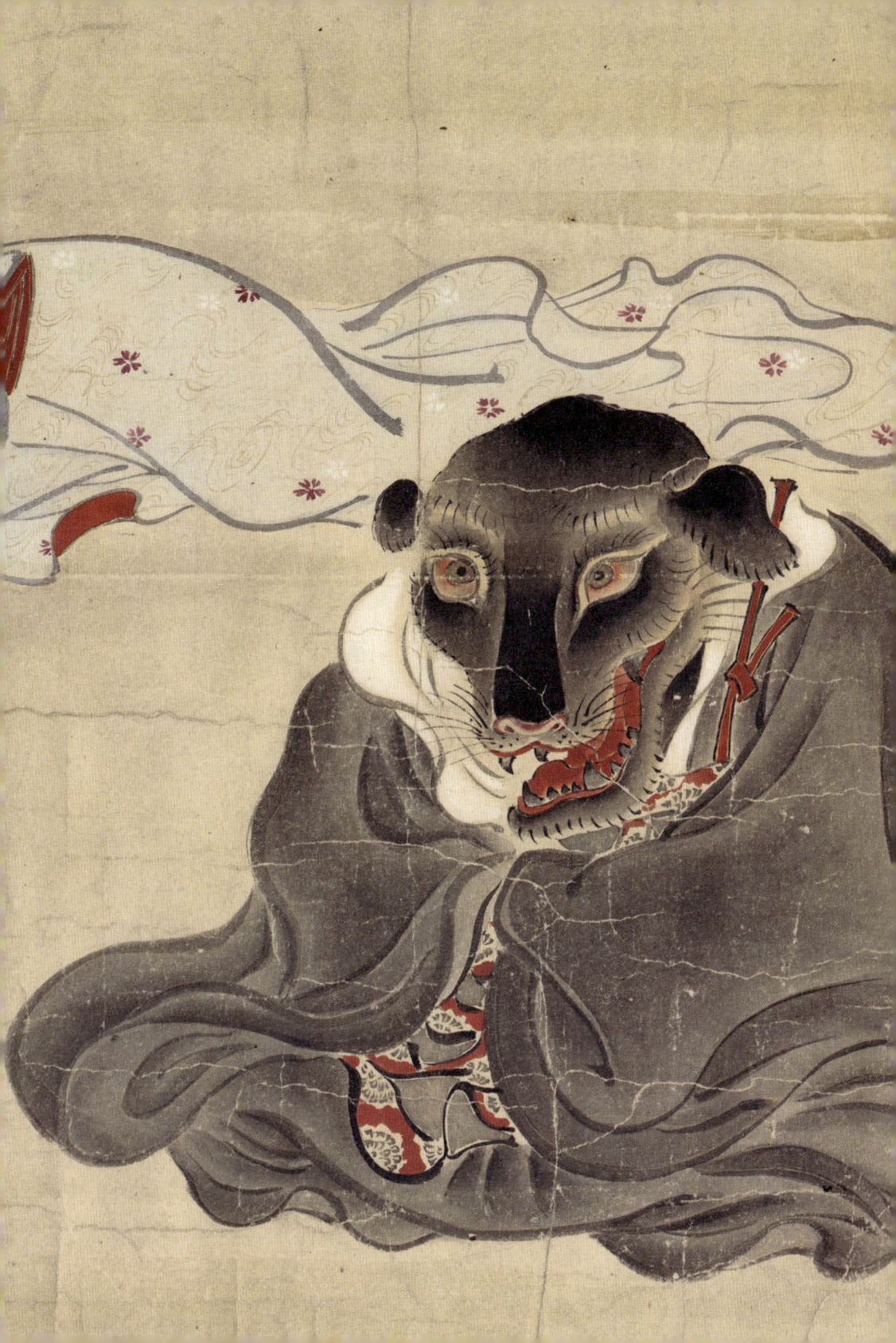

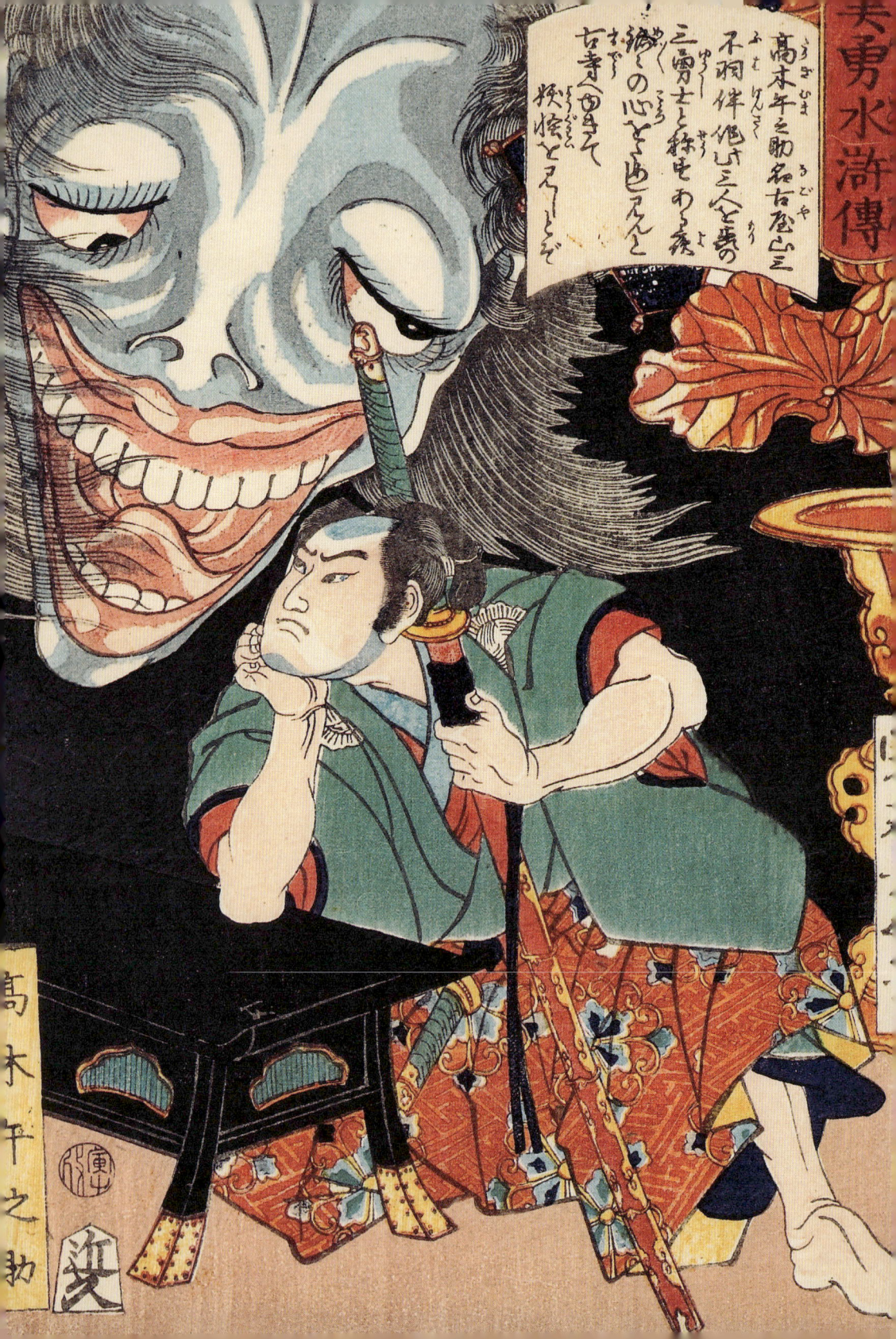

THE SMILE OF DEATH

•

Kuchisake-onna is a *yūrei* of extraordinary beauty, with very pale skin, who hides her face behind a mask, a fan, or a piece of fabric. Before she entered the shadow world, she had been the wife or mistress of a samurai, but his repeated absences had led her to adultery. On learning that she had given herself to passing guests, stable boys, peasants and the like, the samurai returned home determined to kill her. But first he slashed her face from the corners of her mouth to below her ears. Since then, she haunts the dark lanes, watching for lonely travellers so that she can ask them, like an evil sphinx: 'Do you think I am beautiful?' If, on seeing her horrible deformity, the man replies no, she kills him with the pair of scissors or knife she is holding – the very same that was used to wound and then kill her. If he replies yes, she displays her terrifying smile; and if he persists in thinking her beautiful, she mutilates him as she had been, telling him that he, too, will be handsome now.

Tradition says that there are several means of banishing her and warding off the curse. One is to reply 'so-so' instead of yes or no, confusing her and preventing the conversation from taking its course; other options are to offer her sweets or throw down coins in front of her.

p. 136: Tsukioka Yoshitoshi, *Takagi Umanosuke with a Ghost*, detail, 1866 University of Oxford, Ashmolean Museum

pp. 138–139: Katsushika Hokusai, *One Hundred Ghost Tales in a Haunted House* (*Shinpan uki-e bakemono yashiki hyaku monogatari no zu*), detail, ca 1780

pp. 140–141: Utagawa Kunisada I (aka Toyokuni III), Utagawa Hiroshige II, and Kawanabe Kyōsai, *Kataoka Nizaemon VIII as Tamigaya Iemon*, detail, 1863 Los Angeles County Museum of Art

137

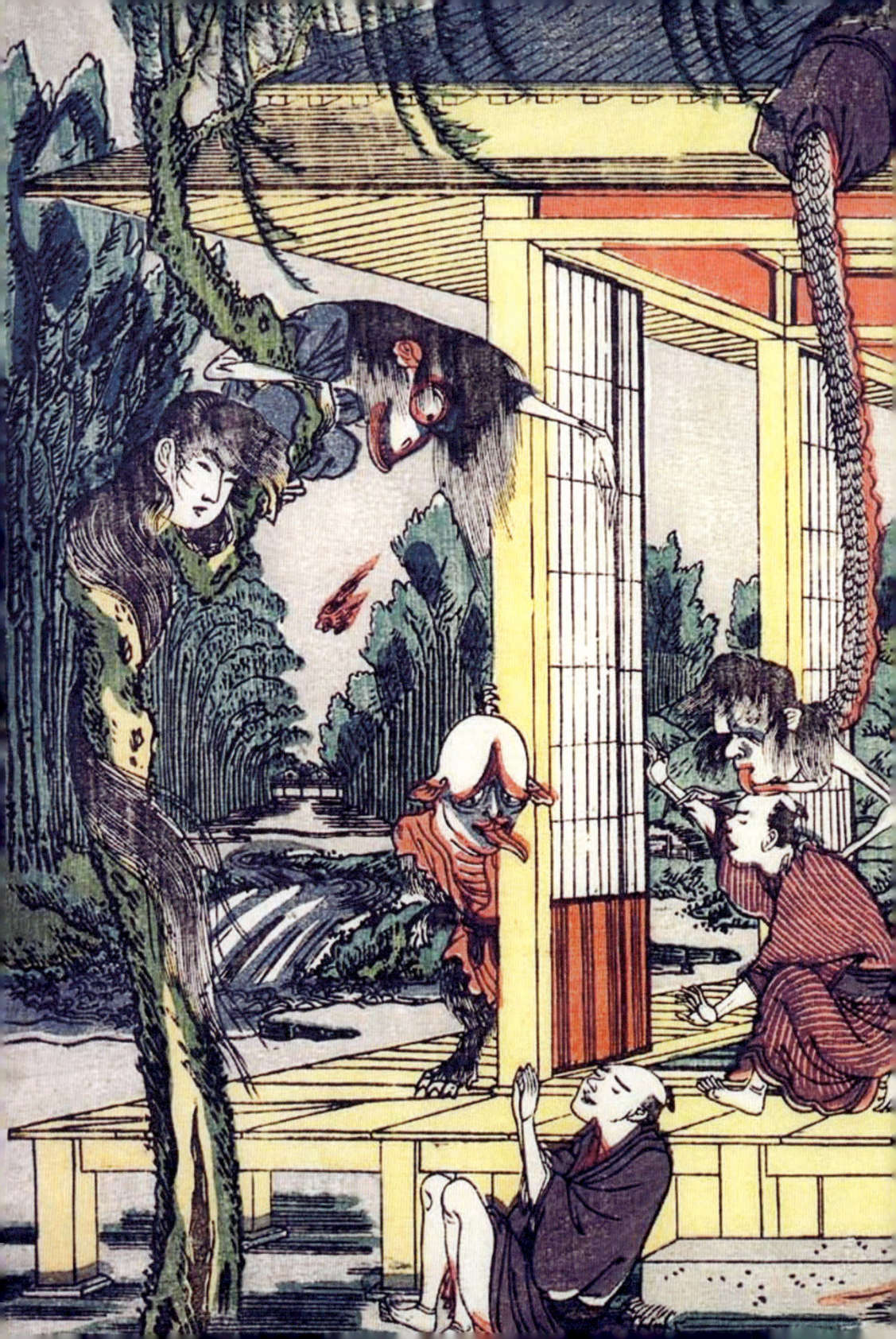

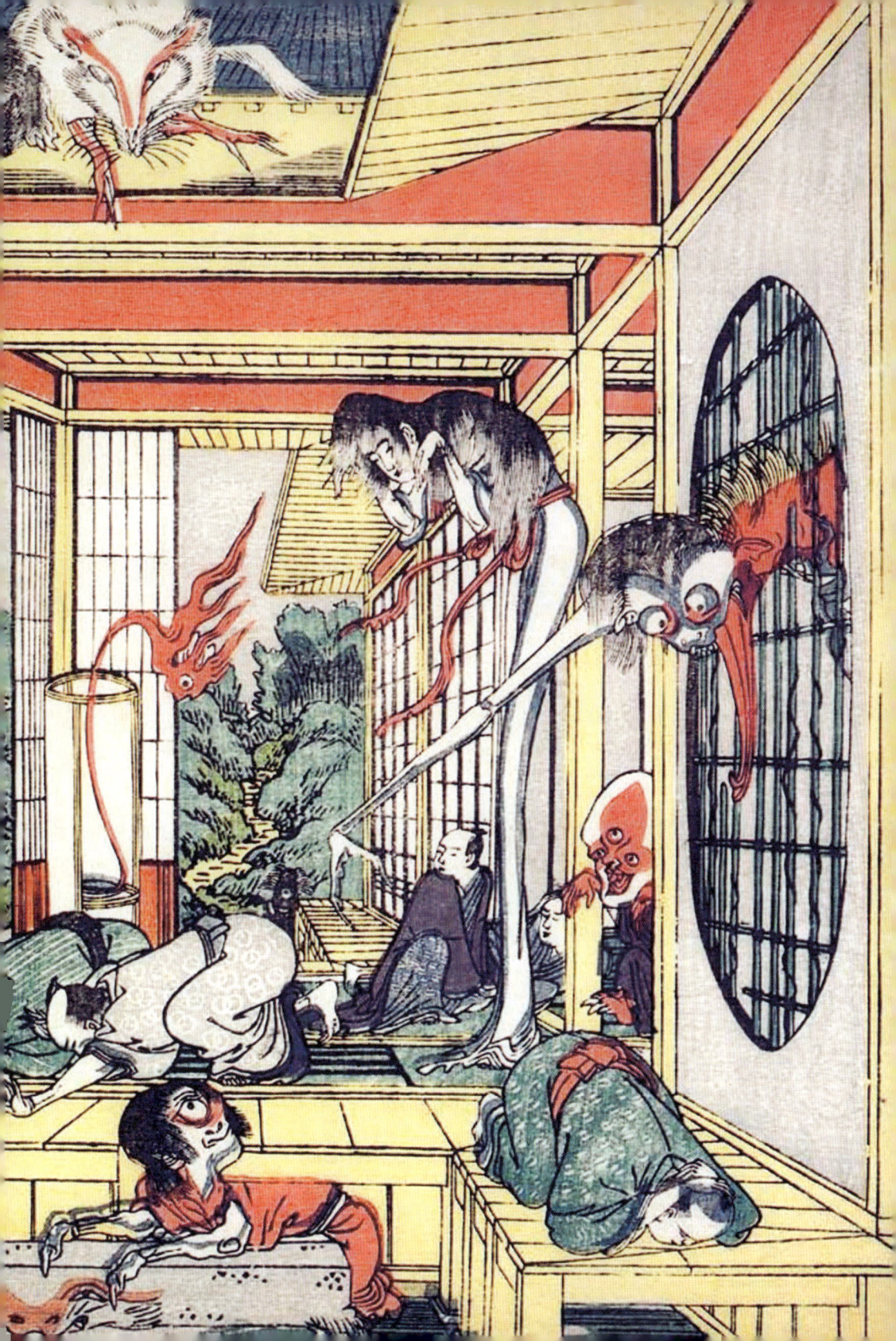

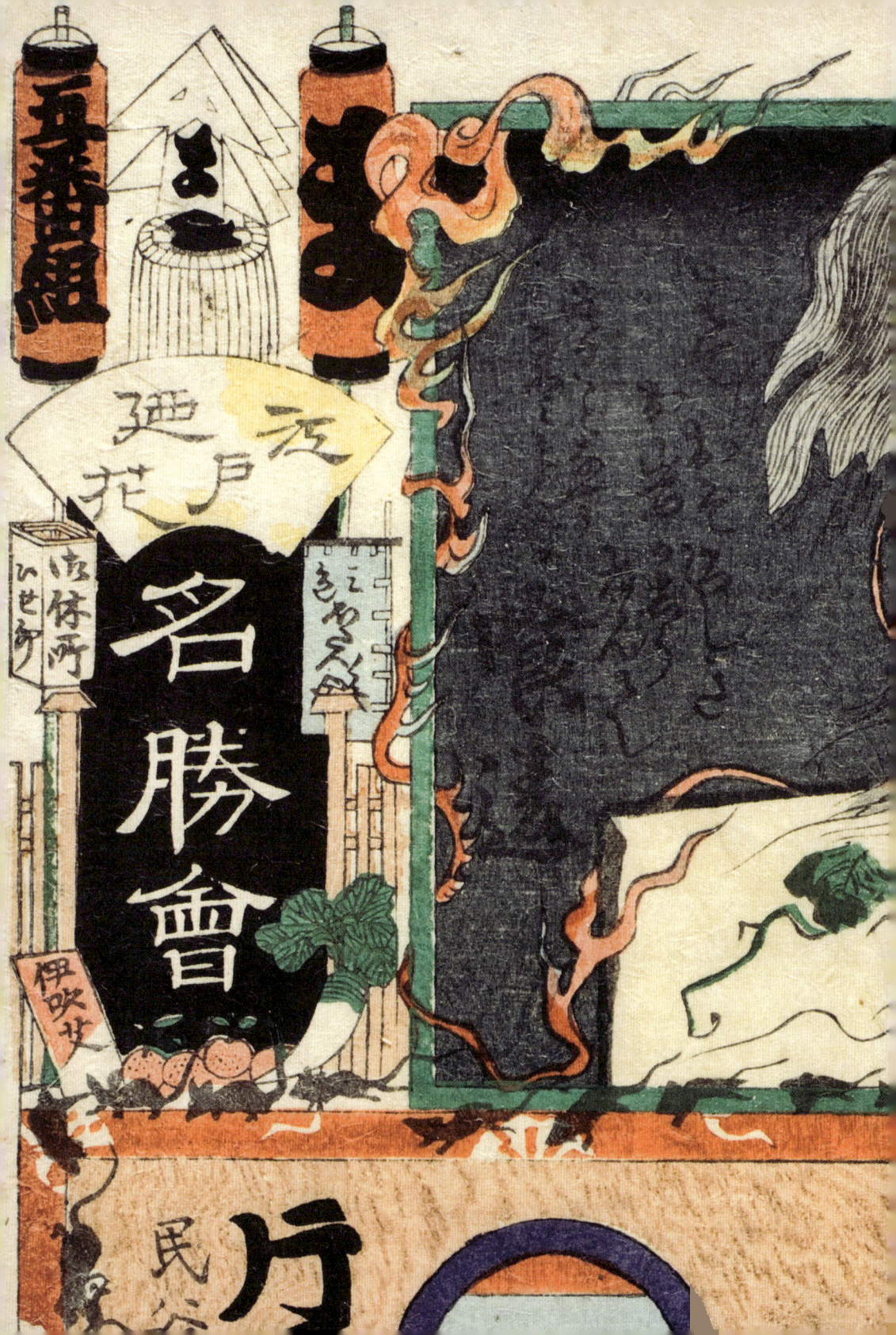

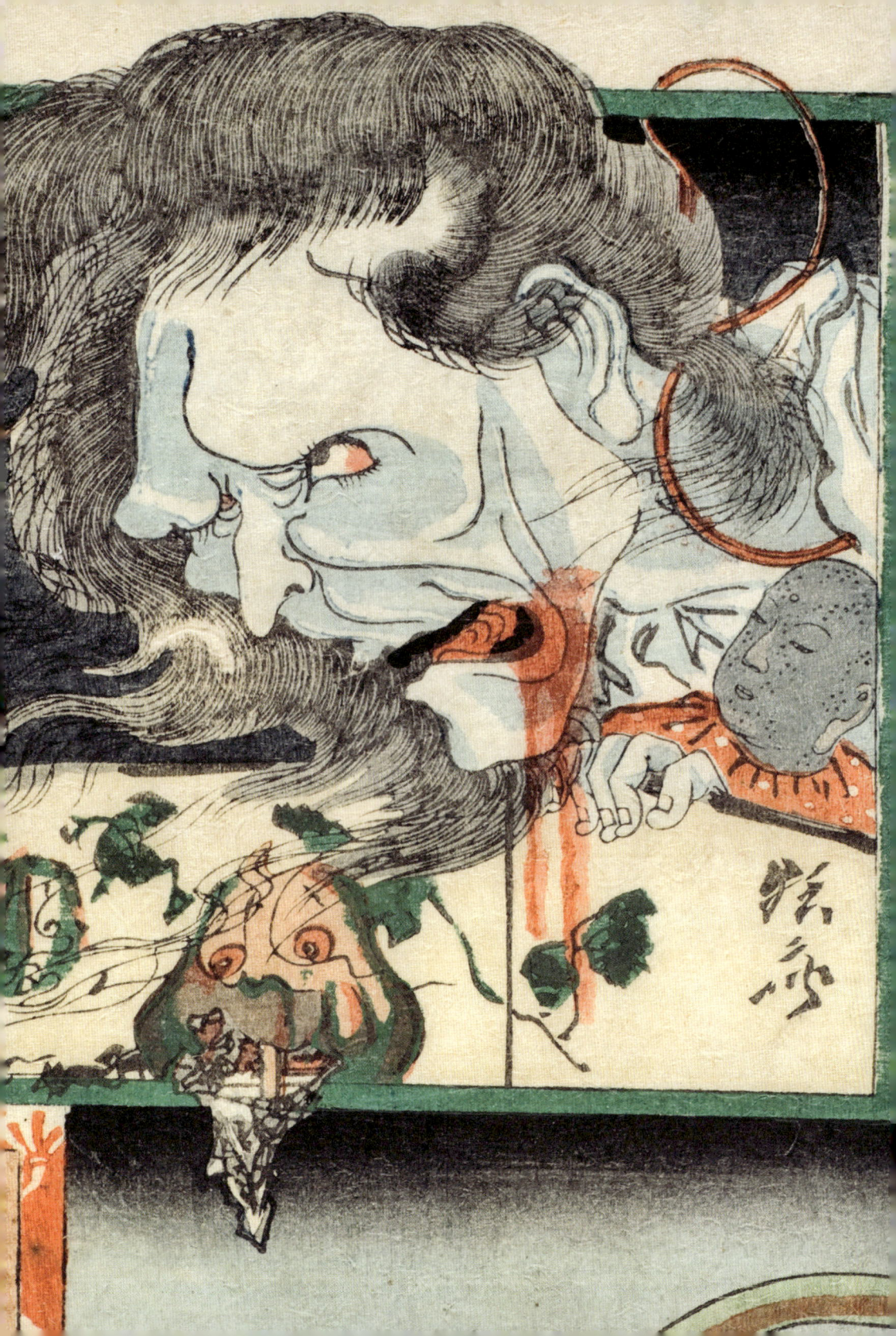

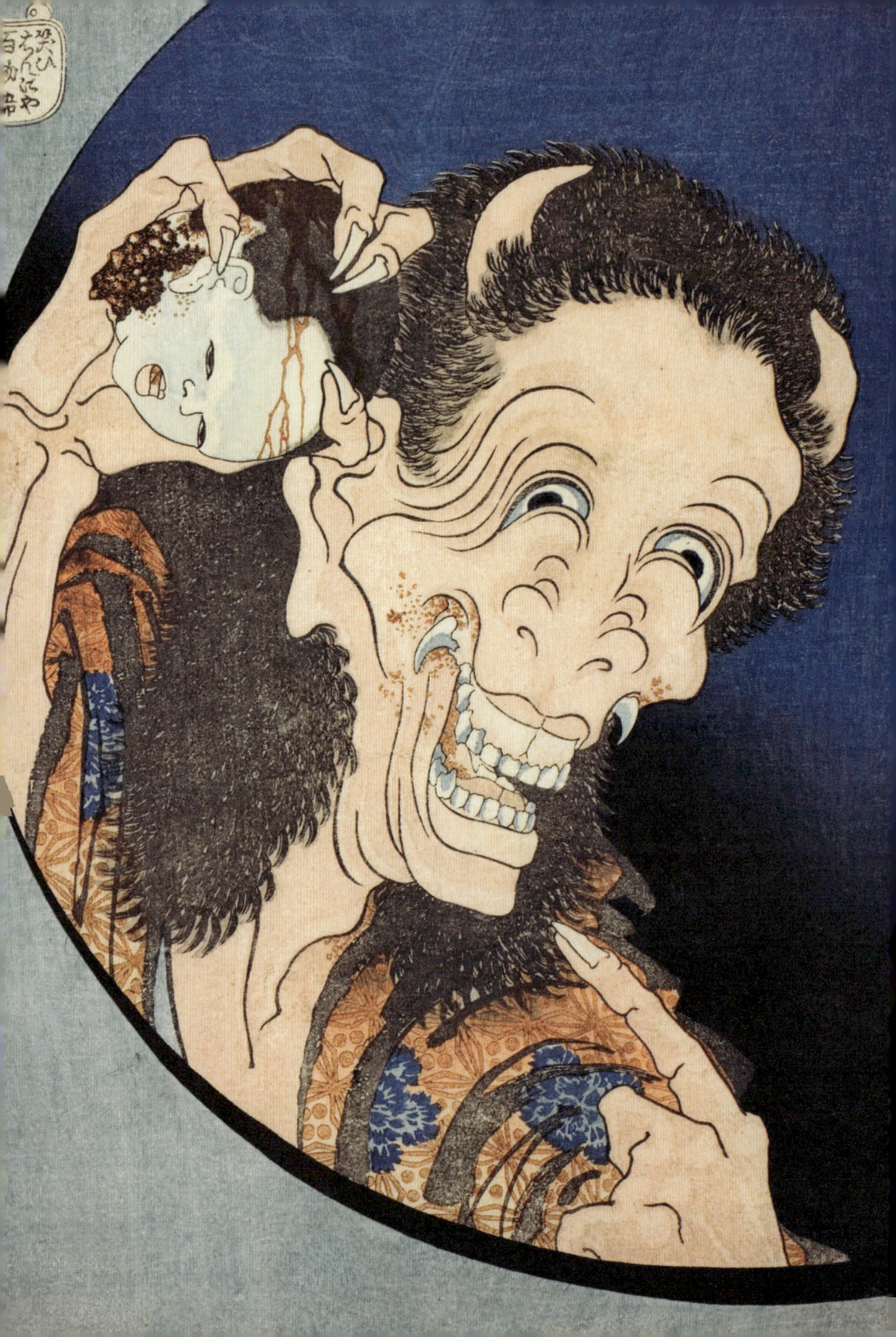

HANNYA

•

There is nothing human left of Hannya. She is perhaps the personification of our most bestial and diabolical urges, of that within us which is most foul and repulsive. In Noh theatre, her mask represents avenging spirits (*onryō*) and has a distorted face, two buffalo horns on the forehead (sometimes gilded), beseeching eyes with metallic glints (again, gilded) and a wide-open mouth filled with fangs. This is the face of jealousy, resentment, rage. The complexion of the ghost (that is, the colour of the mask) varies, indicating the ghost's social origins: white for the aristocracy, red for the peasantry and black for demons. Depending on certain details – a stuck-out tongue, an absence of ears, the shape of her eyes and the site of the horns – a specialist will distinguish various levels of aggression or demonisation. The masks, from *deigan, hashihime, namanari, jya*, to *shinjya* and *adachi onna*, show a gradual progression from abandoned woman to the most dangerous demon imaginable.

Depending on the skill of the actor (the mask-wearer), this face can be repulsive one moment, and pained and tearful the next. One might say that, despite all odds, one hope remains: the hope of redemption.

p. 142: Katsushika Hokusai, *The Laughing Demoness* (*Warai Hannya*), detail, 1831/1832 The Art Institute of Chicago
p. 144: Unknown artist, *Ghost*, detail, Meiji period (1868–1912) Courtesy of Galerie Mingei, Paris
p. 145: Tsukioka Yoshitoshi, *Clearing Weather of the Togakushi Mountains: Taira Koremochi Ason*, detail, 1868 Minneapolis Institute of Art

p. 146: Tsukioka Yoshitoshi, *The Attack of the Ghost of Akugenta Yoshihira at the Nunobiki Waterfall*, detail, 1902 Philadelphia Museum of Art
p. 147: Utagawa Kunisada I (aka Toyokuni III), *Onoe Kikugorō III as the Ghost of Yasukata*, detail, 1852 Amsterdam, Rijksmusem

pp. 148–149: Utagawa Yoshifusa, *The Ghost of Akugenta Yoshihira Takes Vengeance on Nanba Jirō* (centre) *and Taira Kiyomori* (right) *at the Nunobiki Waterfall*, detail, 1856 New York, The Metropolitan Museum of Art

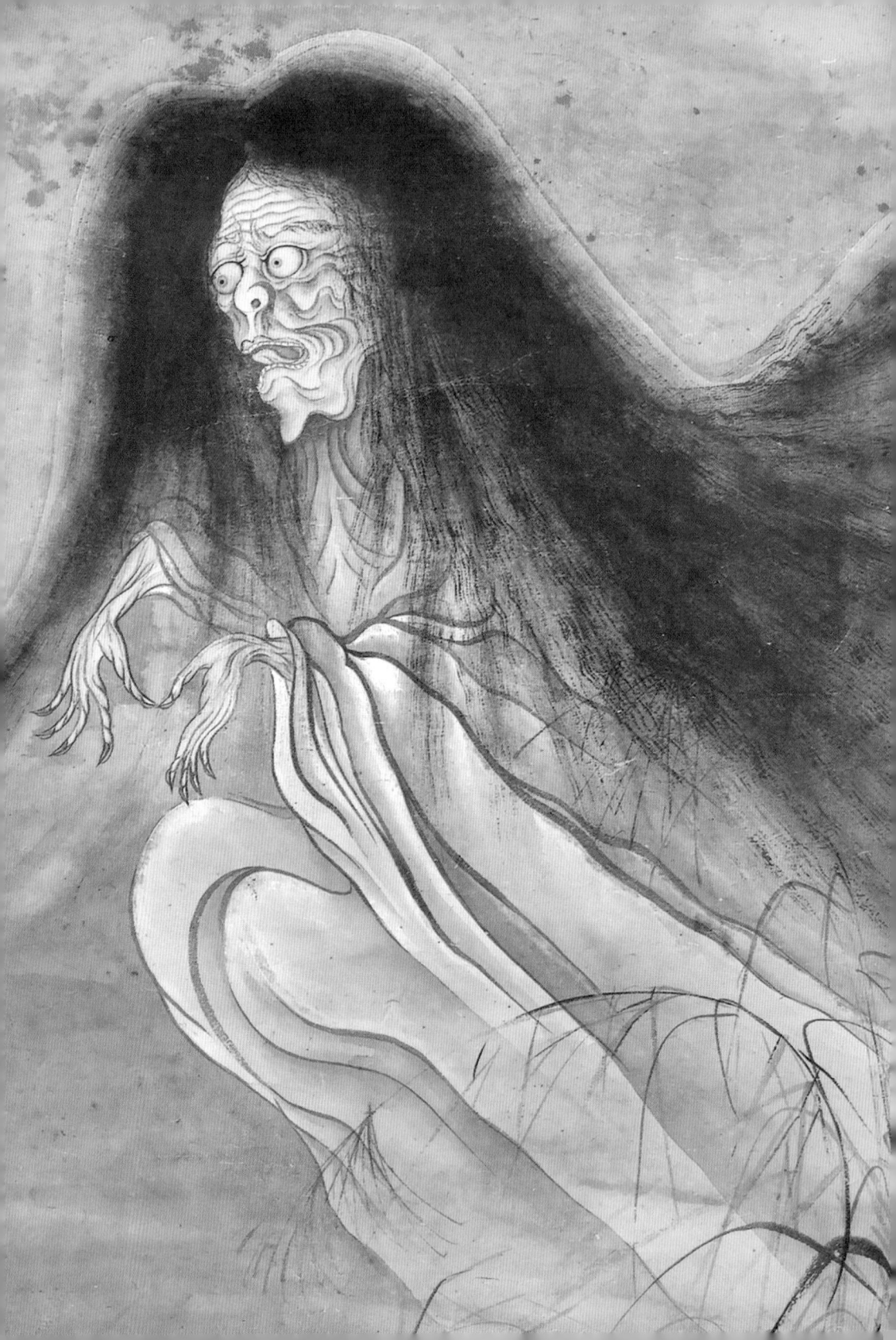

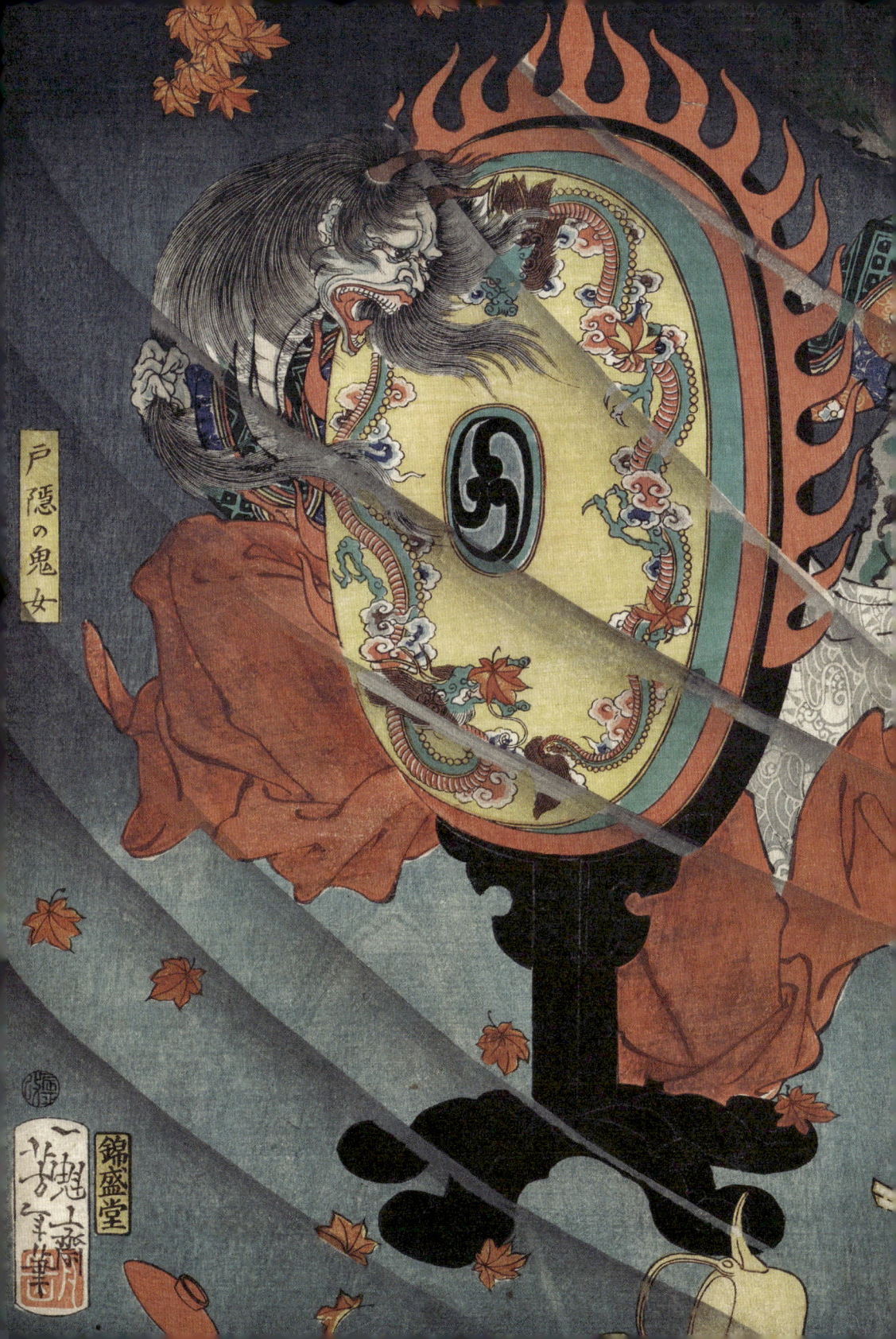

戸隠の鬼女

錦盛堂
一魁斎芳年筆

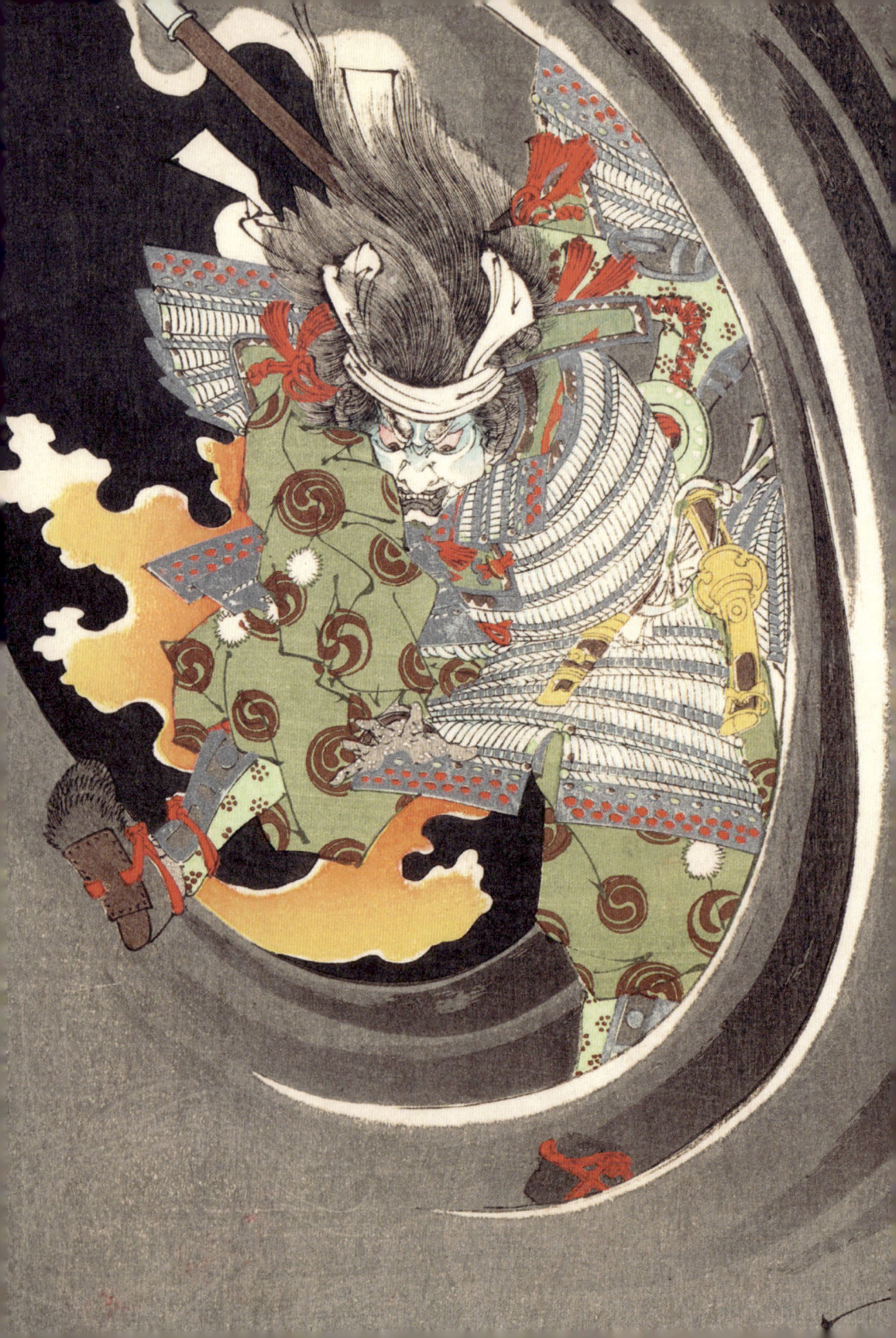

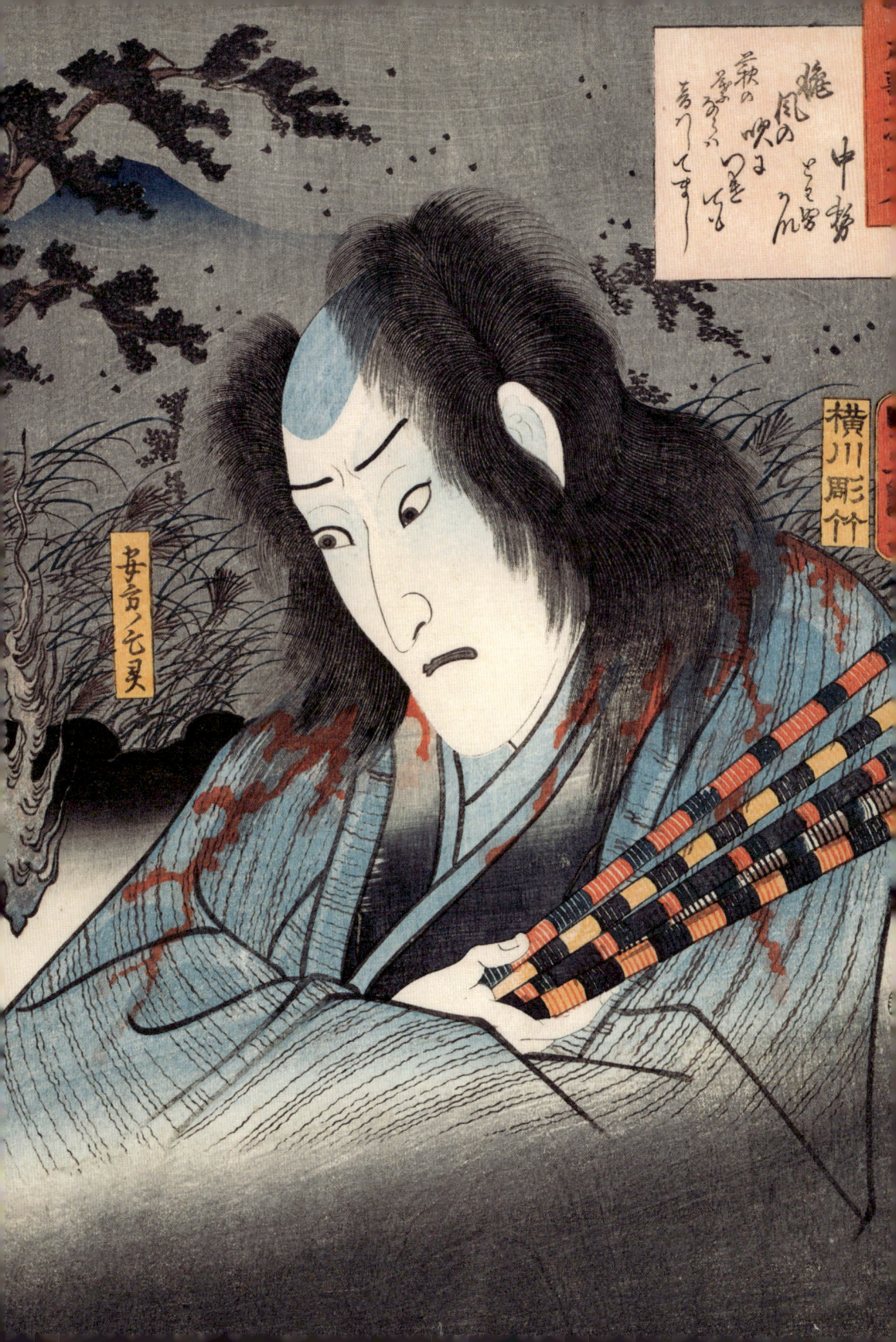

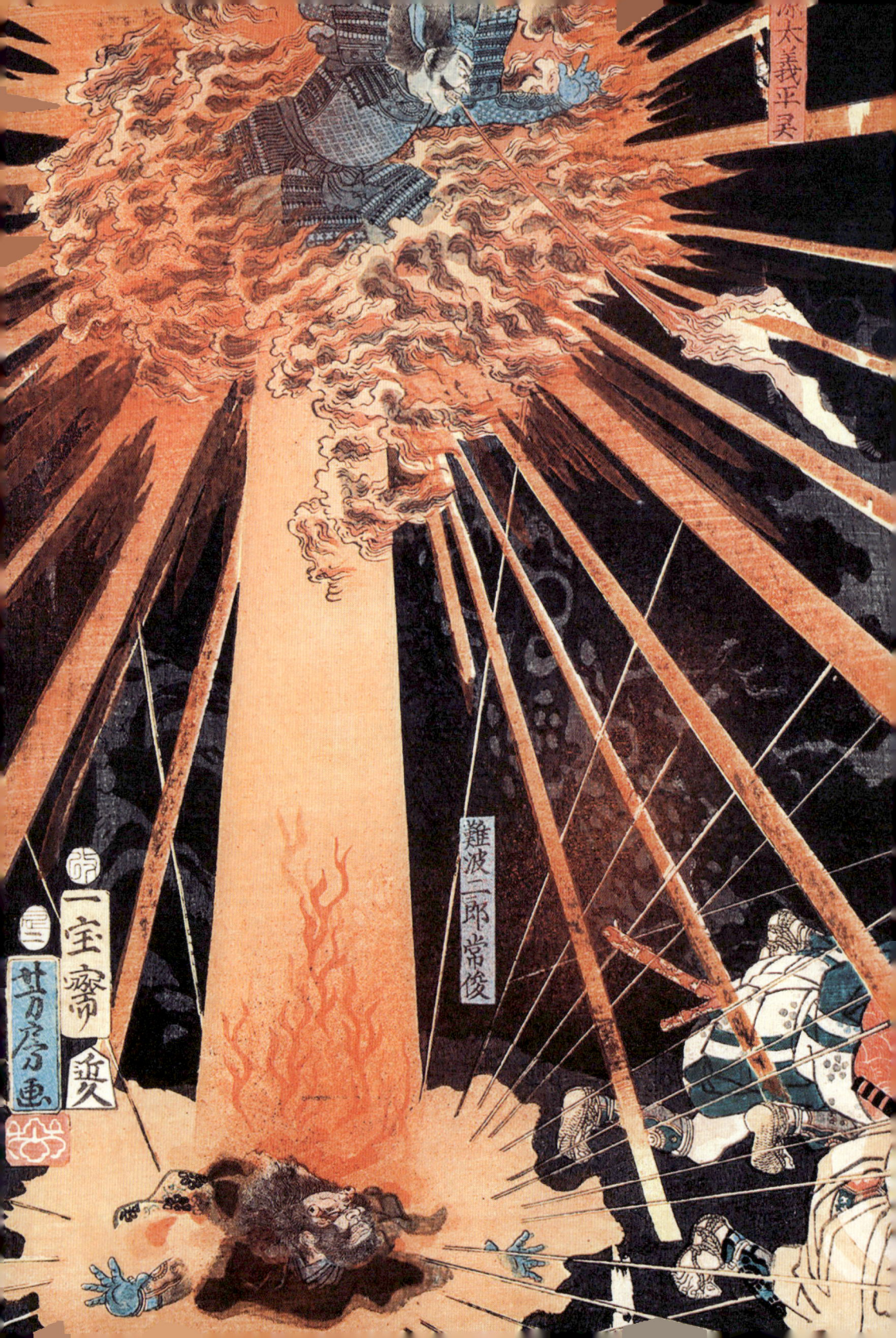

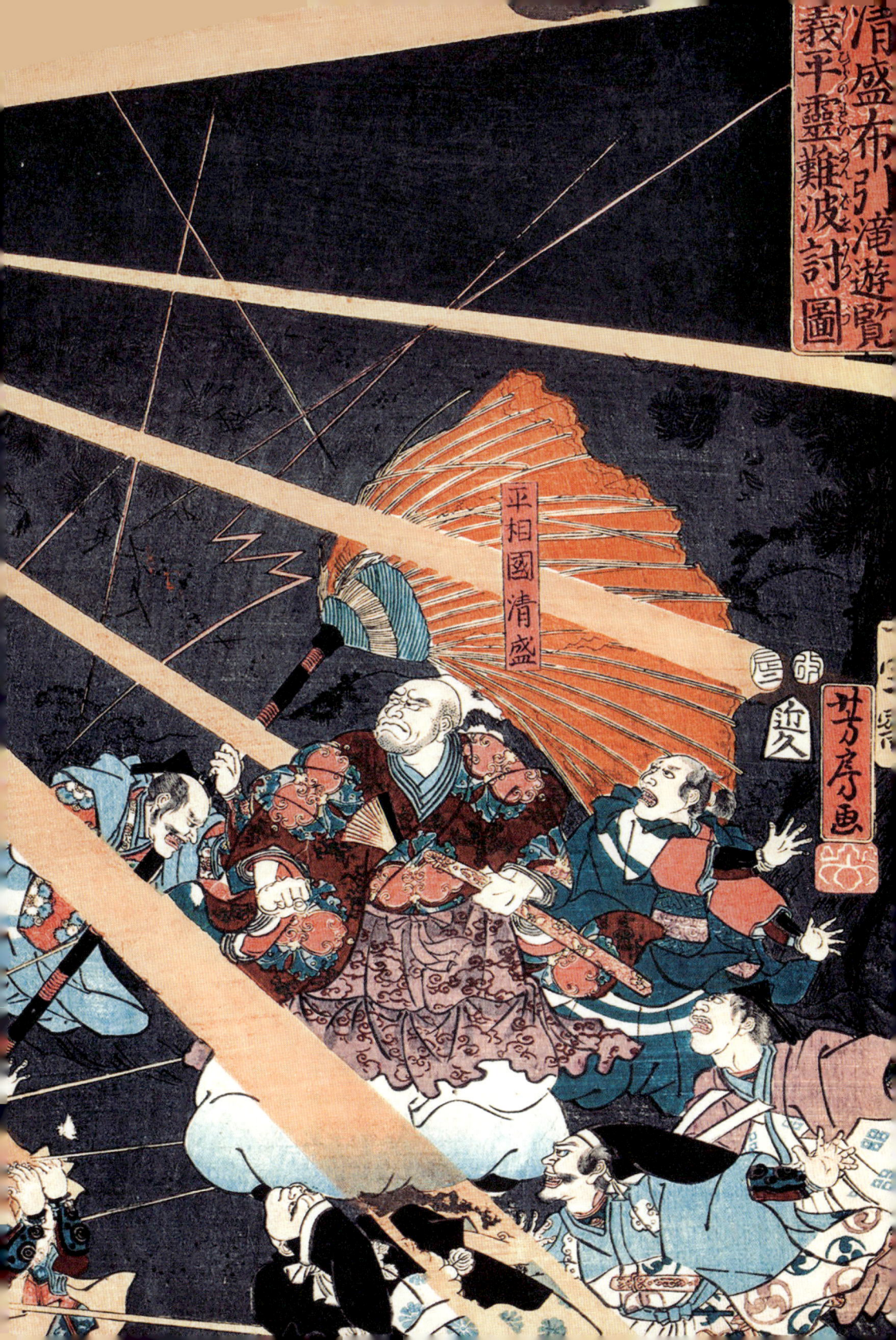

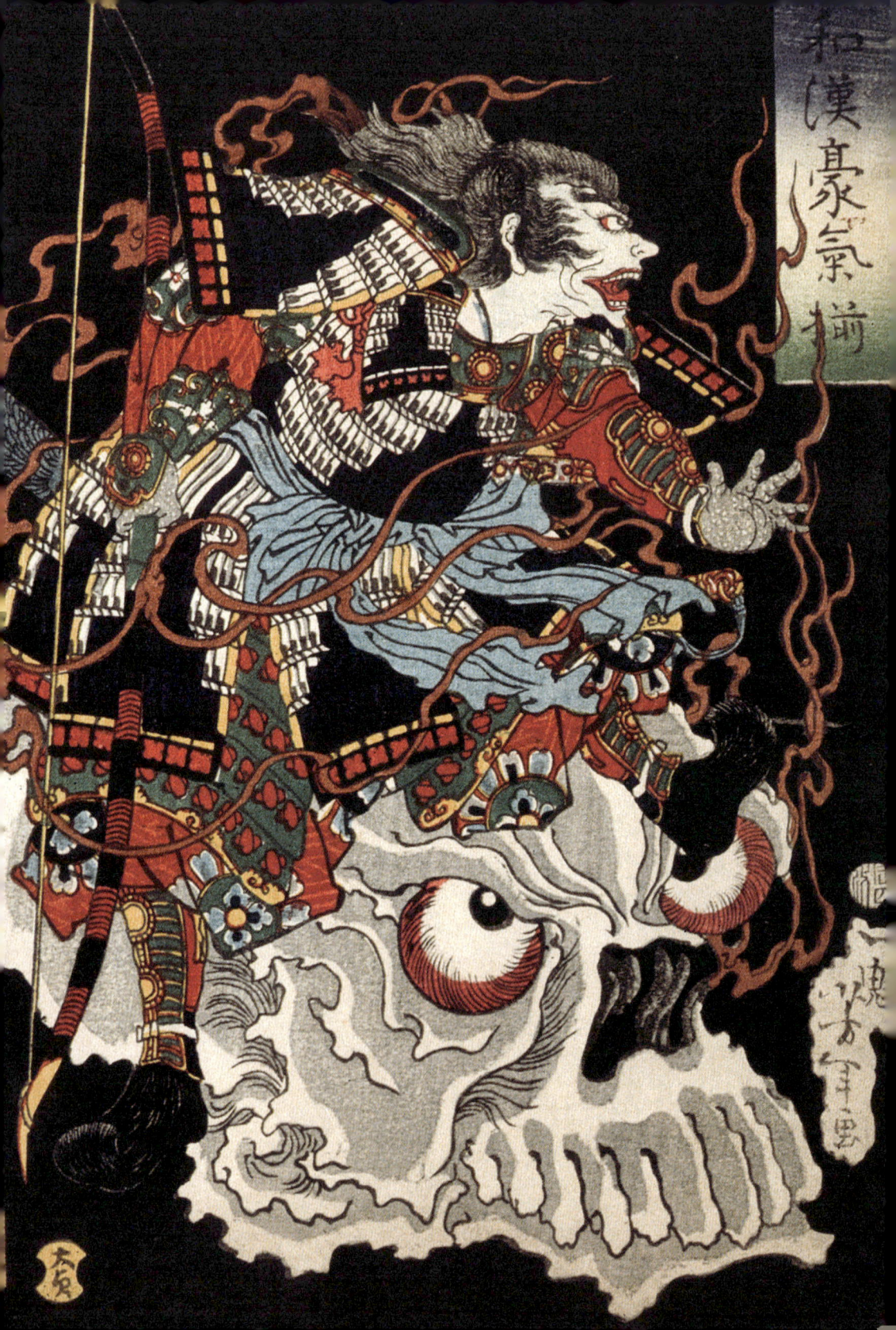

DEMONS OF THE BATTLE-FIELD

•

Death during battle, or in war more generally, is sudden and violent – it is a bad death, especially as the corpse is often mutilated and denied burial. As a result, the dead have great difficulty finding peace and embarking on the path to a new life in the cycle of reincarnation. On becoming *yūrei*, some will haunt the battlefields, while others will haunt the homes, roads or fields of their aggressors. Their appearance varies, depending on their social status at the time of death but also on the degree of resentment that grows within them over the centuries.

The *gashadokuro*, to take one example, are huge skeletons, often dozens of metres high, made up of the carelessly buried bones of fallen soldiers. Their staring eyes pop out of their sockets, and some are covered in shreds of mummified skin. When they appear to the living, they gnash their teeth and devour their victims with their enormous jaws. One of the oldest tales of this *yūrei* dates back to the tenth century. It tells of a warlord, Taira no Mosakado, who was killed and decapitated by two opponents, and then avenged by his daughter Takiyasha Hime, who possessed witch's powers. Using magic spells, she gathered up the bleached bones of her father's former comrades, who had died in battle and remained unburied, and turned them into a monstrous creature, a kind of 'superghost'. The monster ransacked the aggressors' city of Kyoto, and the head of Taira no Masakado rolled as far as a fishing village, which became Tokyo. This head is now interred near the Imperial Palace.

151

Other spirits, *ochimusha*, are the ghosts of samurai who fell in battle. They are as consumed with bitterness over their defeat as they are haunted by the fury of the peasants they bled dry to buy weapons and armour. Recognisable by their tonsure and crown of long hair, they drift across the sites where they committed their atrocities, hotly pursued by the living in 'ghost hunts', frightening livestock and people alike.

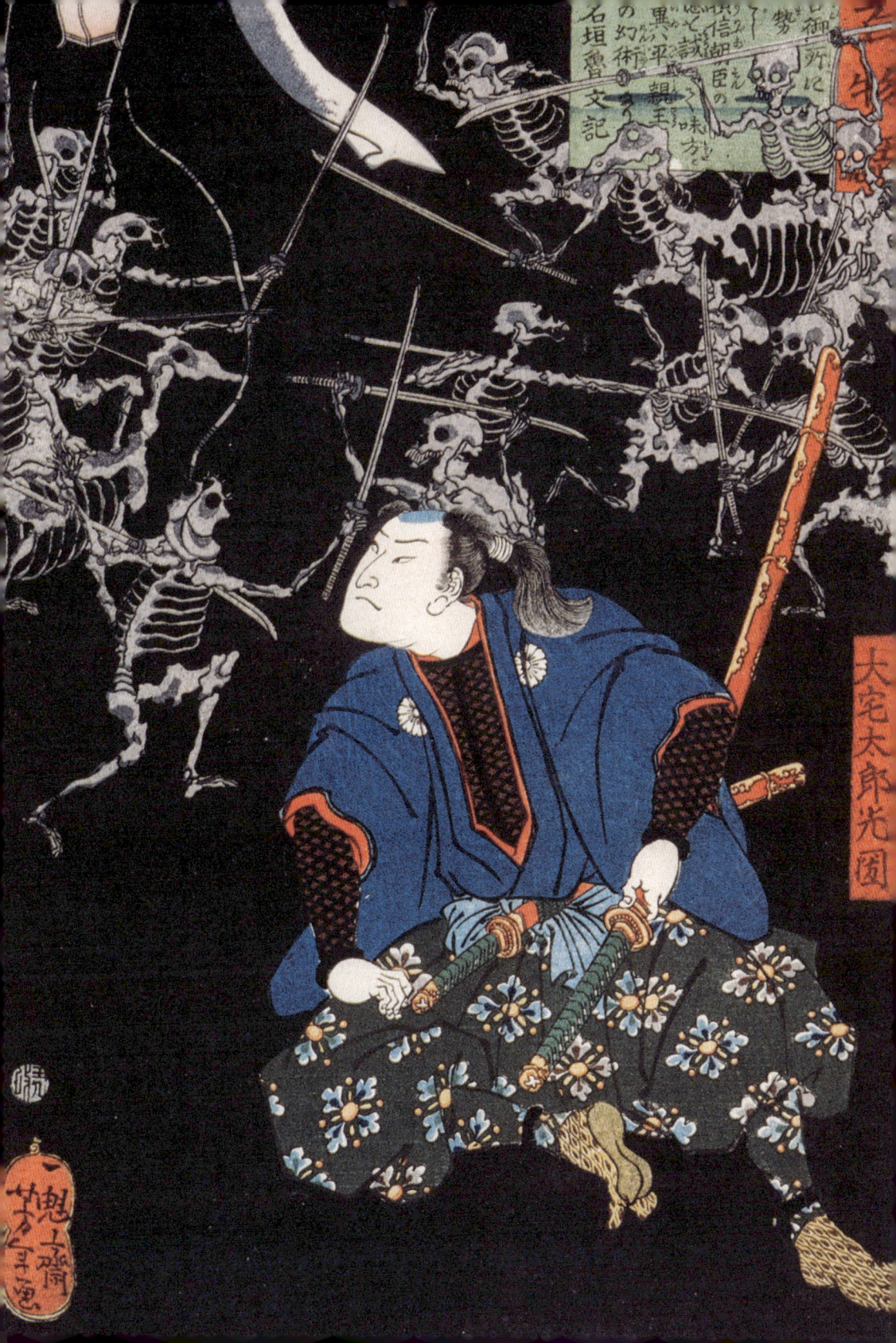

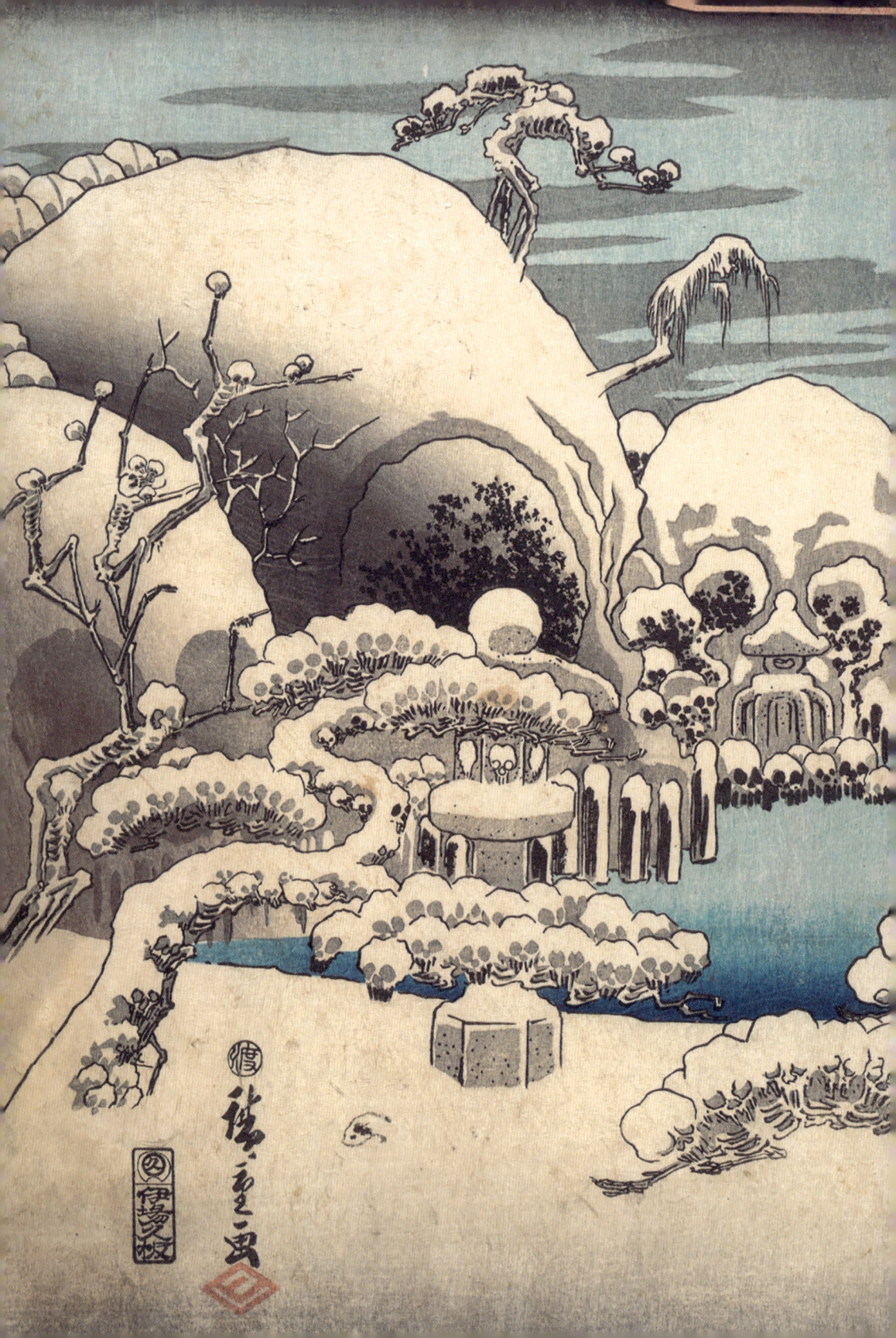

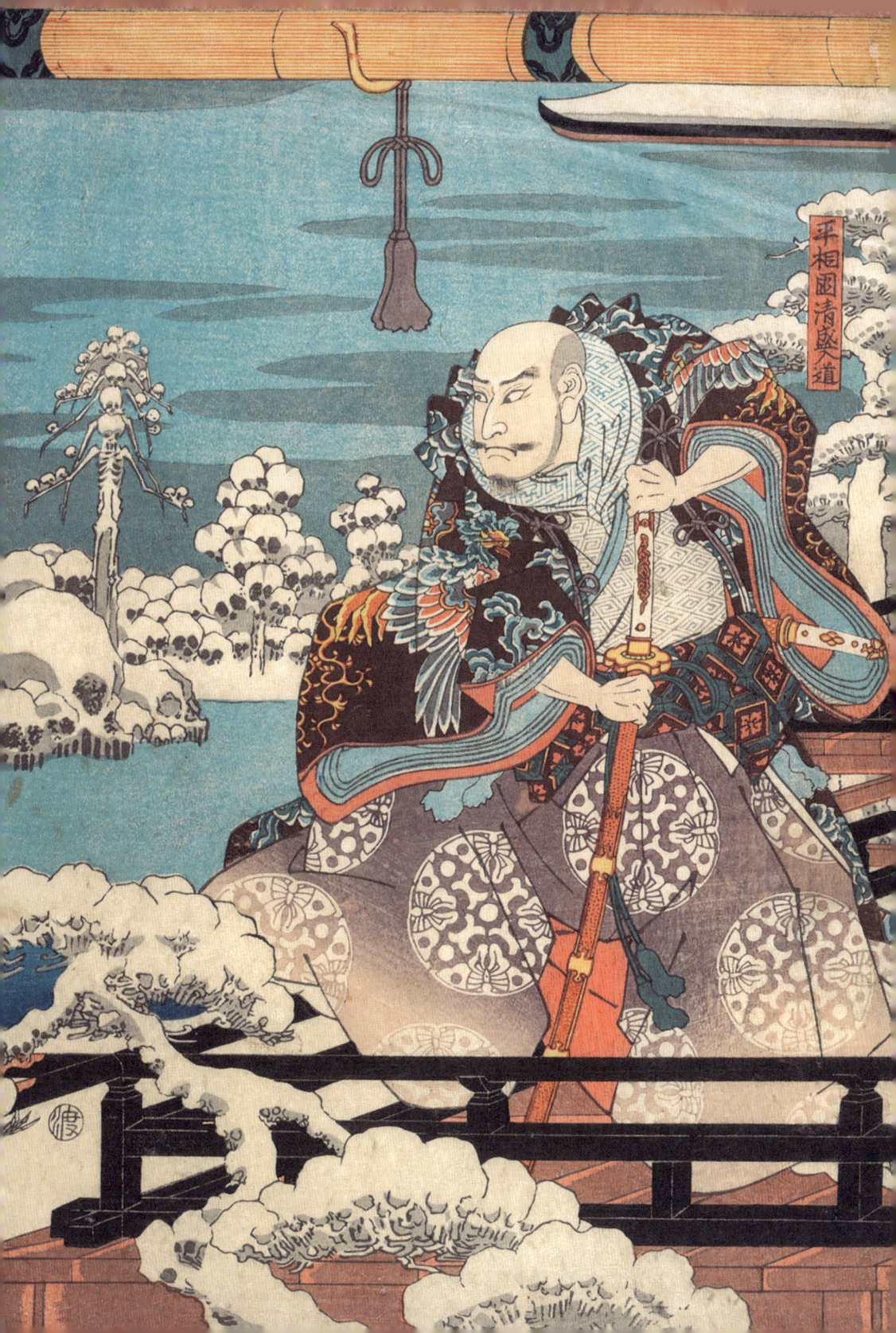

平相國清盛入道

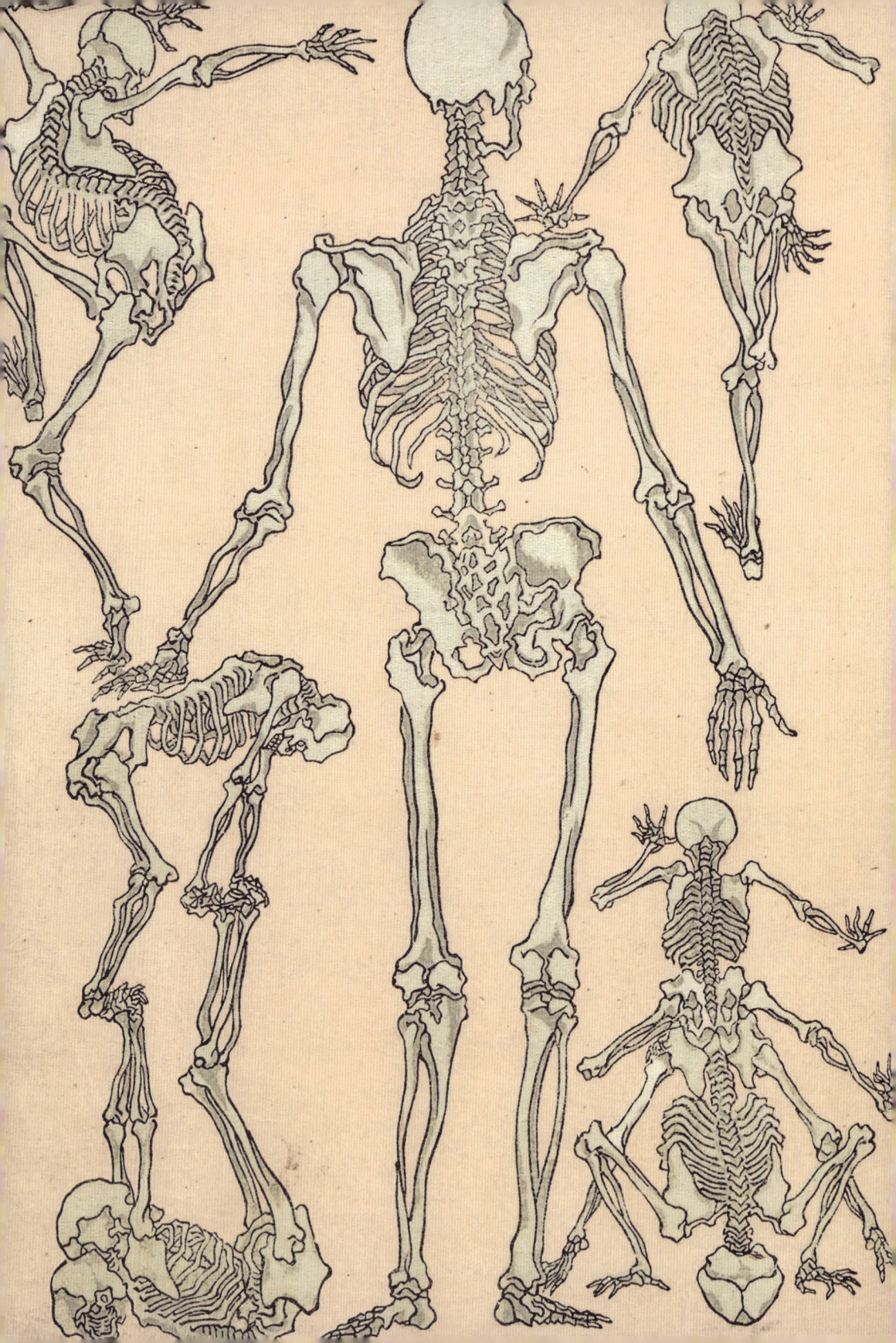

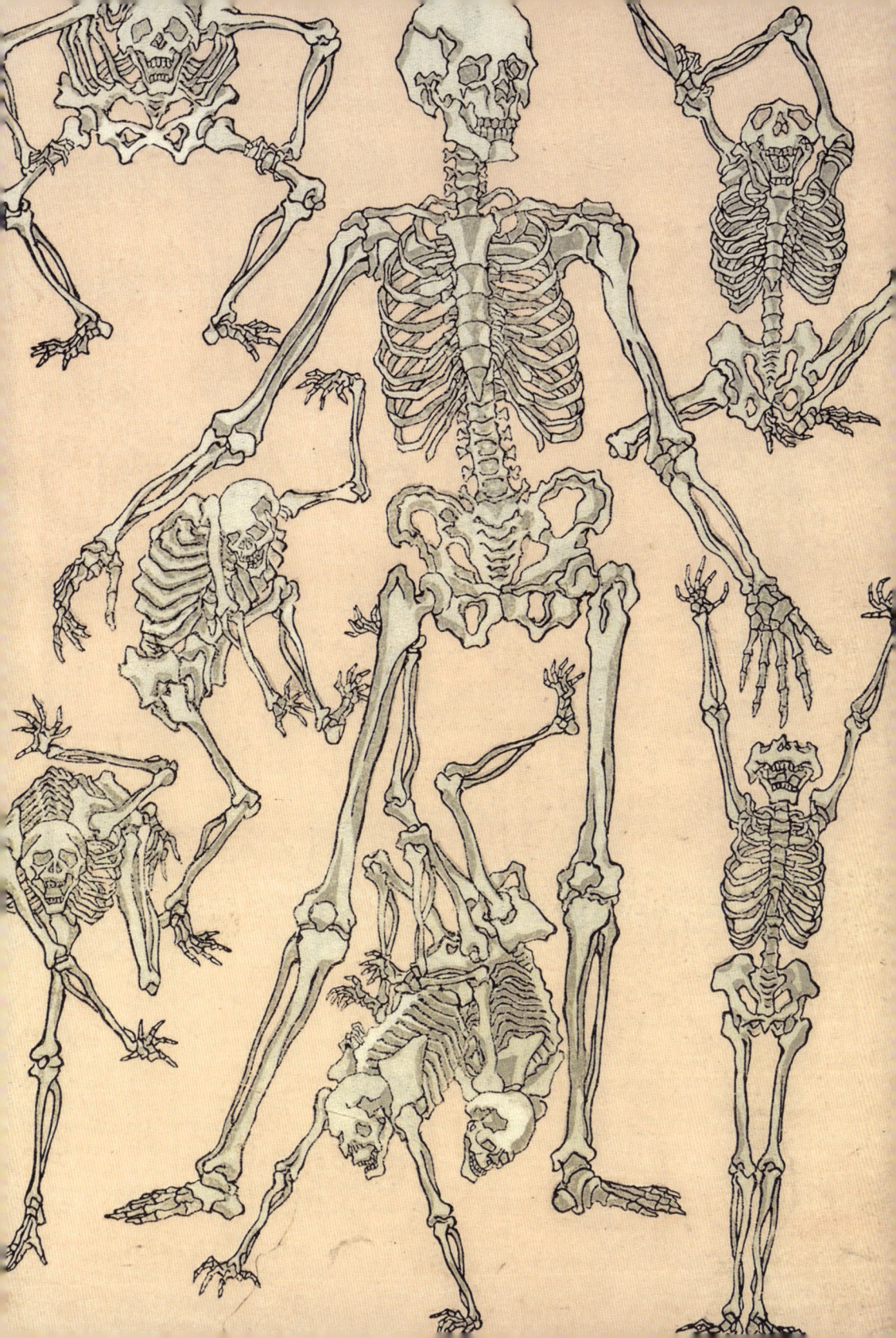

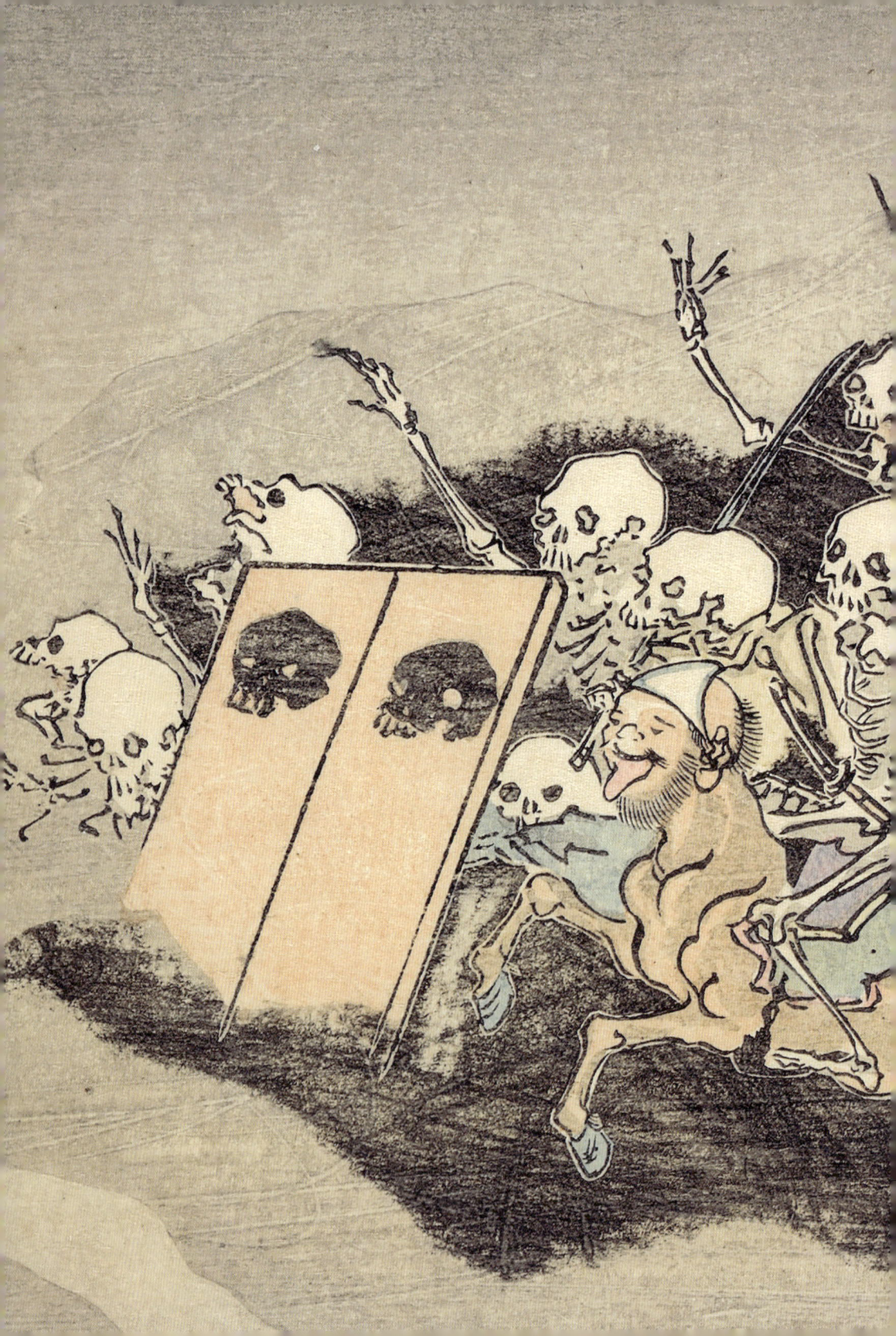

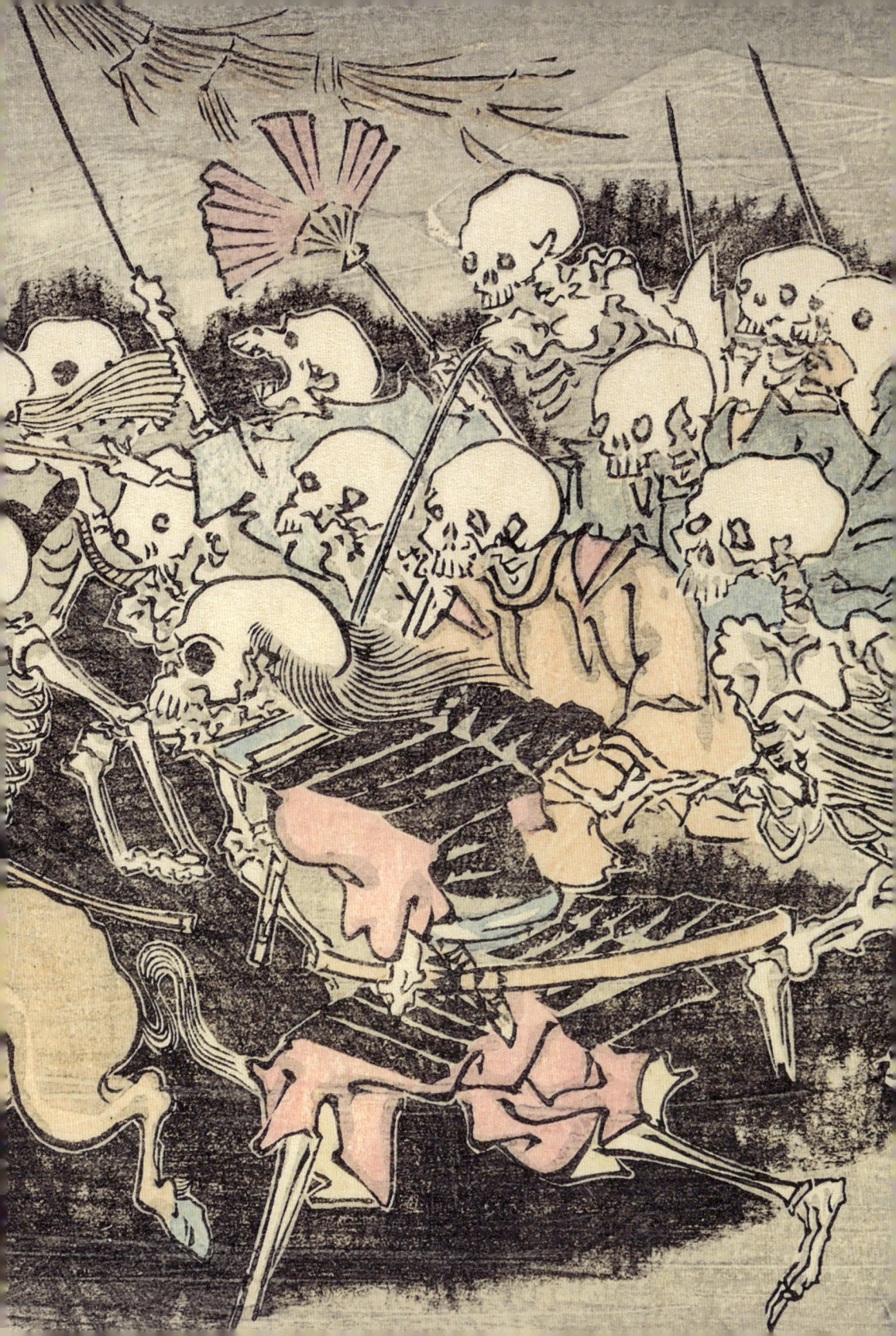

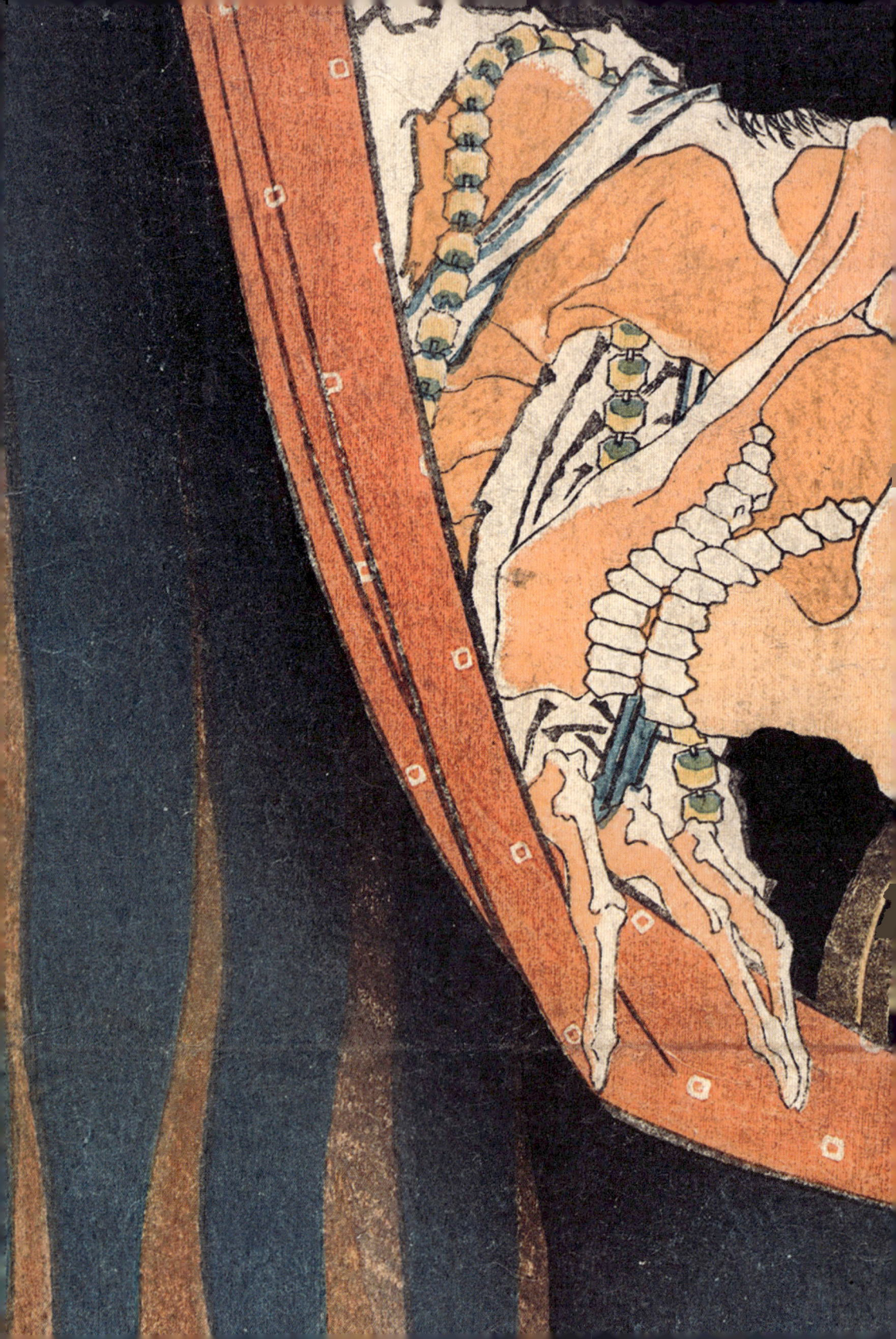

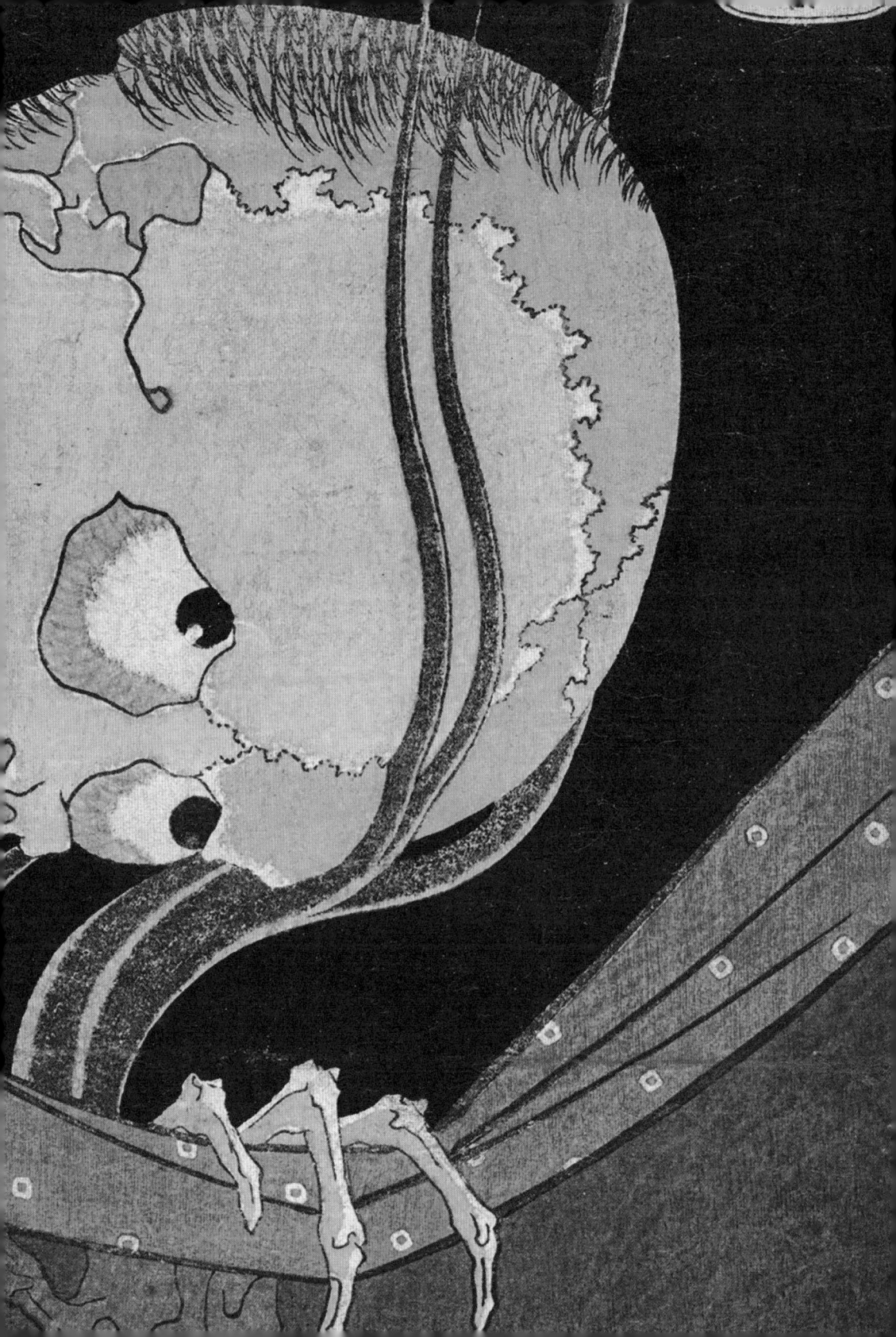

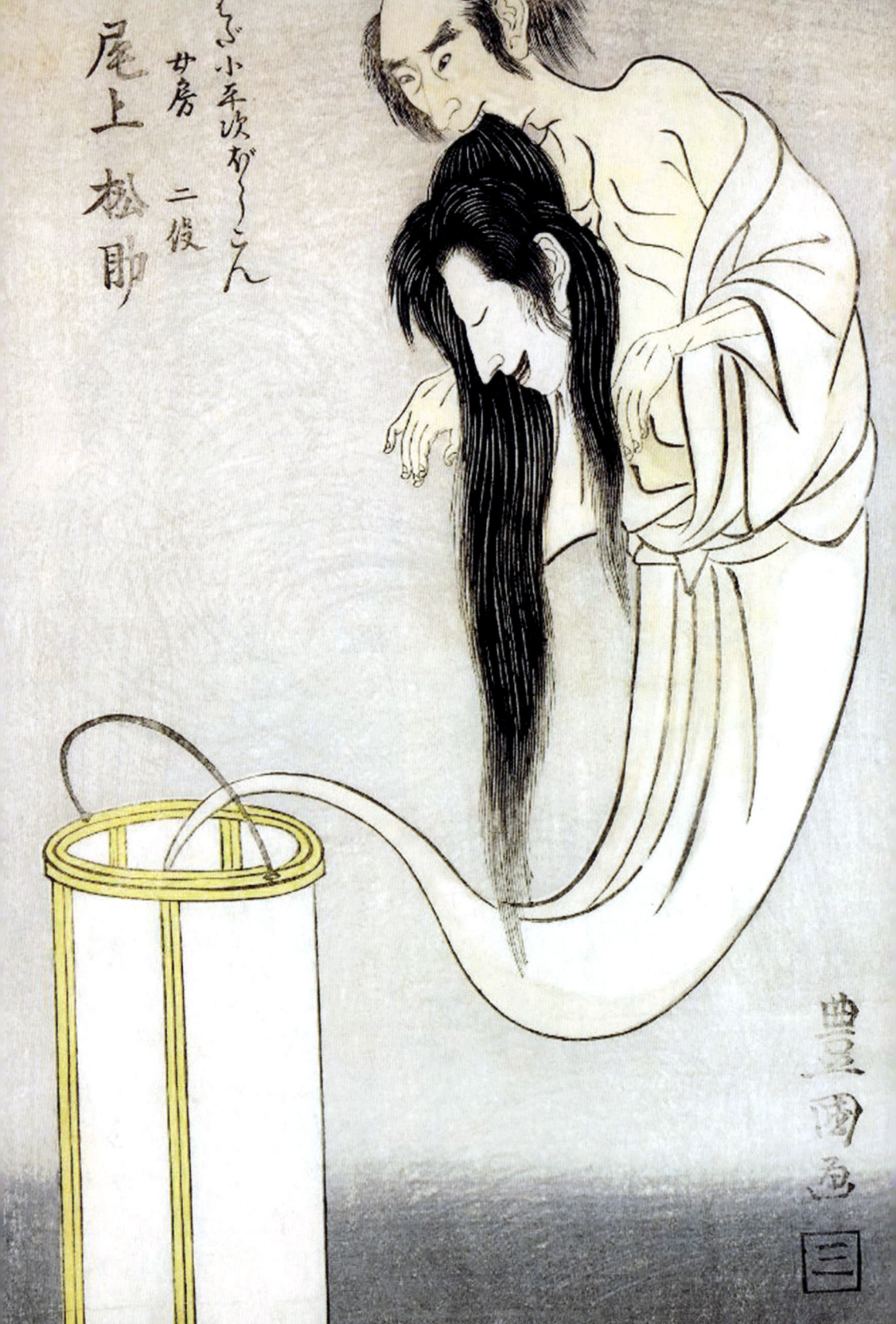

KOHADA KOHEIJI

•

Kohala Koheiji was an Edo-period Kabuki actor at Morita-za theatre, in present-day Tokyo. Lacking great talent, he was restricted to *yūrei* roles – perhaps a foreshadowing of his ultimate fate? His wife, tired of her humble existence, murdered him with the help of her lover (Adachi Sakura, himself an actor) and then tipped the corpse into an isolated marsh.

From that day on, Kohada Koheiji came back again and again to haunt the diabolical lovers, appearing in the form of a hideous skeleton surrounded by small flames. In numerous prints (and some erotic drawings, or *shunga*), his murderers can be seen making love while he himself hides in the bed under a mosquito net or mockingly pulls his unfaithful wife's hair.

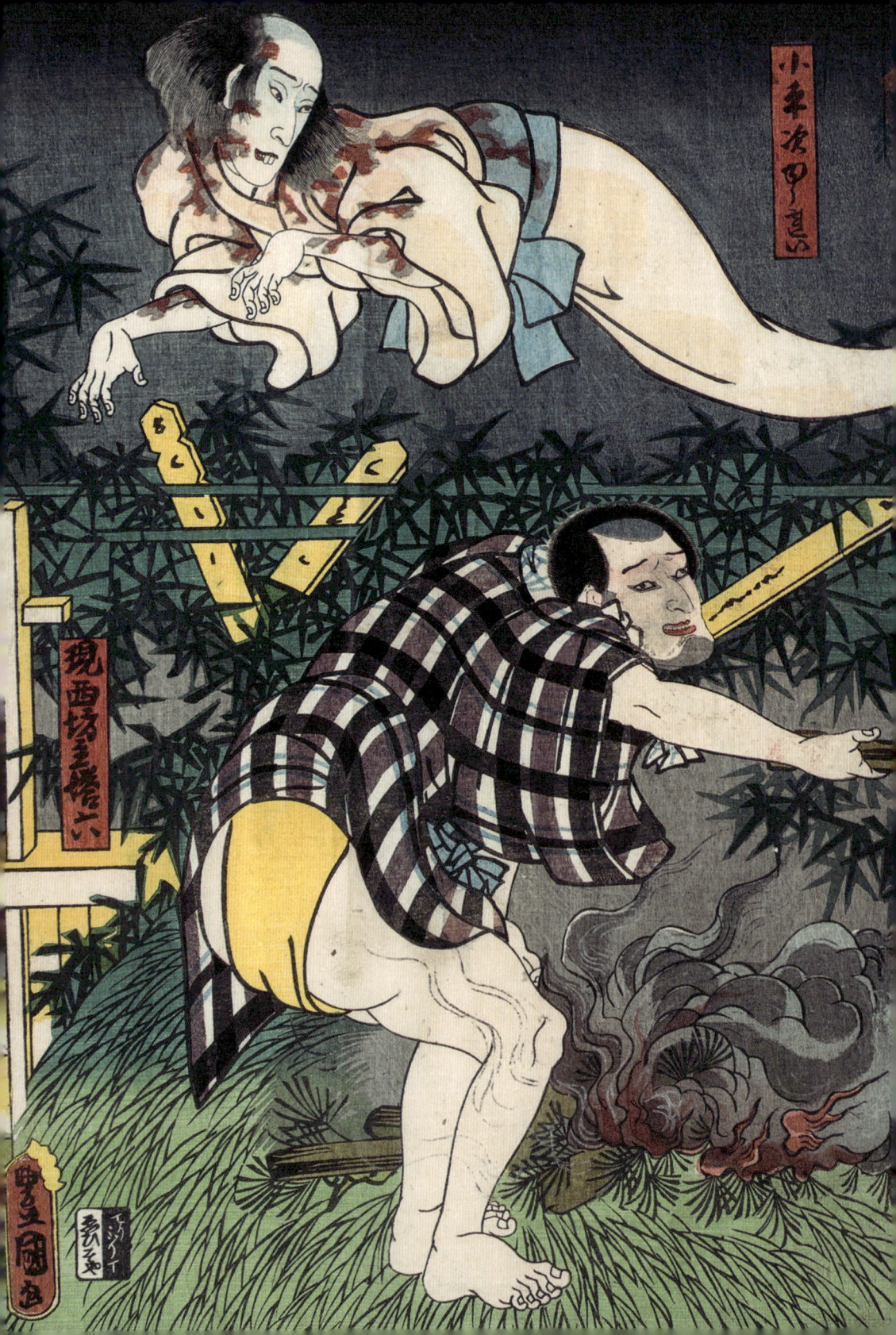

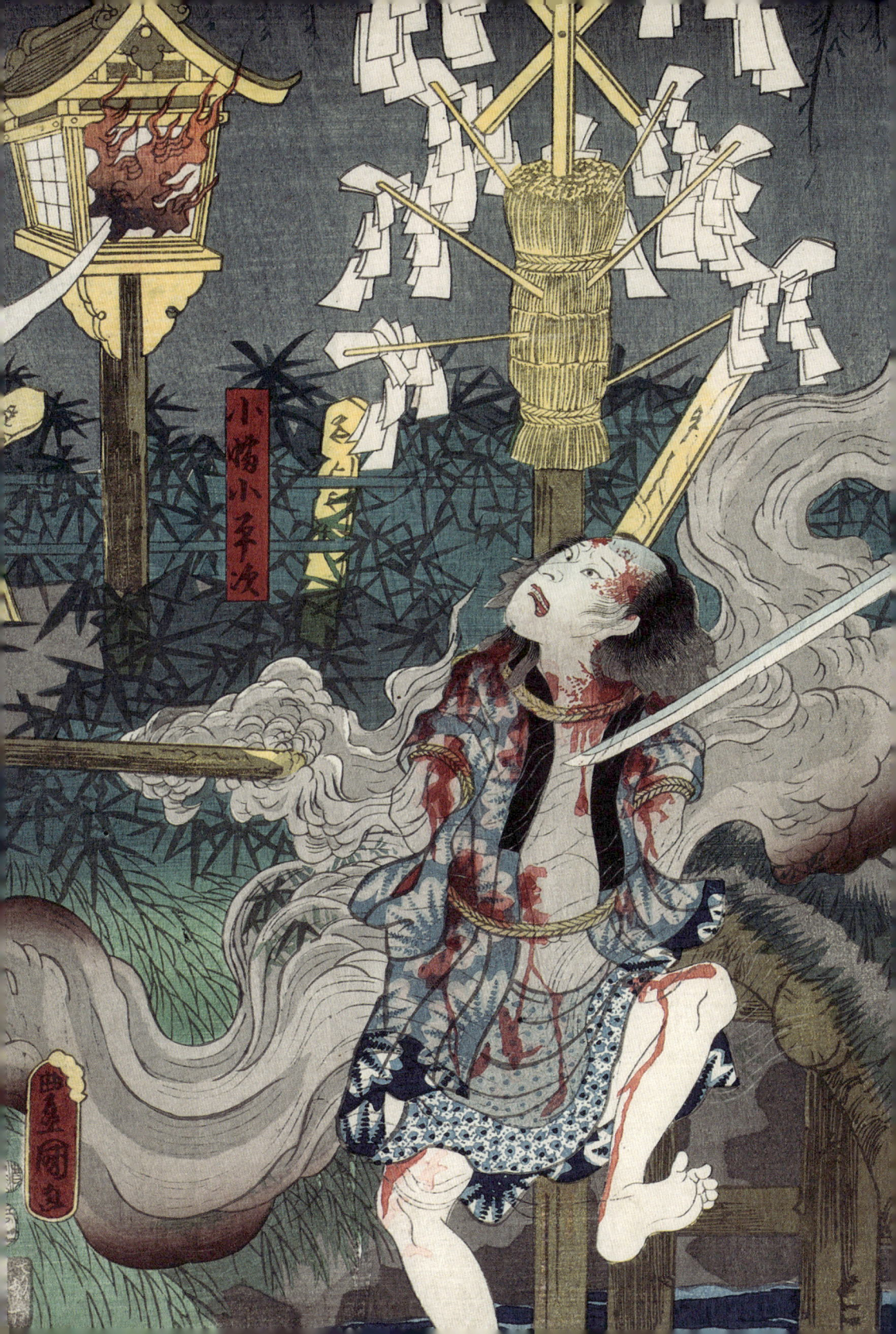

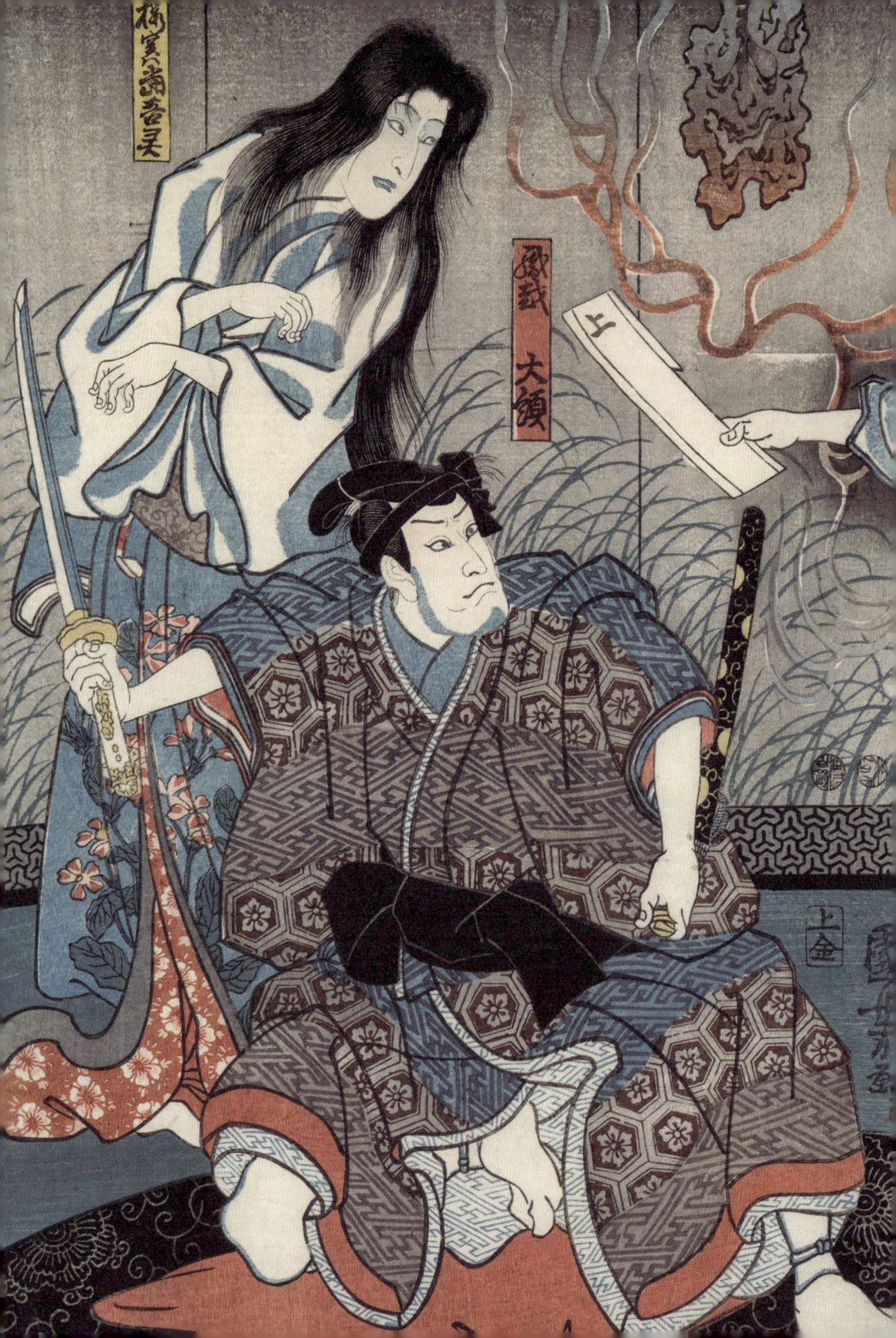

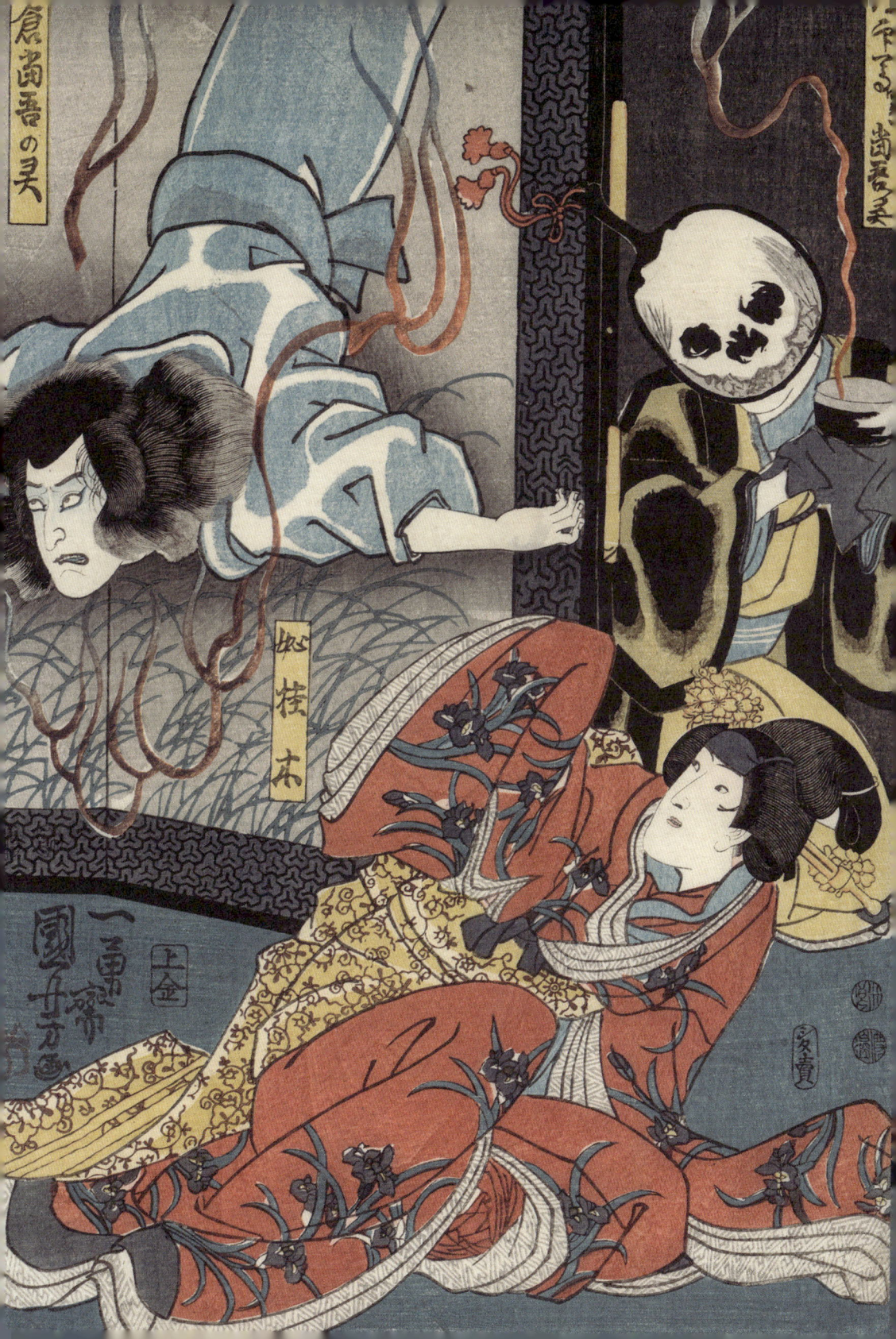

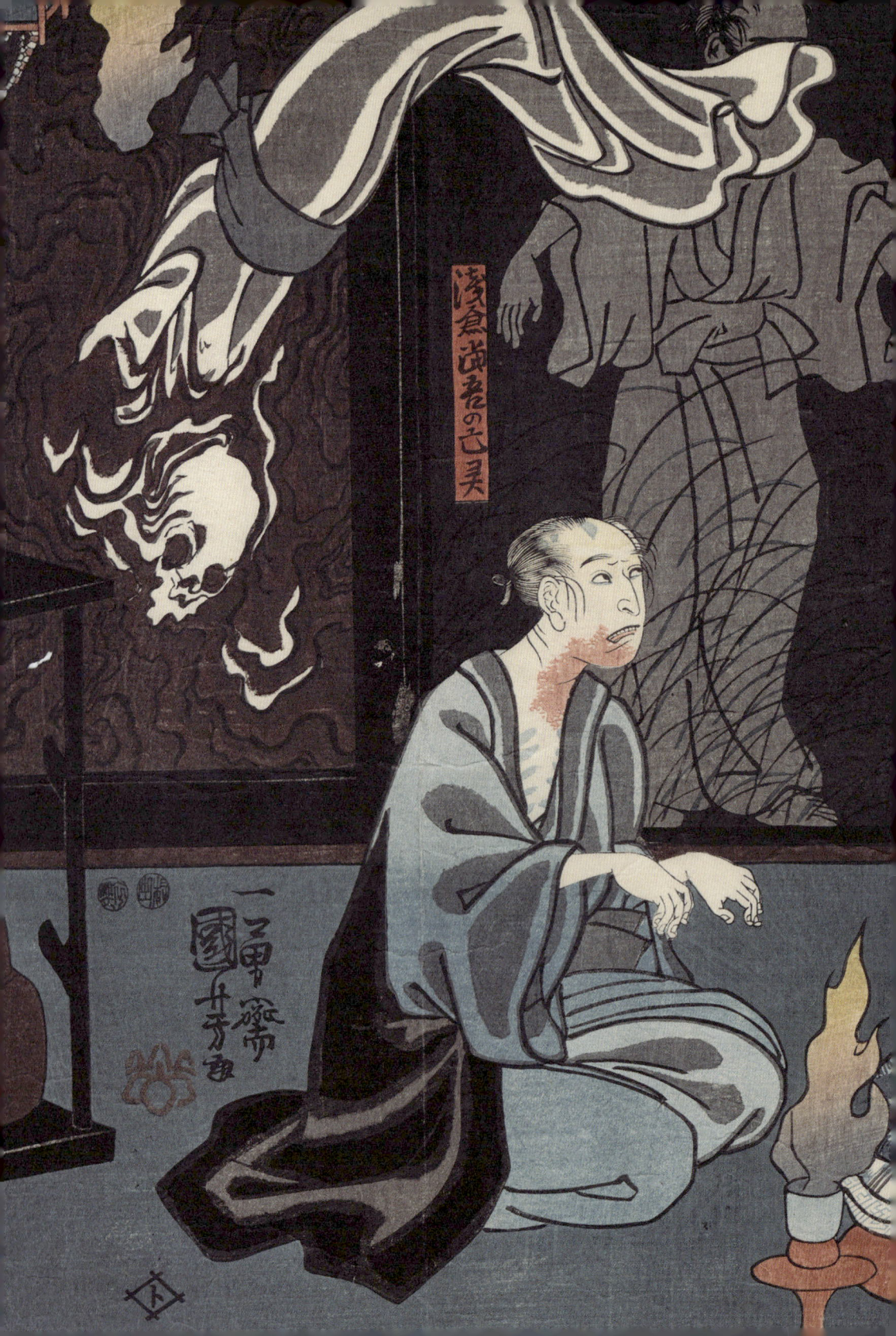

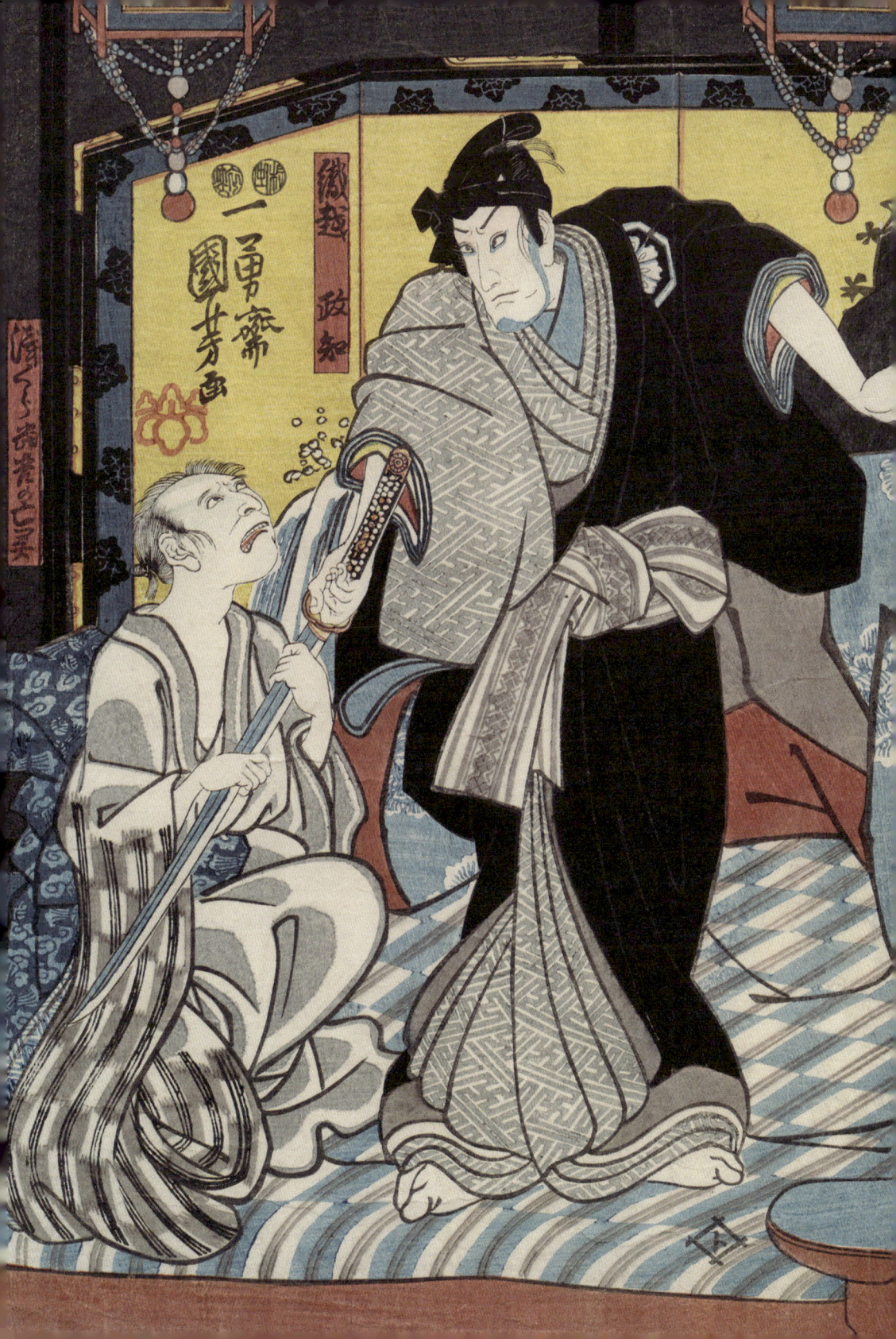

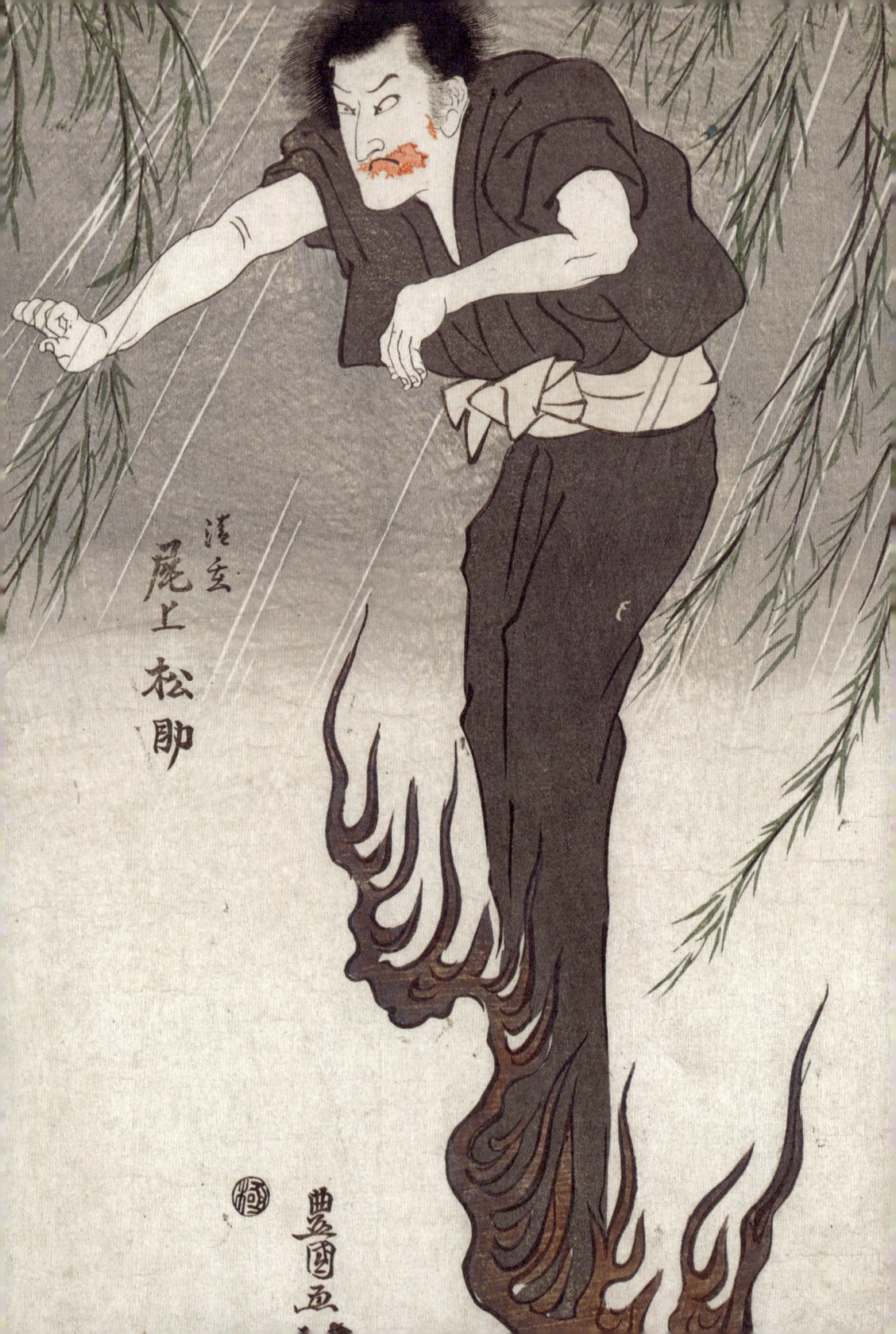

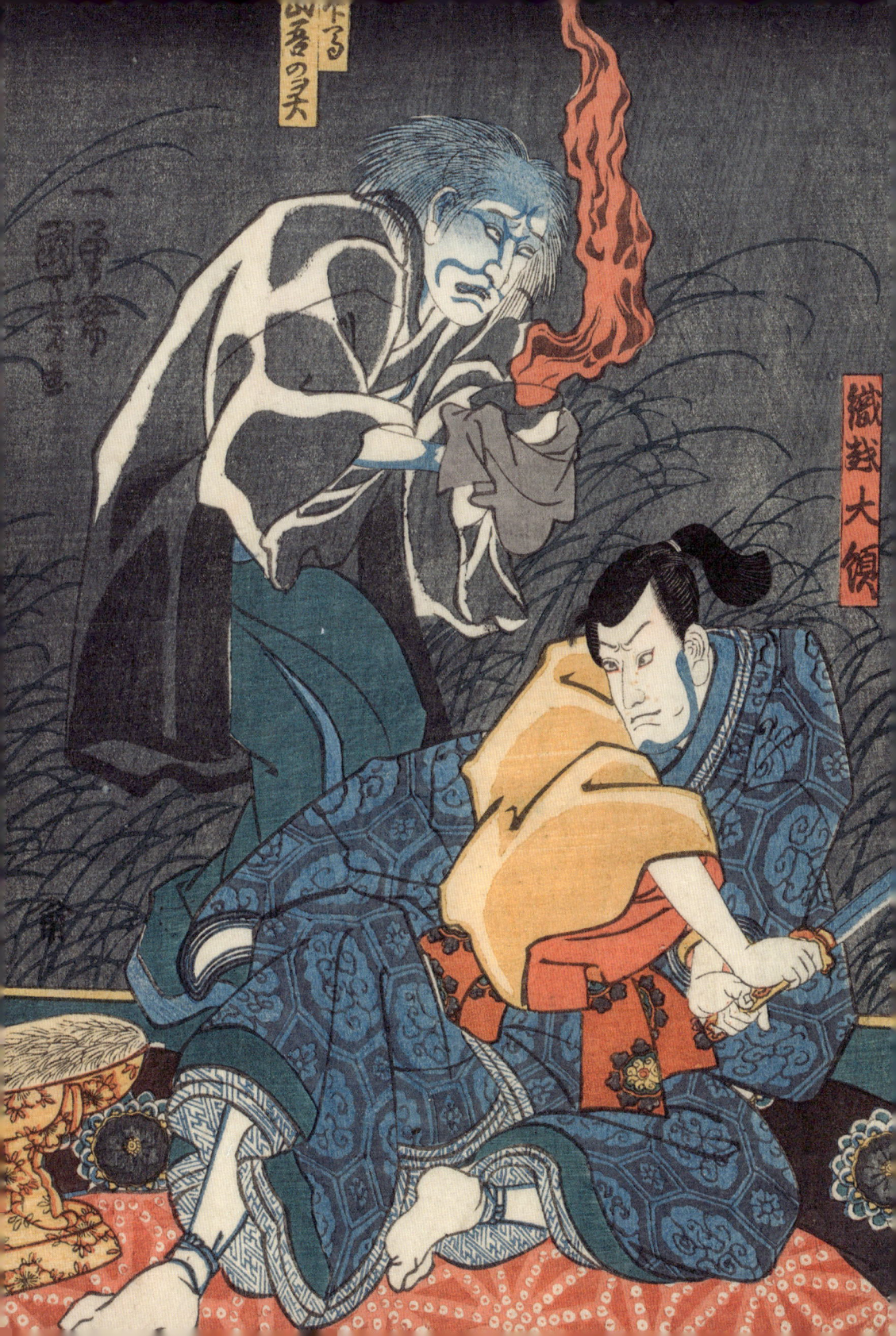

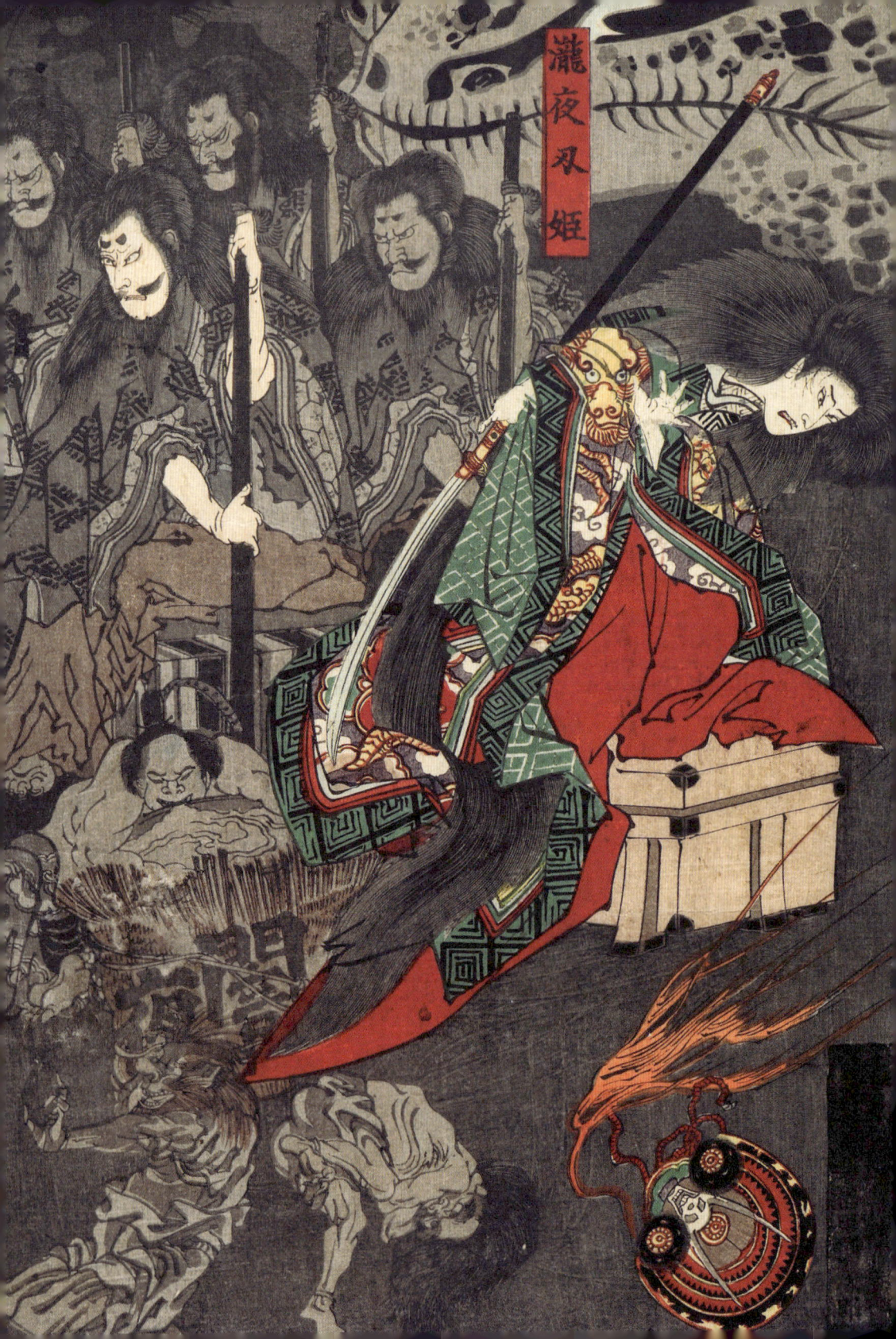
瀧夜叉姫

IMAGES OF TWO INTERLACED WORLDS

•

Many of these paintings are rendered in vibrant color, while others appear deathly pale and cold. Occasionally they are human-sized, like mirrors reflecting a parallel world; and sometimes they are small, like miniatures depicting a land of mysteries and chills. In them, we see the living, the dead, skeletons, shadows, spectres, wills-o'-the-wisp, silhouettes, sketches, ghosts, monsters, pools of blood, and strange shapes that defy reason. The pictures are home to a whole hidden population that speaks of love and death. The motifs are many: We see swords drawn to finish off invisible enemies. A floating head with eyes rolled upwards. An indefinite shape emerging from a dim lantern. A corpse endlessly decomposing. A young girl's *danse macabre* with a sack of bones. Flames outlining a coffin. The hideous lips of a cursed old woman. Phantom boats surging out of raging tides. A snowstorm bringing implacable death. A haunted well vomiting immortal venomous snakes. Horned, grimacing masks. Dead eyes with square pupils. Unhuman hands lacking fingernails. Fatal encounters. Unsolved enigmas. Inns whose beds welcome walking nightmares. Brides with revolting tongues, hanged in a noose of their own hair. Actors made up like ghosts (or ghosts made up like actors?). Dramas endlessly and unfathomably repeating themselves. Child-devouring crabs. Octopuses raping sponge-fisherwomen. Waves as tall as temples and as ravenous as fox-spirits.

173

Implacable armies eviscerating graves. Giant cats crunching on children, the way they toy with mice. Hideously grinning vagabonds baring diabolical teeth. Buddhist divinities and Shinto kamis looking helpless and impotent. Clouds billowing in the shape of skull pyramids. A destitute monk being beaten by bloodstained shrouds. Ruined houses peopled by ghosts. A winged demon screeching his hatred of life and the living. A female spectre exiting the canvas to scare the painter who has come to trace her outlines.

Death, death everywhere. Suffering and fear – above all, fear – ever present. Whoever believes that our eyes are all-seeing and our senses can take it all in is suffering from delusions. This world is far too complex for that.

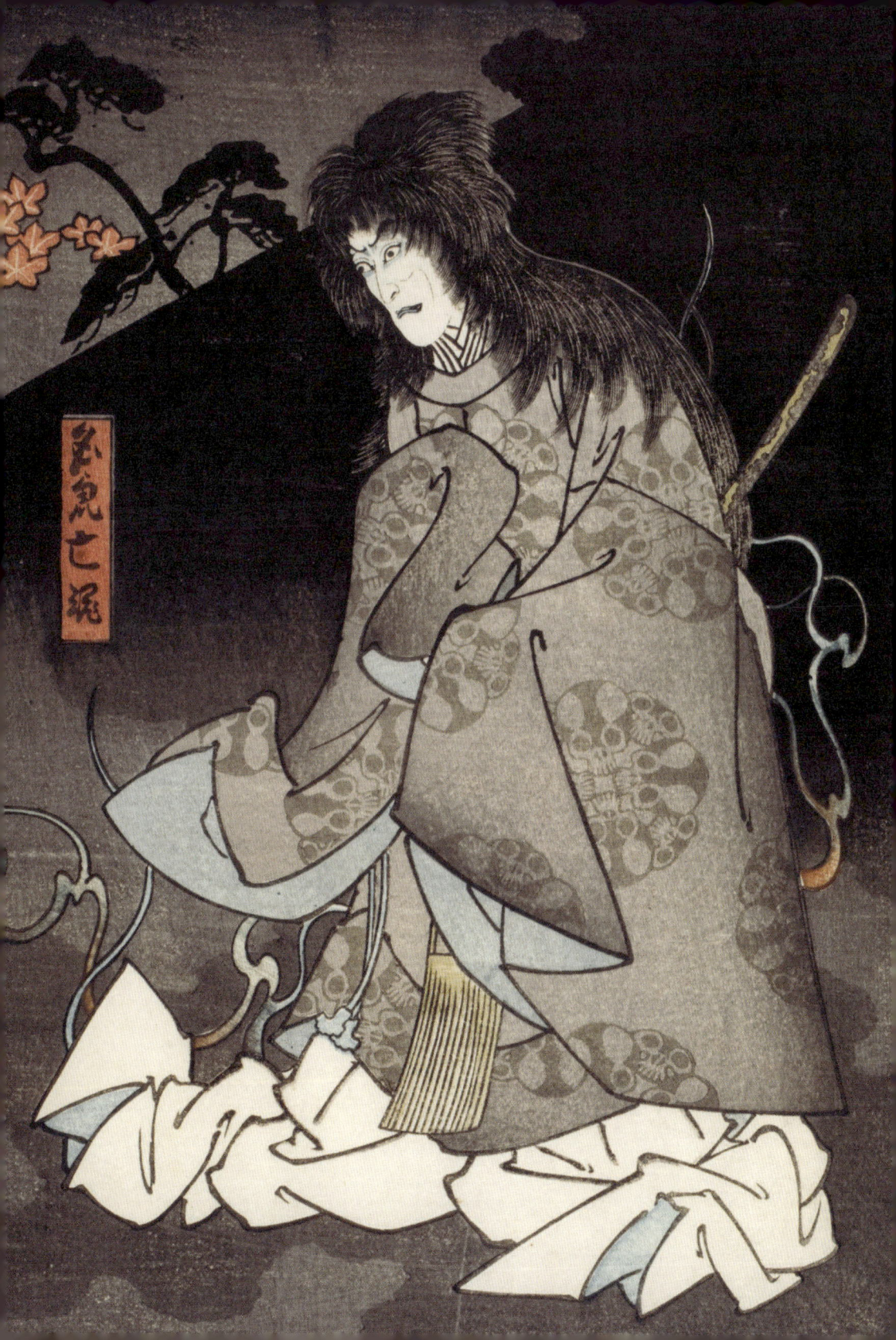

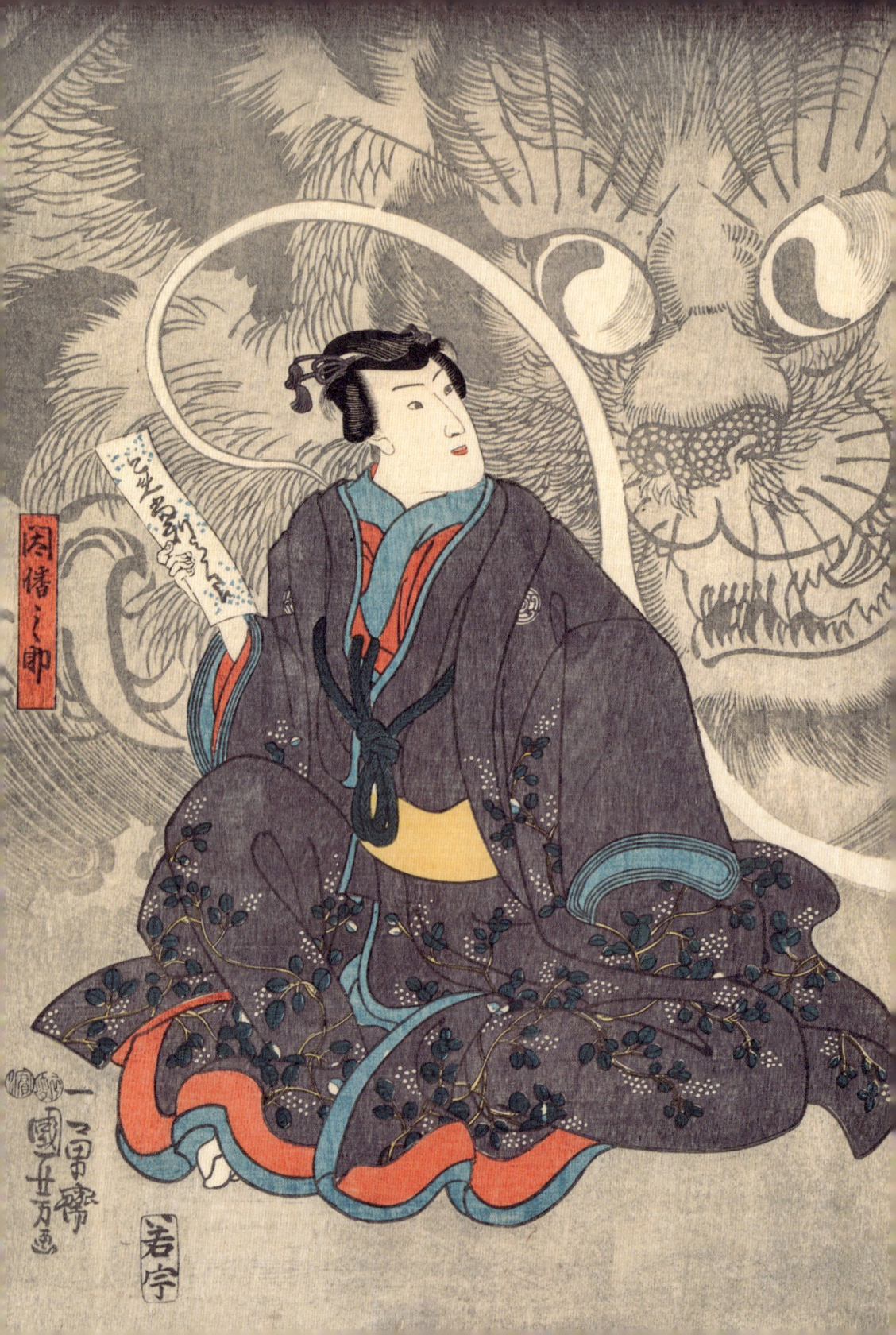

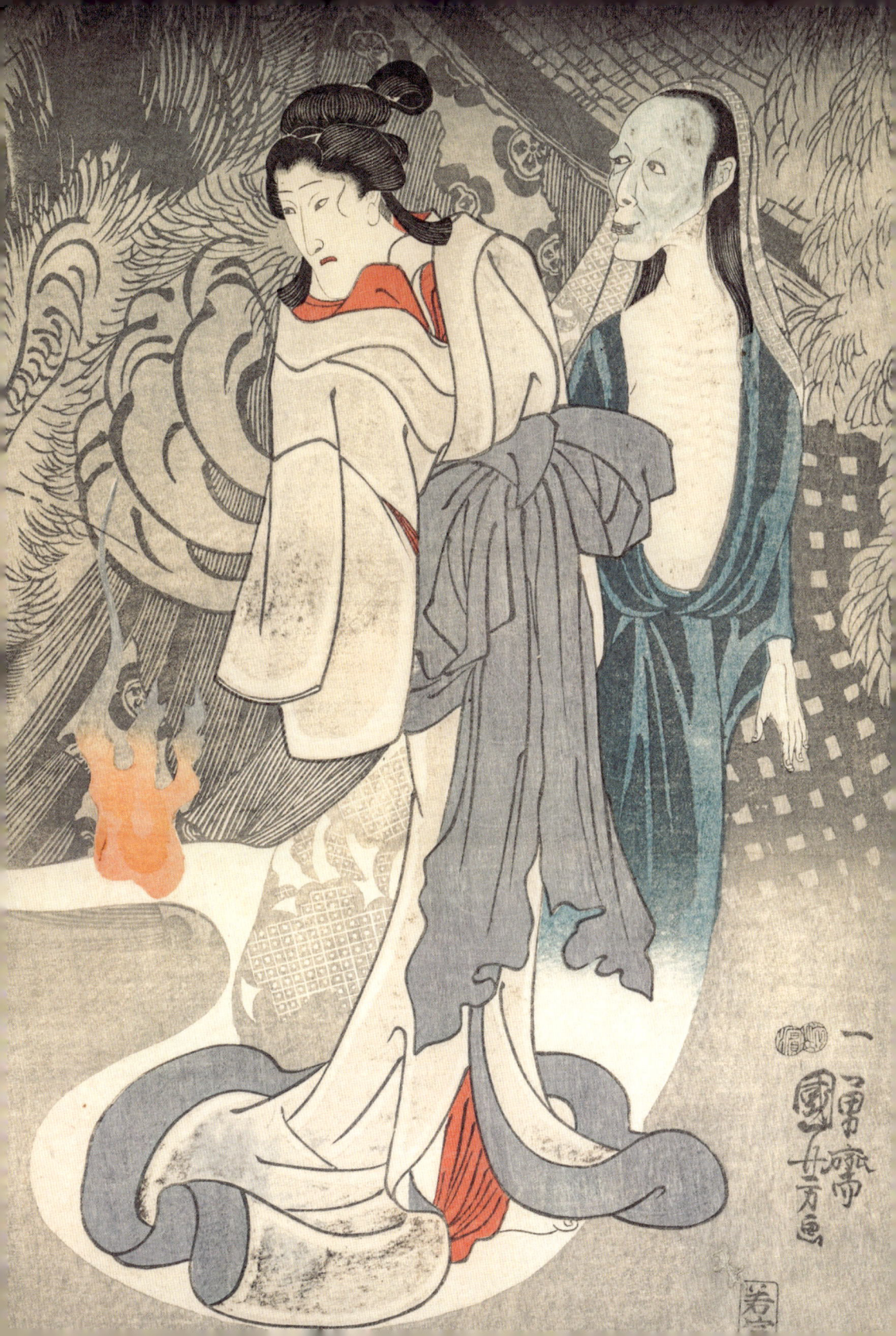

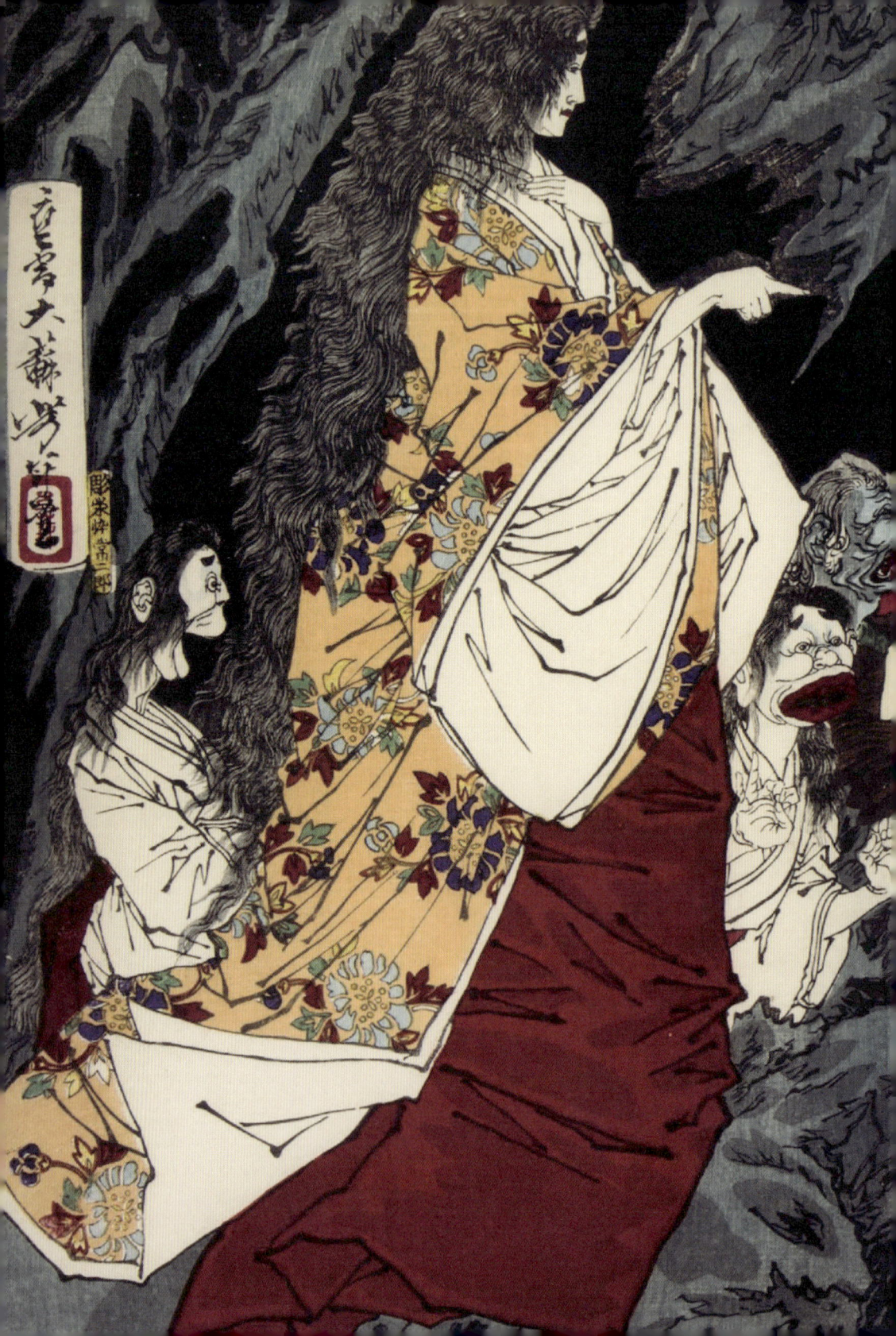

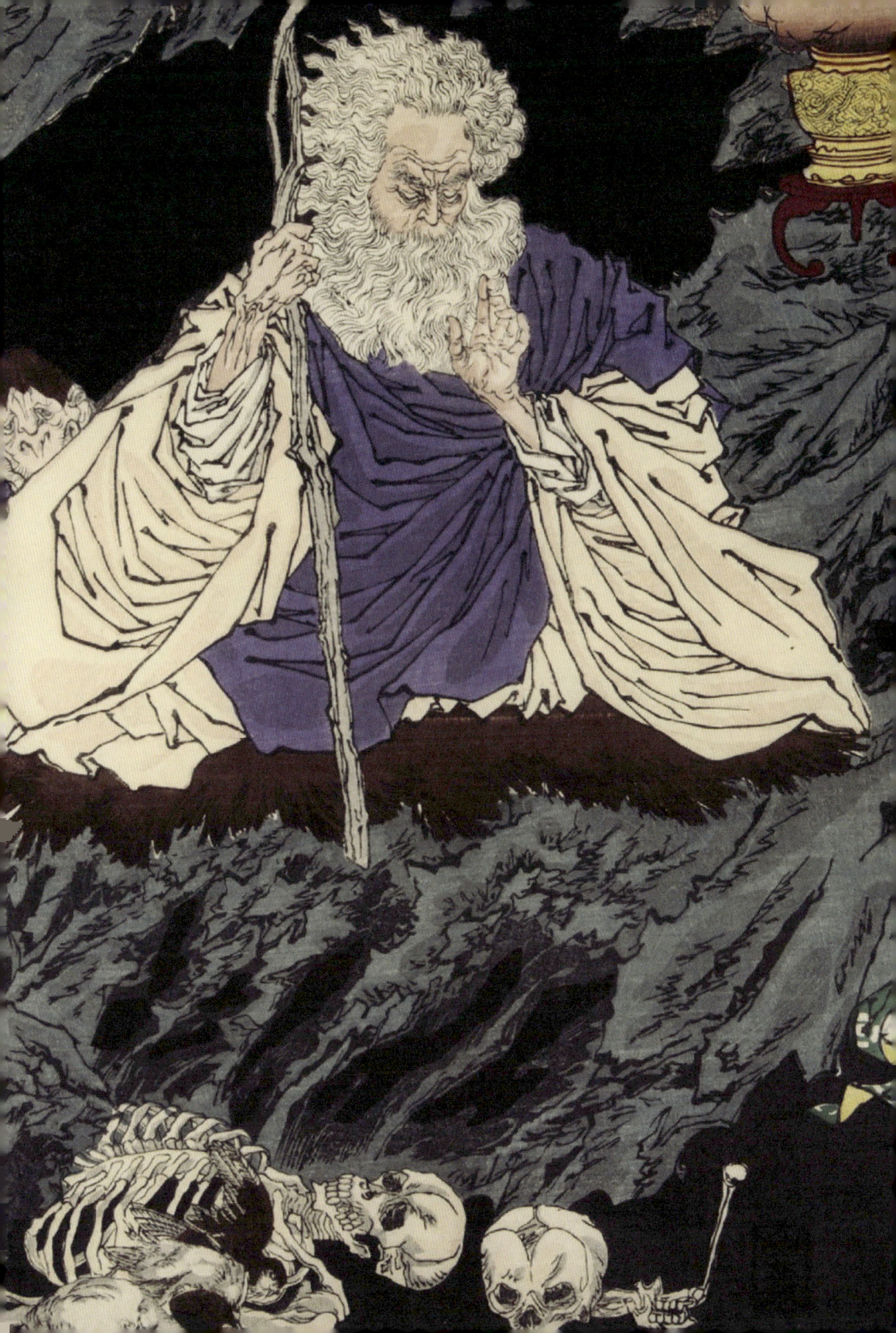

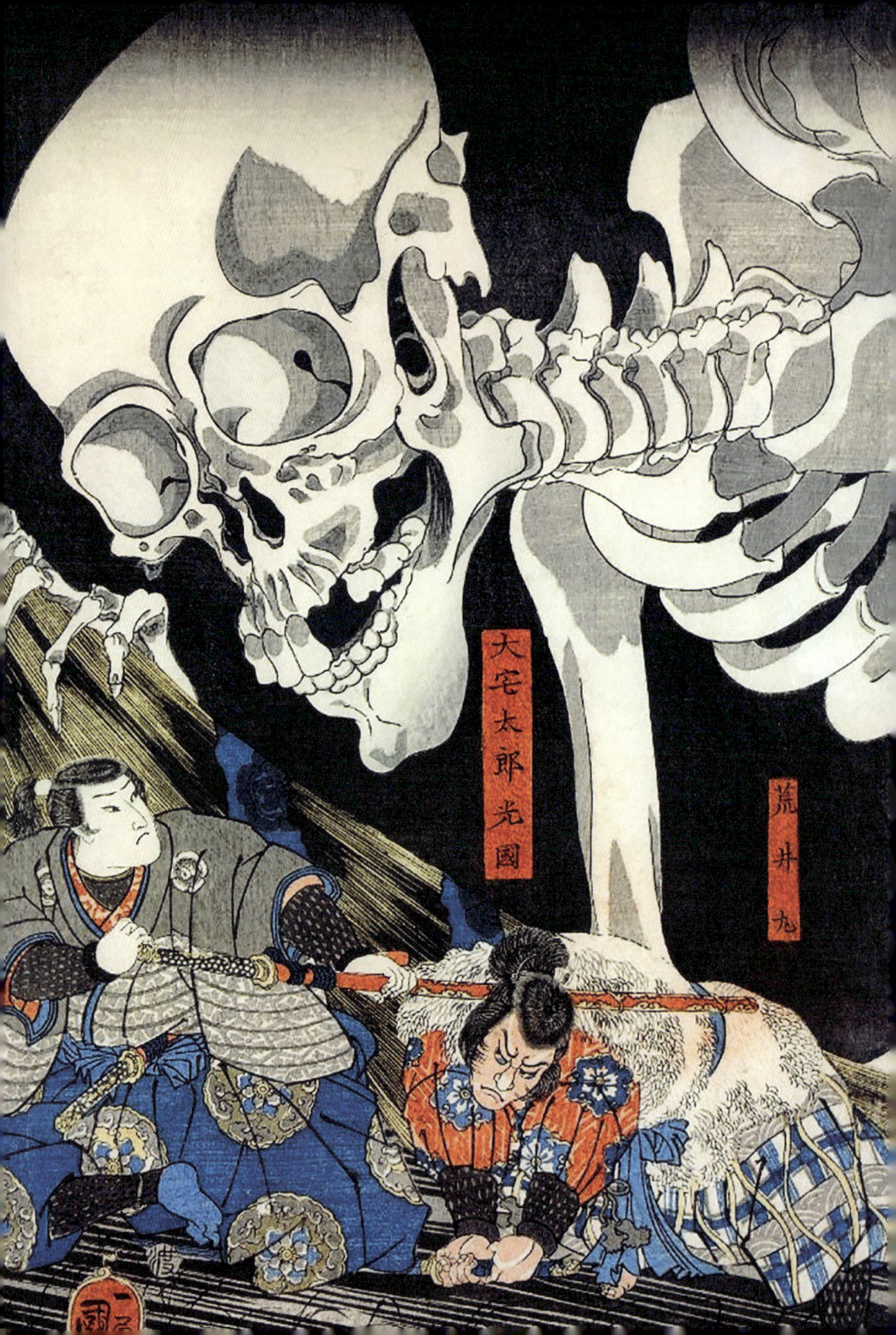

大宅太郎光國

荒井丸

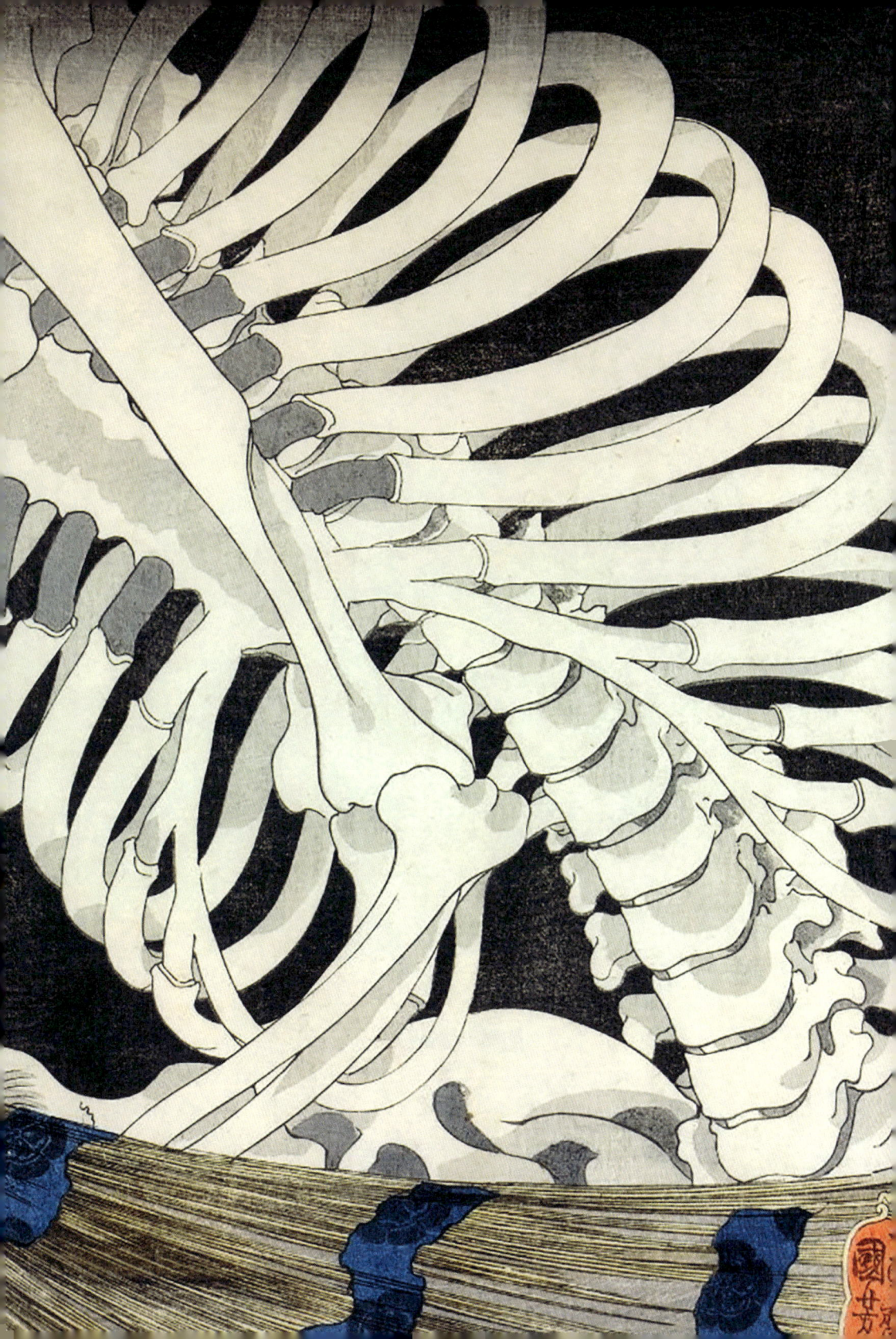

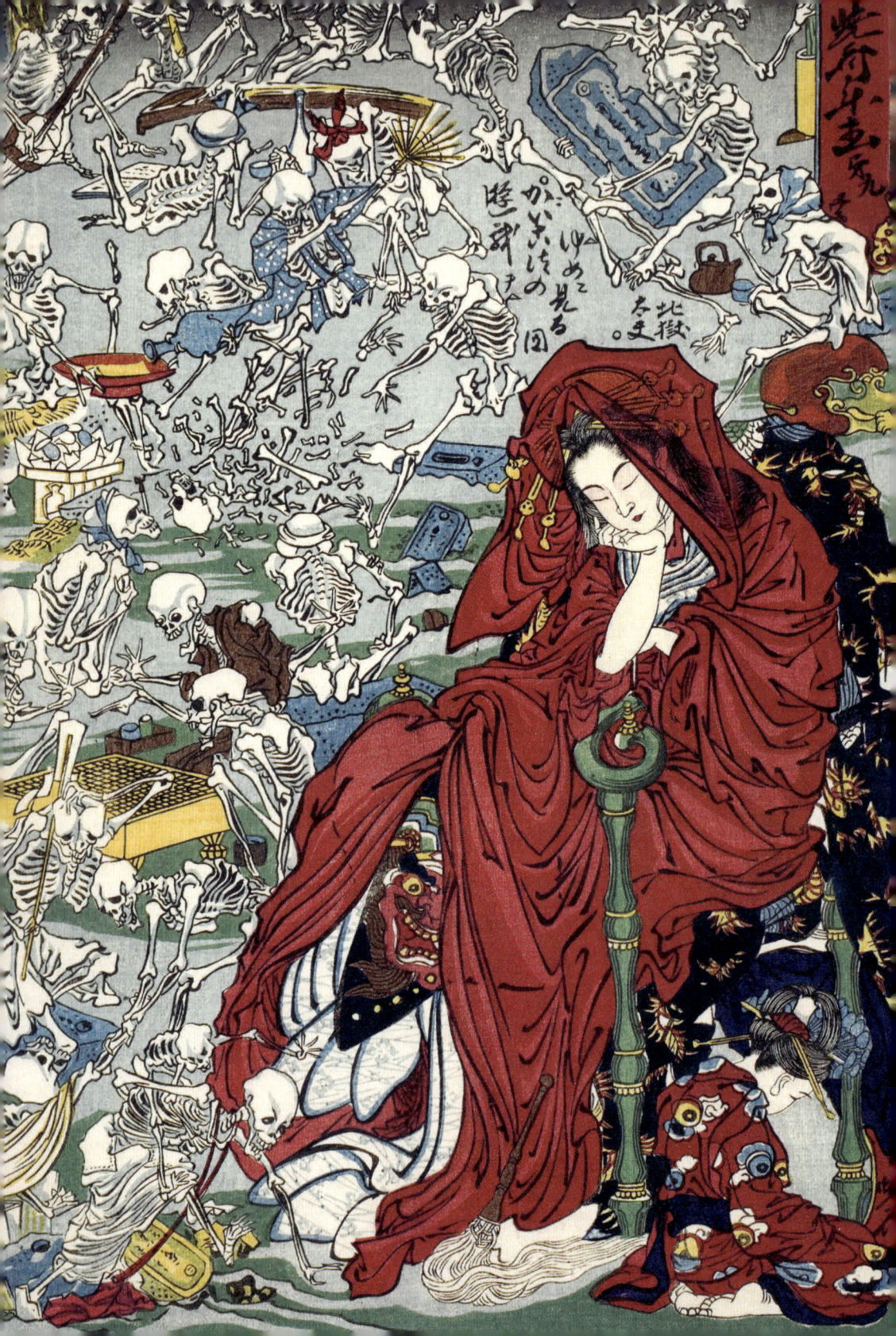

LIST OF ILLUSTRATIONS

Inside cover
Hirabayashi Shūsai (1892–1979), *Ghost of a Courtesan (Yūrei oiran)*, detail, ca 1926—1940, scroll, ink on silk, mounted on silk support, 103 × 48 cm
Courtesy of Galerie Mingei, Paris

p. 2
Tsukioka Yoshitoshi (1839–1892), *Taira Kiyomori Sees Skeletons at Fukuhara*, from the *New Series of Thirty-Six Ghosts (Shinkei sanjūro kaisen)*, 1865, woodblock print (*nishiki-e*), *ōban* format, 35.5 × 23.8 cm

p. 4
Doi Gōga (1817–1881), *Skeleton Father and Son Doing the Bon Dance (Bon odori)*, detail, second half of the 19th century, ink on paper, 174.6 × 59.8 cm
Minneapolis Institute of Art, gift of the Clark Center for Japanese Art & Culture, inv. 2013.29.858

pp. 6–7
Utagawa Yoshitaki (1841–1899), *Soharto Tangondaki Nakamura Sojuro as Otake Goro Mitsokuni (Ghosts)*, detail, date unknown, woodblock print (*nishiki-e*), diptych in *chūban tate-e* format, each 24.9 × 17.5 cm
Philadelphia Museum of Art, gift of Ann E. and Donald W. McPhail, inv. 2017-7-4a,b

p. 8
Tsukioka Yoshitoshi (1839–1892), *Shizunome Ohyaku and Four Hungry Ghosts*, from the series *Hero of the Suikoden (Biyū Suikoden)*, detail, 1866, woodblock print (*nishiki-e*), *chūban* format, 25 × 17.8 cm
Philadelphia Museum of Art, gift of Sidney A. Tannenbaum, inv. 1978-129-72

p. 9
Utagawa Kuniyoshi (1797–1861), *Hosokute Lord Horikoshi*, from the series *Sixty-nine Stations on the Road to Kisokaidō (Kisokaidō rokujūkyū tsugi no uchi)*, detail, 1852,

woodblock print (*nishiki-e*), *ōban* format, 37.8 × 25.5 cm

p. 10
Utagawa School, *Ghost Story*, detail, late 19th century, ink on paper, 213.3 × 71.7 cm
Minneapolis Institute of Art, gift of Willard and Elizabeth Clark, inv. 2015.114.24

pp. 12–13
Utagawa Hiroshige (1797–1858), *New Year's Eve Foxfires at the Changing Tree, Ōji*, from the series *One Hundred Famous Views of Edo (Meisho Edo hyakkei)*, detail, ca 1857, woodblock print (*nishiki-e*), *ōban* format, 32.5 × 21.9 cm
New York, The Metropolitan Museum of Art, Rogers Fund, 1925, inv. JP1470

pp. 14–15
Katsukawa Shun'ei (1762–1819), *Once Upon a Time (Imawa mukashi)*, detail, 1790, woodblock printed book, 22.4 × 15.8 cm
New York, The Metropolitan Museum of Art, purchase, Mary and James G. Wallach Foundation Gift, 2013, inv. 2013.819

p. 16
Anonymous 19th-century master, *Ghost*, detail, painting on silk paper, 198 × 70 cm
Paris, Collection of Philippe Charlier

GATE TO THE UNDERWORLD
p. 19
Iguchi Kashu (1890–1930), *Ghost*, detail, painting on silk, 192 × 53.5 cm
Paris, Musée du quai Branly – Jacques Chirac, inv. 70.2015.40.5.1-2

p. 21
Terasaki Kōgyō (1866–1919), *Ghost*, right-hand scroll of a diptych, detail, July 1900, ink on paper, 217.17 × 48.58 cm
Minneapolis Institute of Art, gift of the Clark Center for Japanese Art & Culture, inv. 2013.29.145.1

p. 22
Kaitu Unrin (1845–1919), *Ghost*, detail, 1882, painting on silk, 193 × 74 cm
Paris, Musée du quai

Branly – Jacques Chirac, inv. 70.2015.40.3.1-2

pp. 24–25
Tsukioka Yoshitoshi (1839–1892), *The Priest Sōgi Notices a Pair of Ghosts in an Abandoned House*, from the 'Thirty-six Supernatural Beings in New Forms (Shinkei sanjūro kaisen)', detail, 1902, woodblock print (*nishiki-e*), *ōban* format, 39.4 × 26.7 cm
Philadelphia Museum of Art, purchased with funds contributed by the E. Rhodes and Leona B. Carpenter Foundation, 1989, inv. 1989-47-628

pp. 26–27
Utagawa Kunisada I (aka Toyokuni III; 1786–1864), *The Ghost of Kamata Matahachi, the Servant, Kamata Matahachi and the Former Mistress of His Brother Tied to a Tree*, detail of the left-hand panel, 1855, woodblock print (*nishiki-e*), diptych in *ōban* format, 37 × 50 cm
Paris, Musée du quai Branly – Jacques Chirac, inv. 70.2015.39.2.1-2

AUTOPSY ON A REVENANT
p. 29
Ōkyo Maruyama (1733–1795), *Ghost*, detail, 1793, painting on silk, 200 × 48 cm
Paris, Musée du quai Branly – Jacques Chirac, inv. 70.2015.40.4.1-2

p. 30
Yūrei, detail from the *Bakemono no e*, late 17th – 18th century, scroll, 44 × 1525 cm
Provo, Brigham Young University Library, inv. 895.63 B17 1863

p. 33
Ikkyo (late 19th – early 20th century), *Ghost of Oiwa*, detail, painting on silk, 173 × 51 cm
Paris, Musée du quai Branly – Jacques Chirac, inv. 70.2015.40.1.1-2

p. 34
Tsukioka Yoshitoshi (1839–1892), *The Ghost of Yūgao from The Tale of Genji*, from the series *One Hundred Aspects of the Moon (Tsuki Hyakushi)*, detail, 1886, woodblock

print (*nishiki-e*), *ōban* format, 39.4 × 26.7 cm
Philadelphia Museum of Art, purchased with funds contributed by the E. Rhodes and Leona B. Carpenter Foundation, 1989, inv. 1989-47-423

p. 37
Tsukioka Yoshitoshi (1839–1892), *Samanosuke Mitsutoshi with Fox Fires*, from the series *One Hundred Tales from China and Japan (Wakan hyaku monogatari)*, detail, 1865, woodblock print (*nishiki-e*), *ōban* format, 37.7 × 25.8 cm
Los Angeles County Museum of Art, Herbert R. Cole Collection, inv. M.84.31.61

p. 38
Utagawa Toyokuni I (1769-1825), *Onoe Matsusuke I as the Ghost of the Wet-Nurse Iohata and Matsumoto Kojiro as Mokuemon in Tokubei of India: Tales of Strange Lands (Tenjiku Tokubei ikoku banashi)*, detail, 1799-1809, woodblock print (*nishiki-e*), *ōban* format, 37.2 × 25.8 cm
The Art Institute of Chicago, Clarence Buckingham Collection, inv. 1925.3159

p. 39
Katsukawa Shunshō (1726–1792), *Man Falling Backward, Startled by a Woman's Ghost over a River*, detail of the ghost, ca 1782, print, *hosoban* diptych, 31.7 × 14.2 cm (left-hand panel), 31.5 × 14.2 cm (right-hand panel)
The Art Institute of Chicago, Clarence Buckingham Collection, inv. 1938.497

p. 40
Utagawa Toyokuni I (1769–1825), *Onoe Shoroku as a Ghost*, detail, date unknown, woodblock print (*nishiki-e*), *ōban* format, 38.6 × 26 cm
Washington DC, Arthur M. Sackler Gallery, Smithsonian Institution, Anne van Biema Collection, inv. S2004.3.120

p. 41
Kitagawa Utamaro (1753–1806), *Child's Nightmare of Ghosts*, detail, ca 1800/01, woodblock print (*nishiki-e*), *ōban* format

The Art Institute of Chicago, gift of Mr. and Mrs. Richard M. Weissman, inv. 1997.743

pp. 42–43
Katsukawa Shunshō (1726–1792), *Ichikawa Danjuro V as a Skeleton, Spirit of the Priest Seigen* (left), *and Iwai Hanshiro IV as Princess Sakura* (right), detail, 1783, print, diptych in *hosoban* format, 32.9 × 15.2 cm (left-hand panel), 32.9 × 15 cm (right-hand panel)
The Art Institute of Chicago, Clarence Buckingham Collection, inv. 1938.491

OKIKU

p. 44
Katsushika Hokusai (1760–1849), *The Mansion of the Plates*, from the series *One Hundred Tales* (*Hyaku monogatari*), detail, 1831/32, woodblock print (*nishiki-e*), *chūban* format, 25.5 × 18.6 cm
The Art Institute of Chicago, Clarence Buckingham Collection, inv. 1943.604

p. 46
Kiyosada (active ca 1848), *Arashi Rikaku II as the Ghost of Okiku*, detail, August 1848, woodblock print (*nishiki-e*), *chūban* format, 252. × 17.2 cm
Amsterdam, Rijksmuseum, acquired with the support of the F. G. Waller-Fonds, inv. RP-P-2009-136

p. 49
Tsukioka Yoshitoshi (1839–1892), *The Ghost of Okiku in the Play 'The Dish Mansion'* (*Sarayashiki*), from the series *Thirty-six Supernatural Beings in New Forms* (*Shinkei sanjūro kaisen*), detail, 1902, woodblock print (*nishiki-e*), *ōban* format, 39.4 × 26.7 cm
Philadelphia Museum of Art, purchased with funds contributed by the E. Rhodes and Leona B. Carpenter Foundation, 1989, inv. 1989-47-613

p. 50
Kawanabe Kyōsai (1831–1889), *Manga*, detail of Okiku, 1881, 22.3 × 15 cm
New York, The Metropolitan Museum of Art, purchase, Mary and James G.

Wallach Foundation Gift, 2013, inv. 2013.765

p. 51
Toyohara Kunichika (1835–1900), *The Samurai Aoyama with the Ghost of Okiku*, detail of the ghost of Okiku, 1892, *nishiki-e* stamp, vertical triptych in *ōban* format, each 35.5 × 25.5 cm
Amsterdam, Rijksmuseum, inv. RP-P-1994-55

pp. 52–53
Utagawa Kunisada I (aka Toyokuni III; 1786–1864), *Actors with the Ghost of Okiku in the Play 'The Dish Mansion'* (*Sarayashiki*), detail, 1857, woodblock print (*nishiki-e*), *ōban* format, 35.2 × 24.3 cm
Amherst College, Mead Art Museum, inv. AC 2004.71

pp. 54–55
Utagawa Kunisada I (aka Toyokuni III; 1786–1864), *Ichikawa Kodanji IV as the Ghost of Iwafuji* (*Iwafuji no bōrei*) (right) *and Iwai Kumesaburō III as Second Onoe* (*Nidai no Onoe*) (left), detail, 1860, woodblock print (*nishiki-e*), *ōban* diptych, 36.3 × 50 cm
Boston, Museum of Fine Arts, William Sturgis Bigelow Collection, inv. 11.40911a-b

OTSUYU

p. 56
Tsukioka Yoshitoshi (1839–1892), *The Ghost of the Courtesan Otsuyu and the Peony Lantern* (*Botan Dōrō*), from the series *Thirty-six Supernatural Beings in New Forms* (*Shinkei sanjūro kaisen*), detail, 1902, woodblock print (*nishiki-e*), *ōban* format, 39.4 × 26.7 cm
Philadelphia Museum of Art, purchased with funds contributed by the E. Rhodes and Leona B. Carpenter Foundation, 1989, inv. 1989-47-623

p. 58
Suzuki Harunobu (1725–1770), *Woman Admiring Plum Blossoms at Night*, detail, ca 1766, woodblock print (*nishiki-e*) with embossing (*karazuri*), *aiban* format, 32.4 × 21 cm

New York, The Metropolitan Museum of Art, Fletcher Fund, 1929, inv. JP1506

p. 61
Utagawa Kuniyoshi (1797–1861), *The Ghost of Oiwa*, detail, 1847/1848, woodblock print (*nishiki-e*), 36 × 24 cm
University of Oxford, Ashmolean Museum, inv. EA1971.61

pp. 62–63
Utagawa Kunisada II (1823–1880), *Main Street of the Yoshiwara on a Starlight Night*, detail, 1852–1864, woodblock print (*surimono*), 20.6 × 18.1 cm
New York, The Metropolitan Museum of Art, The Howard Mansfield Collection, purchase, Rogers Fund, 1936, inv. JP2632

pp. 64–65
Utagawa Toyokuni I (1769–1825), *Two Actors*, detail, date unknown, woodblock print (*nishiki-e*), diptych in *aiban* format, 35.5 × 4.87 cm
Amsterdam, Rijksmuseum, bequest of S. Emmering, Amsterdam, inv. RP-P-201526-1898

UBUME

p. 66
Ubume, detail of the *Bakemono no e*, late 17th – 18th century, scroll, 44 × 1525 cm
Provo, Brigham Young University Library, inv. 895.63 B17 1863

p. 69
Utagawa Kunisada I (aka Toyokuni III; 1786–1864), *Ghost of Wet-Nurse Igarashi*, detail, 1852, woodblock print (*nishiki-e*), *ōban* format, 35.2 × 24.4 cm
Amsterdam, Rijksmuseum, gift of H. J. Herwig and A. H. Herwig-Kempers, inv. RP-P-2017-6140

p. 70
Suzuki Kason (1860–1919), *Ghost*, left-hand scroll of a diptych, detail, July 1900, ink on paper, 220.9 × 54.6 cm
Minneapolis Institute of Art, gift of the Clark Center for Japanese Art & Culture, inv. 2013.29.145.1

p. 71
Tsukioka Yoshitoshi (1839–1892), *Oiwa and the Sash Serpent in the Tale of the Ghost of Yotsuya*, from the series *Thirty-six Supernatural Beings in New Forms* (*Shinkei sanjūro kaisen*), detail, 1902, woodblock print (*nishiki-e*), *ōban* format, 39.4 × 26.7 cm
Philadelphia Museum of Art, purchased with funds contributed by the E. Rhodes and Leona B. Carpenter Foundation, 1989, inv. 1989-47-632

p. 72
Tsukioka Yoshitoshi (1839–1892), *Shume Urabe Suetake Meeting a Ghost with a Child*, from the series *One Hundred Tales from China and Japan* (*Wakan hyaku monogatari*), detail, 1865, woodblock print (*nishiki-e*), *ōban* format, 37.3 × 25.2 cm
Los Angeles County Museum of Art, Herbert R. Cole Collection, inv. M.84.31.54

p. 73
Tsukioka Yoshitoshi (1839–1892), *A Widower Witnesses His Wife's Ghost Nursing Their Child*, series published in the newspaper *Yūbin hōchi shinbun*, detail, April 1875, woodblock print (*nishiki-e*), *ōban* format, 34.7 × 23.5 cm
Los Angeles County Museum of Art, Herbert R. Cole Collection, inv. M.84.31.170

p. 74
Kawanabe Kyōsai (1831–1889), *Manga*, detail of an *ubume*, 1881, 22.3 × 15 cm
New York, The Metropolitan Museum of Art, purchase, Mary and James G. Wallach Foundation Gift, 2013, inv. 2013.765

p. 75
Konishi Hirosada (aka Gosōtei Hirosada; ca 1819–1863), *Actor as Ghost Holding an Infant in an Unidentified Play*, detail, ca 1847–1853, woodblock print (*nishiki-e*), *chūban* format, 24.8 × 17.8 cm
Philadelphia Museum of Art, gift of Jack Shear in memory of Anne d'Harnoncourt, 2008, inv. 2008-62-101

NOH

p. 76
Mask from Noh theatre depicting the character of *zo-onna* (young girl), late 18th century, wood and pigments, 21 × 13.5 × 6.5 cm
Paris, Collection of Philippe Charlier

pp. 80–81
Two masks from Noh theatre depicting the character of *zo-onna* (young girl) and young servant (or youth), first half of the 20th century, wood and pigments, 21 × 13.5 × 6.5 cm
Paris, Collection of Philippe Charlier

pp. 82–83
Tsukioka Yoshitoshi (1839–1892), *Onoe Kikugorō V as the Ghost of the Cormorant-Fisher*, from the series *A Barometer of the Emotions* (*Seiu kandankei*), detail, 1876, woodblock print (*nishiki-e*), *ōban* format, 39.4 × 26.7 cm
Philadelphia Museum of Art, purchased with funds contributed by the E. Rhodes and Leona B. Carpenter Foundation, 1989, inv. 1989-47-25

pp. 84–85
Tsukioka Yoshitoshi (1839–1892), *Kodembō no Shōshichi, an Osaka Thief, Tormented by Ghosts*, series published in the newspaper *Yūbin hōchi shinbun*, detail, April 1875, woodblock print (*nishiki-e*), *ōban* format, 34.7 × 23.5 cm
Los Angeles County Museum of Art, Herbert R. Cole Collection, inv. M.84.31.183

FUNAYŪREI

p. 86
Utagawa Kuniyoshi (1797–1861), *The Ghosts of the Heike Attack the Clan of Minamoto Yoshitsune in the Bay of Daimotsu*, from the series *Mirror of the Life of Minamoto Yoshitsune* (*Hodo Yoshitsune koi no Minamoto ichidai kagami, sanryakuden*), detail, 1853, woodblock print (*nishiki-e*), *ōban* format, 36 × 24.2 cm

pp. 89, 90–91
Utagawa Kuniyoshi (1797–1861), *Ghosts of the Taira at Daimotsu Bay*, detail, 1843–1847, woodblock print (*nishiki-e*), triptych in *ōban* format, each 37.5 × 25.1 cm
New York, The Metropolitan Museum of Art, Fletcher Fund, 1929, inv. JP1565

pp. 92–93
Utagawa Kuniyoshi (1797–1861), *Benkei Fighting the Ghost of Taira Tomomori*, detail, 1818, woodblock print (*nishiki-e*), diptych in *ōban* format, 36.3 × 51 cm

pp. 94–95
Ichiyusai Kuniyoshi (1797–1861), *The Ghosts of the Taira Attack the Boat of Yoshitsune*, detail of the left-hand and centre panels, 1843–1845, woodblock print (*nishiki-e*), triptych in *aiban* format, 32.5 × 67.9 cm
University of Oxford, Ashmolean Museum, inv. EA1971.161

pp. 96–97
Katsukawa Shun'ei (1762–1819), *Once Upon a Time* (*Imawa mukashi*), detail, 1790, woodblock printed book, 22.4 × 15.8 cm
New York, The Metropolitan Museum of Art, purchase, Mary and James G. Wallach Foundation Gift, 2013, inv. 2013.819

YUKI-ONNA

p. 98
Ōkyo Maruyama (1733–1795), *Ghost of Oyuki*, detail, coloured ink, painting on silk, 149 × 44 cm
Paris, Musée du quai Branly – Jacques Chirac, inv. 70.2015.31.1

p. 101
Uemura Shōen (1875–1949), *Yuki-onna*, detail, ca 1926, print, 45.5 × 28.4 cm
Courtesy of Galerie Mingei, Paris

p. 103
Yuki-onna, detail of the *Bakemono no e*, late 17th–18th century, scroll, 44 × 1525 cm
Provo, Brigham Young University Library, inv. 895.63 B17 1863

pp. 104–105
Katsukawa Shun'ei (1762–1819), *Once Upon a Time* (*Imawa mukashi*), detail, 1790, book, 22.4 × 15.8 cm

New York, The Metropolitan Museum of Art, purchase, Mary and James G. Wallach Foundation Gift, 2013, inv. 2013.819

pp. 106–107
Utagawa Kunisada I (aka Toyokuni III; 1786–1864), *Seki Sanjūrō II as Tamiya Iemon* (right) *and Onoe Kikugorō III of Kamigata* (*Kudari*) *as the Ghost of the Lantern* (left), detail, 1831, woodblock print (*nishiki-e*), diptych in *ōban* format, 35.8 × 48.8 cm
Boston, Museum of Fine Arts, William Sturgis Bigelow Collection, inv. 11.40700a-b

OIWA, THE FACE OF DEATH

p. 108
Katsushika Hokusai (1760–1849), *Oiwa*, from the series *One Hundred Tales* (*Hyaku monogatari*), detail, 1831/32, woodblock print (*nishiki-e*), *chūban* format, 25.6 × 16.1 cm
The Art Institute of Chicago, Clarence Buckingham Collection, inv. 1943.603

p. 111
Taiju (14th century), *Ghost of Oiwa*, detail, painting on silk, 168.5 × 35 cm
Paris, Musée du quai Branly – Jacques-Chirac, inv. 70.2015.40.2.1-2

p. 112
Unknown artist, *Ichikawa Yonezō as the Ghost of Oiwa*, detail, 1864, woodblock print (*nishiki-e*), *chūban* format, 19.7 × 18.2 cm
Philadelphia Museum of Art, purchased with the Lola Downin Peck Fund and with funds contributed by various donors, inv. 1969-208-416

p. 113
Utagawa Toyokuni I (1769–1825), *Onoe Matsusuke as the Ghost of the Murdered Wife Oiwa, in 'A Tale of Horror from the Yotsuya Station on the Tokaido Road'*, detail, 1812, print, 37.5 × 25.7 cm
New York, The Metropolitan Museum of Art, gift of Louis V. Ledoux, 1927, inv. JP1492

p. 114
Shunbaisai Hokuei (active 1829–1837), *Kabuki Actor Arashi Rikan II as Tamiya Iemon Confronted by an Image of His Murdered Wife, Oiwa, on a Broken Lantern, Referring to Katsushika Hokusai's One Hundred Tales* (*Hyaku monogatari*), detail, 1832, woodblock print (*nishiki-e*), *ōban* format, 37.8 x 25.7 cm
New York, The Metropolitan Museum of Art, purchase, Friends of Asian Art Gifts, in honor of James C. Y. Watt, 2011, inv. 2011.135

p. 115
Utagawa Kuniyoshi (1797–1861), *Kamiya Iemon and the Ghost-Lantern of Oiwa*, from the series *One Hundred Poets After Ogura* (*Ogura nazorae hyakunin isshu*), detail, 1845–1848, woodblock print (*nishiki-e*), *ōban* format, 34 × 22.5 cm

pp. 116–119
Utagawa Kuniyoshi (1797–1861), *Ichikawa Danjūrō VIII as Kamiya Iemon Holding Panels Representing His Servant, Kohei, and His Wife, Oiwa*, detail, ca 1850, *shikake-e* print, 35.5 × 22.8 cm
Lyon Collection

KASANE

p. 120
Utagawa Kuniyoshi (1797–1861), *Unuma: Yoemon and His Wife Kasane*, from the series *Sixty-Nine Stations on the Kisokaidō Road* (*Kisokaidō rokujūkyū-tsugi*), detail, 1852, woodblock print (*nishiki-e*), *ōban* format, 36.2 × 27.5 cm
Paris, Musée Cernuschi – Musée des Arts de l'Asie de la Ville de Paris

pp. 122–123
Utagawa Kunisada I (aka Toyokuni III; 1786–1864), *Onoe Kikugorō III as the Ghost of Kasane* (*Kasane shiryō*) (right) *and Ichimura Uzaemon XII as Shiozawa Tanzaburō* (left), detail, 1836, woodblock print (*nishiki-e*), diptych in *ōban* format, 35.8 × 49.2 cm
Boston, Museum of Fine Arts, William Sturgis

Bigelow Collection, inv. 11.40685a-b

p. 124
Toyohara Kunichika (1835–1900), *Ichikawa Udanji I as the Ghost of the Wife of Sōgo and Nakamura Kangoro XII as Yamazumi Goheita in 'The Legend of Sakura Sōgo' (Sakura Sōgo den)*, detail, 1893, woodblock print (*nishiki-e*), vertical triptych in *ōban* format, each 37 × 25.7 cm Amsterdam, Rijksmuseum, purchased with the support of the F. G. Waller-Fonds, inv. RP-P-2009-973

p. 125
Utagawa Kunisada I (aka Toyokuni III; 1760–1864), *Ichikawa Kodanji IV as the Ghost of Kasane, Poem by Fujiwara no Toshiyuki Ason*, from the series *Comparison of Thirty-six Selected Poems (Mitate sanjūrok kaisen no uchi)*, detail, 1852, woodblock print (*nishiki-e*), *ōban* format, 35.56 × 24.7 cm Minneapolis Institute of Art, bequest of Louis W. Hill, Jr., inv. 96.146.104.17

HEADS THAT FLY

p. 126
Kawanabe Kyōsai (1831–1889), *Manga*, detail of a *rokurokubi*, 1881, 22.3 × 15 cm New York, The Metropolitan Museum of Art, purchase, Mary and James G. Wallach Foundation Gift, 2013, inv. 2013.765

p. 129
Kawanabe Kyōsai (1831–1889), *The Yokai Rokurokubi and Mikoshinyūdō Accosting a Noodle Shop Customer*, illustration of the proverb 'resistance is futile', from the series *One Hundred Illustrations from Kyōsai's Hand (Kyōsai hyakuzu)*, detail, [1863] Washington DC, Library of Congress, LC-USZC4-8651

pp. 130–131
Utagawa Kunisada I (aka Toyokuni III; 1786–1864), *Bandō Actors Hikosaburō IV as the Hunter (Ryōshi) Amizō* (right), *Onoe Tamizō II, from Kamigata (Kudari), as Koshimoto*

Otsuru in the Scene of the Long-necked Ghost (Rokorokubi Ōatari, centre), and Onoe Tamizō II in a Double Role (Futayaku) of Nitta Umejirō (left), detail of the centre and right-hand panels, 1841, woodblock print (*nishiki-e*), *ōban* format, 37.2 × 76.1 cm Boston, Museum of Fine Arts, William Sturgis Bigelow Collection, inv. 11.43459a-c

pp. 132–133
Katsushika Hokusai (1760-1849), *Manga*, two *rokurokubi*, vol. XII, detail, 1834

pp. 134–135
Rokurokubi, detail of the *Bakemono no e*, late 17th – 18th century, scroll, 44 × 1525 cm Provo, Brigham Young University Library, inv. 895.63 B17 1863

THE SMILE OF DEATH

p. 136
Tsukioka Yoshitoshi (1839–1892), *Takagi Umansuke with a Ghost*, from the series *Hero of Suikoden (Biyū Suikoden)*, detail, 1866, woodblock print (*nishiki-e*), *chūban* format, 24.92 × 18.26 cm University of Oxford, Ashmolean Museum, inv. EA1971.215

pp. 138–139
Katsushika Hokusai (1760–1849), *One Hundred Ghost Tales in a Haunted House (Shinpan uki-e bakemono yashiki hyaku monogatari no zu)*, detail, ca 1780, woodblock print (*nishiki-e*), *ōban* format, 23.7 × 35.4 cm

pp. 140–141
Utagawa Kunisada I (aka Toyokuni III; 1786–1864), Utagawa Hiroshige II (1826–1869) and Kawanabe Kyōsai (1831–1889), *Kataoka Nizaemon VIII as Tamigaya Iemon; 'Ma' Brigade, Fifth Squad; Earthen Bridge by Kuitachi in Asakusa*, from the series *Flowers of Edo and Views of Famous Places (Edo no hana meishō awase)*, detail, 1863, woodblock print (*nishiki-e*), *ōban* format, 35.7 × 23.5 cm

Los Angeles County Museum of Art, gift of Arthur and Fran Sherwood, inv. M.2007.152.50

HANNYA

p. 142
Katsushika Hokusai (1760–1849), *The Laughing Demoness (Warai Hannya)*, from the series *One Hundred Tales (Hyaku monogatari)*, detail, 1831/32, woodblock print (*nishiki-e*), *chūban* format, 25.3 × 18 cm The Art Institute of Chicago, Clarence Buckingham Collection, inv. 1943.605

p. 144
Unknown artist, *Ghost*, Meiji period (1868–1912), detail, scroll, ink on paper, montage on silk, 115 × 43.5 cm Courtesy of Galerie Mingei, Paris

p. 145
Tsukioka Yoshitoshi (1839–1892), *Clearing Weather of the Togakushi Mountains: Taira Koremochi Ason*, from the series *Eight Views and Stories of Warriors (Bidan musha hakkei)*, detail from the left-hand panel, 1868, woodblock print (*nishiki-e*), triptych in *ōban* format, each 36.6 × 24 cm Minneapolis Institute of Art, The Mary Griggs Burke Endowment Fund established by the Mary Livingston Griggs and Mary Griggs Burke Foundation, gifts of various donors, by exchange, and gift of Edmond Freis in memory of his parents, Rose and Leon Freis, inv. 2017.106.84a-c

p. 146
Tsukioka Yoshitoshi (1839–1892), *The Attack of the Ghost of Akugenta Yoshihira at the Nunobiki Waterfall*, from the series *Thirty-six Supernatural Beings in New Forms (Shinkei sanjūro kaisen)*, detail, 1902, woodblock print (*nishiki-e*), *ōban* format, 39.4 × 26.7 cm Philadelphia Museum of Art, purchased with funds contributed by the E. Rhodes and Leona B. Carpenter Foundation, 1989, inv. 1989-47-615

p. 147
Utagawa Kunisada I (aka Toyokuni III; 1786–1864), *Onoe Kikugorō III as the Ghost of Yasukata*, from the series *Comparison of the Thirty-six Immortal Poets (Mitate sanjūro kaisen no uchi)*, detail, 1852, woodblock print (*nishiki-e*), *ōban*, format, 34.8 × 24.3 cm Amsterdam, Rijksmuseum, gift of H. J. Herwig-Kempers, inv. RP-P-2017-6144

pp. 148–149
Utagawa Yoshifusa (active between 1837 and 1860), *The Ghost of Akugenta Yoshihira Takes Vengeance on Nanba Jirō* (centre) *and Taira Kiyomori* (right) *at the Nunobiki Waterfall*, detail of the centre and left-hand panels, 1856, woodblock print (*nishiki-e*), *ōban* triptych, 36.8 × 24.8 cm New York, The Metropolitan Museum of Art, purchase, Arnold Weinstein Gift, 2001, inv. 2001.715.11a–c

DEMONS OF THE BATTLEFIELD

p. 150
Tsukioka Yoshitoshi (1839–1892), *Warrior on a Skull*, from the series *Valor in China and Japan (Wakan gōki zoroi)*, detail, 1868, woodblock print (*nishiki-e*), *ōban* format, 37.4 × 25.4 cm Los Angeles County Museum of Art, Herbert R. Cole Collection, inv. M.84.31.197

p. 153
Tsukioka Yoshitoshi (1839–1892), *Ōya Tarō Mitsukune Watching Skeletons*, from the series *One Hundred Tales of China and Japan (Wakan hyaku monogatari)*, detail, 1865, woodblock print (*nishiki-e*), *ōban* format, 35.5 × 24.4 cm Los Angeles County Museum of Art, Herbert R. Cole Collection, inv. M.84.31.443

pp. 154–155
Utagawa Hiroshige (1797–1868), *Taira no Kiyomori's Spectral Vision*, detail from the left-hand and centre panels, ca 1845, woodblock print

(*nishiki-e*), ōban triptych, 38.1 × 73.7 cm
New York, The Metropolitan Museum of Art, The Howard Mansfield Collection, purchase, Rogers Fund, 1936, inv. JP2540

pp. 156–157
Kawanabe Kyōsai (1831–1889), *Manga*, detail, 1881, 22.3 × 15 cm
New York, The Metropolitan Museum of Art, purchase, Mary and James G. Wallach Foundation Gift, 2013, inv. 2013.765

pp. 158–159
Kawanabe Kyōsai (1831–1889), *Kyōsai's Pictures of One Hundred Demons (Kyōsai hyakki gadan)*, detail, 1890, woodblock printed book, leporello binding (*orihon*), 19.8 × 12 cm
New York, The Metropolitan Museum of Art, purchase, gift of Mary and James G. Wallach Foundation Gift, 2013, inv. 2013.767

pp. 160–161
Katsushika Hokusai (1760–1849), *Kohada Koheiji*, from the series *One Hundred Tales (Hyaku monogatari)*, detail, ca 1831, print, *chūban* format, 25.6 × 18.1 cm
The Art Institute of Chicago, Clarence Buckingham Collection, inv. 1943.602

KOHADA KOHEIJI

p. 162
Utagawa Toyokuni I (1769–1825), *The Ghost of Kohada Koheiji Emerging from a Lantern with the Head of His Wife*, detail, 1808, woodblock print (*nishiki-e*), ōban format, 38 × 24 cm

pp. 164–165
Utagawa Kunisada I (aka Toyokuni III; 1786–1864), *Bandō Shūka I as Koheiji's Wife (Nyōbō) Otsuka and Bandō Hikosaburō IV as Adachi Sakurō* (right); *Ichikawa Kodanji IV as Kohada Koheiji* (centre); *Ichikawa Kodanji IV as Koheiji's Ghost and Asao Okuyama III as Gensai Bōzu Tōroku* (left), detail of the left-hand and centre panels, 1853, woodblock print (*nishiki-e*), triptych in

ōban format, 35.2 × 73 cm
Boston, Museum of Fine Arts, William Sturgis Bigelow Collection, inv. 11.29193-5

pp. 166–167
Utagawa Kuniyoshi (1797–1861), *Ichikawa Kodanji IV as the Tea Server (Chadō) Inma, Actually the Ghost (Rei) of Tōgo, Iwai Kumesaburō III as the Shirabyōshi Dancer Katsuragi, and Ichikawa Kodanji IV as the Ghost of Asakura Tōgo* (right), *Bandō Hikosaburō IV as Orikoshi Tairyō, Ichikawa Kodanji IV as Koshimoto Kozakura, Actually the Ghost of Tōgo* (left), detail, 1851, woodblock print (*nishiki-e*), diptych in ōban format, 35.3 × 49.8 cm
Boston, Museum of Fine Arts, William Sturgis Bigelow Collection, inv. 11.38353a-b

pp. 168–169
Utagawa Kuniyoshi (1797–1861), *Bandō Hikosaburō IV as Orikoshi Masatomo* (right) *and Ichikawa Kodanji IV as the Ghost of Asakura Tōgo* (right and left), detail, 1851, woodblock print (*nishiki-e*), ōban diptych, 36.1 × 49.7 cm
Boston, Museum of Fine Arts, William Sturgis Bigelow Collection, inv. 11.38371a-b

p. 170
Utagawa Toyokuni I (1769–1825), *Onoe Matsusuke II as the Ghost of Seigen*, ca 1810, *woodblock print* (*nishiki-e*), ōban format, 35.5 × 24 cm
Minneapolis Institute of Art, bequest of Richard P. Gale, inv. 74.1.184

p. 171
Utagawa Kuniyoshi (1797–1861), *Orikoshi Tairyō Tormented by the Ghost of Sakura Sōgo*, scene from the Kabuki play *The History of Sakura (Sakura sōshi)*, detail of the right-hand panel, 1851, woodblock print (*nishiki-e*), triptych in ōban format, each 34.4 × 24.3 cm
Amsterdam, Rijksmuseum, gift of H. J. Herwig and A. H. Herwig-Kempers, inv. RP-P-2019-219

IMAGES OF TWO INTERLACED WORLDS

p. 172
Utagawa Yoshiiku (1833–1904), *Nocturnal Parade of One Hundred Demons at Sōma Palace, Takiyasha Hime*, detail of the right-hand panel, 1893, woodblock print (*nishiki-e*), triptych in ōban format, 37.5 × 75.3 cm
University of Oxford, Ashmolean Museum, inv. EA1971.237

p. 175
Konishi Hirosada (aka Gosōtei Hirosada; ca 1819–1863), *Ichikawa Ebizō V as the Ghost of Natora in the Play 'Comparison of Flowers' in The Tales of Ise (Hanakurabe Ise Monogatari)*, detail of the right-hand panel, 1849, woodblock print (*nishiki-e*), triptych, *chūban* format, each 24.8 × 17.8 cm
Philadelphia Museum of Art, gift of Jack Shear in memory of Anne d'Harnoncourt, 2008, inv. 2008-62-176a

pp. 176–177
Utagawa Kuniyoshi (1797–1861), *Scene from a Ghost Story: The Okazaki Cat Demon*, detail, ca 1850, woodblock print (*nishiki-e*), diptych in ōban format, each 36.5 × 25.4 cm
New York, The Metropolitan Museum of Art, Fletcher Fund, 1929, inv. JP1563

pp. 178–179
Tsukioka Yoshitoshi (1839–1892), *Supernatural Beings at Shirazunoyabu in Yawata*, detail of the left-hand and centre panels, 1881, woodblock print (*nishiki-e*), triptych in ōban format, 39.4 × 80 cm
Philadelphia Museum of Art, purchased with funds contributed by the E. Rhodes and Leona B. Carpenter Foundation, 1989, inv. 1989-47-266a-c

pp. 180–181
Utagawa Kuniyoshi (1797–1861), *Ōya Tarō Mistukuni Investigates the Skeleton Invoked by Taira Masakado's Daughter Takiyasha Hime, in Sōma Palace*, detail of the centre and right-hand panel, ca 1844, woodblock print

(*nishiki-e*), ōban triptych, 36.2 × 74.1 cm
Boston, Museum of Fine Arts, William Sturgis Bigelow Collection, inv. 11.30468-70

p. 182
Kawanabe Kyōsai (1831–1889), *Hell Courtesan*, from the series *Kyōsai's Drawings for Pleasure (Kyōsai Rakuga)*, detail, 1874, woodblock print (*nishiki-e*), ōban format, 36.2 × 24.8 cm
Wellesley College, Davis Museum and Cultural Center, inv. 2005.137

p. 188
Utagawa Kuniyoshi (1797–1861), *Poem by Dainagon Tsunenobu*, from the series *One Hundred Poems by One Hundred Poets (Hyakunin isshu no uchi)*, detail, ca 1840–1842, woodblock print (*nishiki-e*), ōban format, 37.5 × 25 cm
Boston, Museum of Fine Arts, William Sturgis Bigelow Collection, inv. 11.34934

pp. 190–191
Tsukioka Yoshitoshi (1839–1892), *A Painting of a Ghost Comes to Life in the Studio of the Painter Ōkyo*, from the series *Drawings by Yoshitoshi for Pleasure (Yoshitoshi ryakuga)*, detail, 1880s, print, *chūban* format, 17.8 × 24.8 cm
Philadelphia Museum of Art, purchased with funds contributed by the E. Rhodes and Leona B. Carpenter Foundation, 1989, inv. 1989-47-283

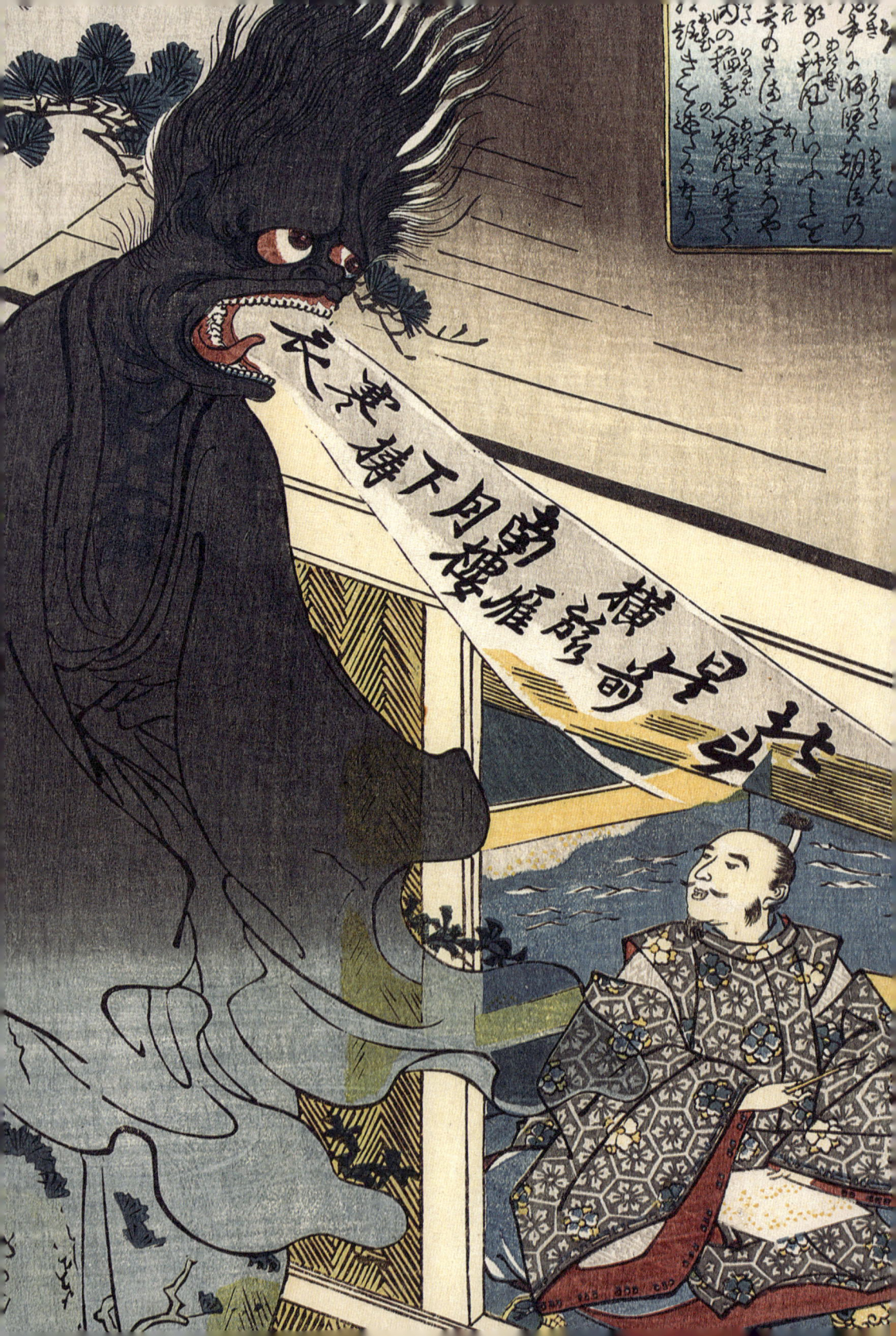

BIBLIOGRAPHY

Anonymous, *Histoires d'amour et de mort de la Chine ancienne: Chefs-d'œuvre de la nouvelle (Dynastie des Tang, 618–907)*, translation and introduction by André Lévy, Paris: Flammarion, 1997

Anonymous, *L'Antre aux fantômes des collines de l'ouest: Sept contes chinois anciens (xiie-xive siècle)*, introduction, notes and commentaries by André Lévy; Unesco, Connaissance de l'Orient, translated by André Lévy and René Goldman, Paris: Gallimard, 1972

Karen Brazell, *Traditional Japanese Theater: An Anthology of Plays*, New York: Columbia University Press, 1998

Laurence C. Bush, *Asian Horror Encyclopedia: Asian Horror Culture in Literature, Manga and Folklore*, New York: Writers Club Press, 2001

Laurence Caillet, *Démons et Merveilles: Nuits japonaises*, Nanterre: Société d'Ethnologie, 2018

Philippe Charlier, *Comment faire l'amour avec un fantôme? Anthropologie de l'invisible*, Paris: Éditions du Cerf, 2021

Philippe Charlier, *Rituels*, Paris: Éditions du Cerf, 2020

Supranatural: Dokuro, Bakemono, Yūrei (exhib. cat.), Paris: Galerie Mingei, 2018

Michael Dylan Foster, *Pandemonium and Parade: Japanese Monsters and the Culture of Yōkai*, Berkeley: University of California Press, 2008

Karl Friday, *The First Samurai: The Life and Legend of the Warrior Rebel Taira Masakado*, Hoboken: John Wiley & Sons, 2008

Henry Joseph Glassman, "The Religious Construction of Motherhood in Medieval Japan", PhD diss., Stanford University, 2001

Maurice Godelier (ed.), *La Mort et ses au-delà*, Paris: CNRS Éditions, 2014

Allan G. Grapard, "Religious practices", in: Donald H. Shively and William H. McCullough (eds.), The Cambridge History of Japan, vol. 2, *Heian Japan*, Cambridge: Cambridge University Press, 1999.

Lafcadio Hearn, *Kwaidan: Stories and Studies of Strange Things*, Boston and New York: Houghton Mifflin and Company, 1904

Michiko Iwasaka and Barre Toelken, *Ghosts and the Japanese: Cultural Experience in Japanese Death Legends*, Logan: Utah State University Press, 1994

Henri L. Joly, *Legend in Japanese Art: A Description of Historical Episodes, Legendary Characters, Folklore, Myths, Religious Symbolism, Illustrated in the Arts of Old Japan*, London: John Lane, 1908

Donald Keene, *Seeds in the Heart: Japanese Literature from Earliest Times to the Late Sixteenth Century*, New York: Henry Holt & Co, 1993

Ayako Nishino, *Paul Claudel, le nō et la synthèse des arts*, Paris: Classiques Garnier, 2013

Herbert H. Plutschow, *Chaos and Cosmos: Ritual in Early and Medieval Japanese Literature*, Leiden: E. J. Brill, 1990

Philippe Pons and Pierre-François Souyri, *L'Esprit de plaisir: Une histoire de la sexualité et de l'érotisme au Japon (xviie-xxe siècle)*, Paris: Payot, 2020

Julien Rousseau and Stéphane du Mesnildot (eds.), *Enfers et fantômes d'Asie* (exhib. cat.), Paris: Musée du Quai Branly – Jacques Chirac and Flammarion, 2018

Pu Songling, *Contes fantastiques du pavillon des Loisirs*, translated by Li Fengbai and Denise Ly-Lebreton, Beijing: Éditions en langues étrangères, 1986

Pu Songling, *Chroniques de l'étrange*, translation and introduction by André Lévy, Paris: Philippe Picquier, 2 vols, 1996, repr. 2010

Jacqueline I. Stone and Mariko Namba Walter (eds.), *Death and the Afterlife in Japanese Buddhism*, Honolulu: University of Hawai'i Press, 2008

Haruko Wakita, *Women in Medieval Japan: Motherhood, Household Management and Sexuality*, translated by Alison Tokita, Clayton: Monash University Press and University of Tokyo Press, 2006

189

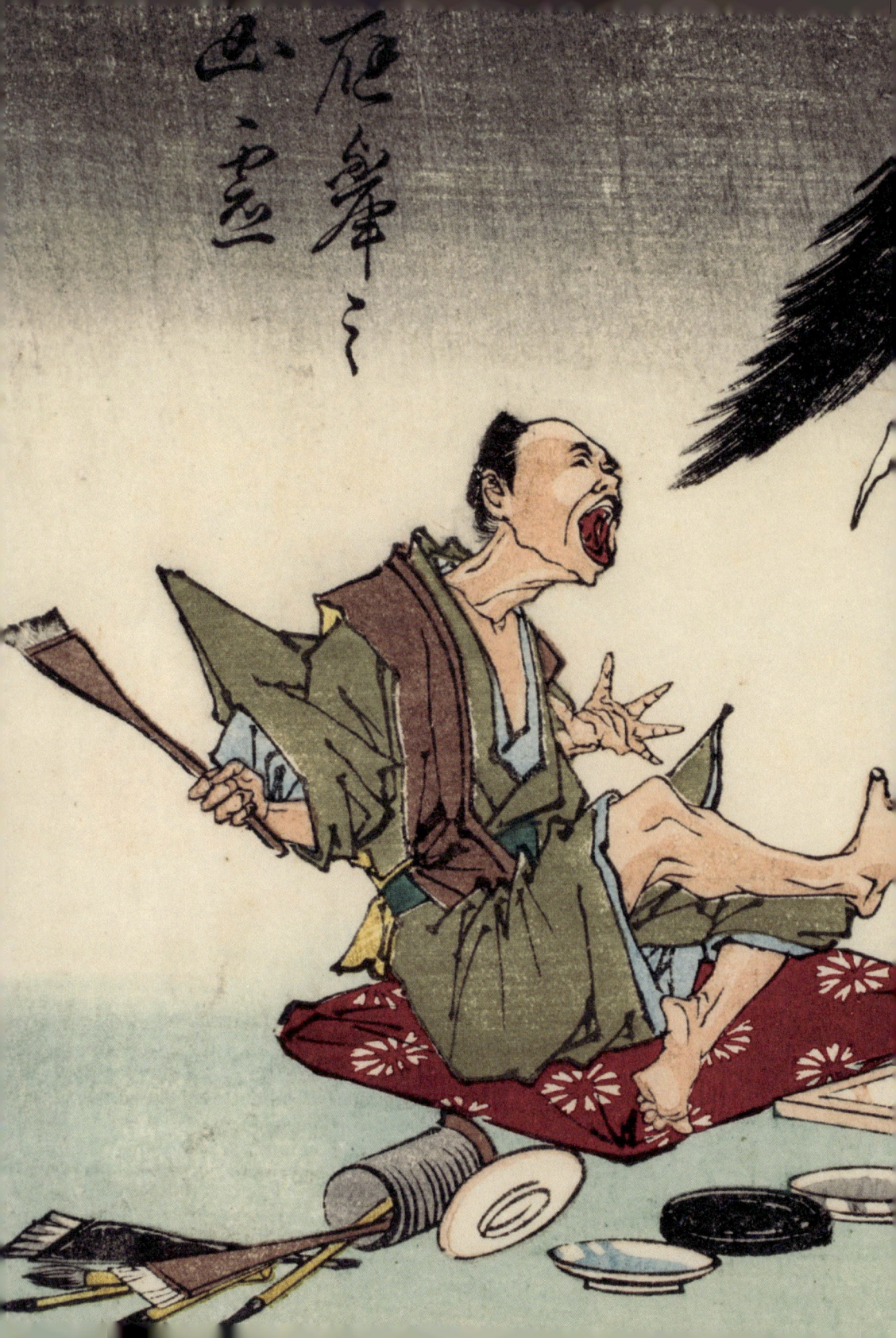

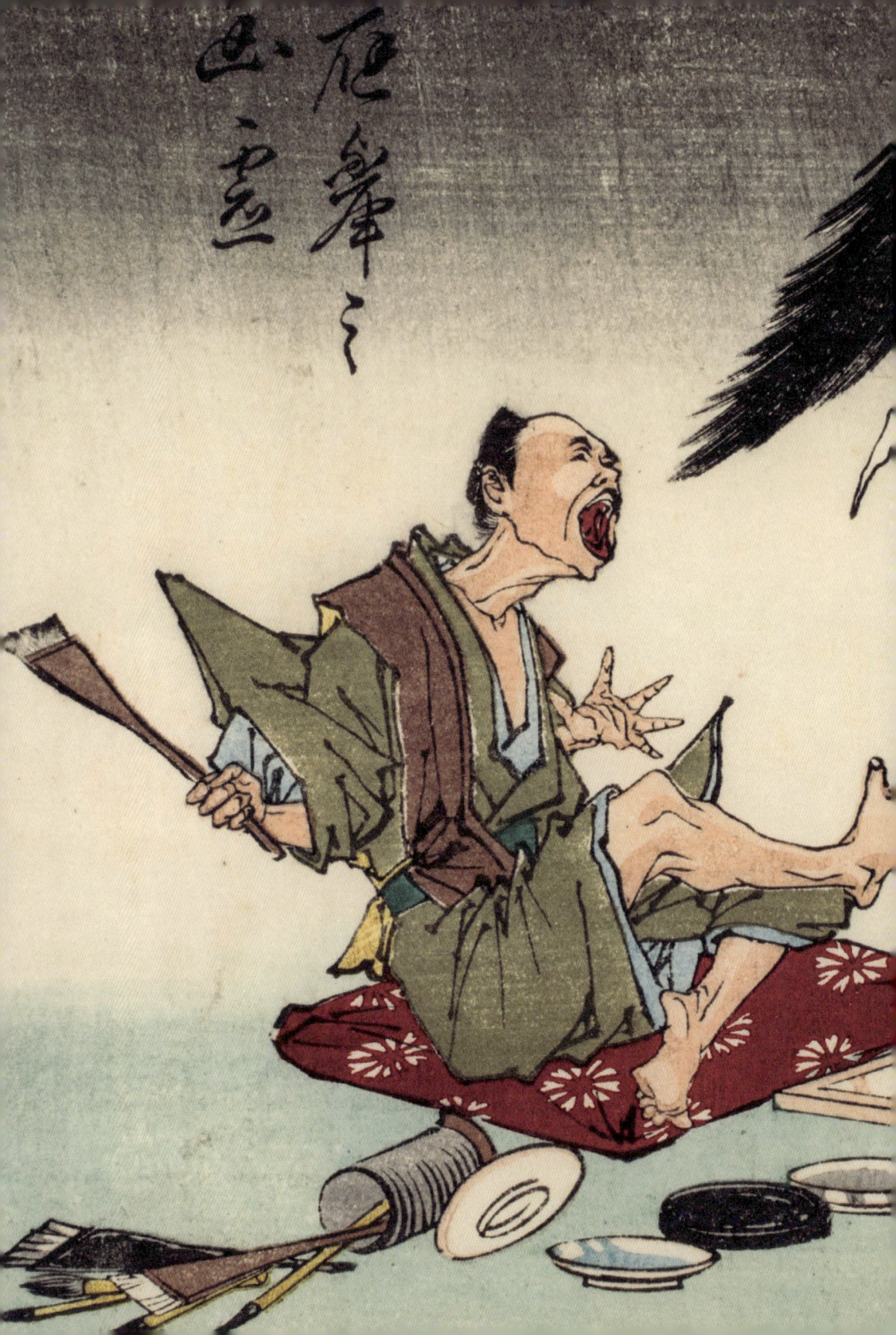

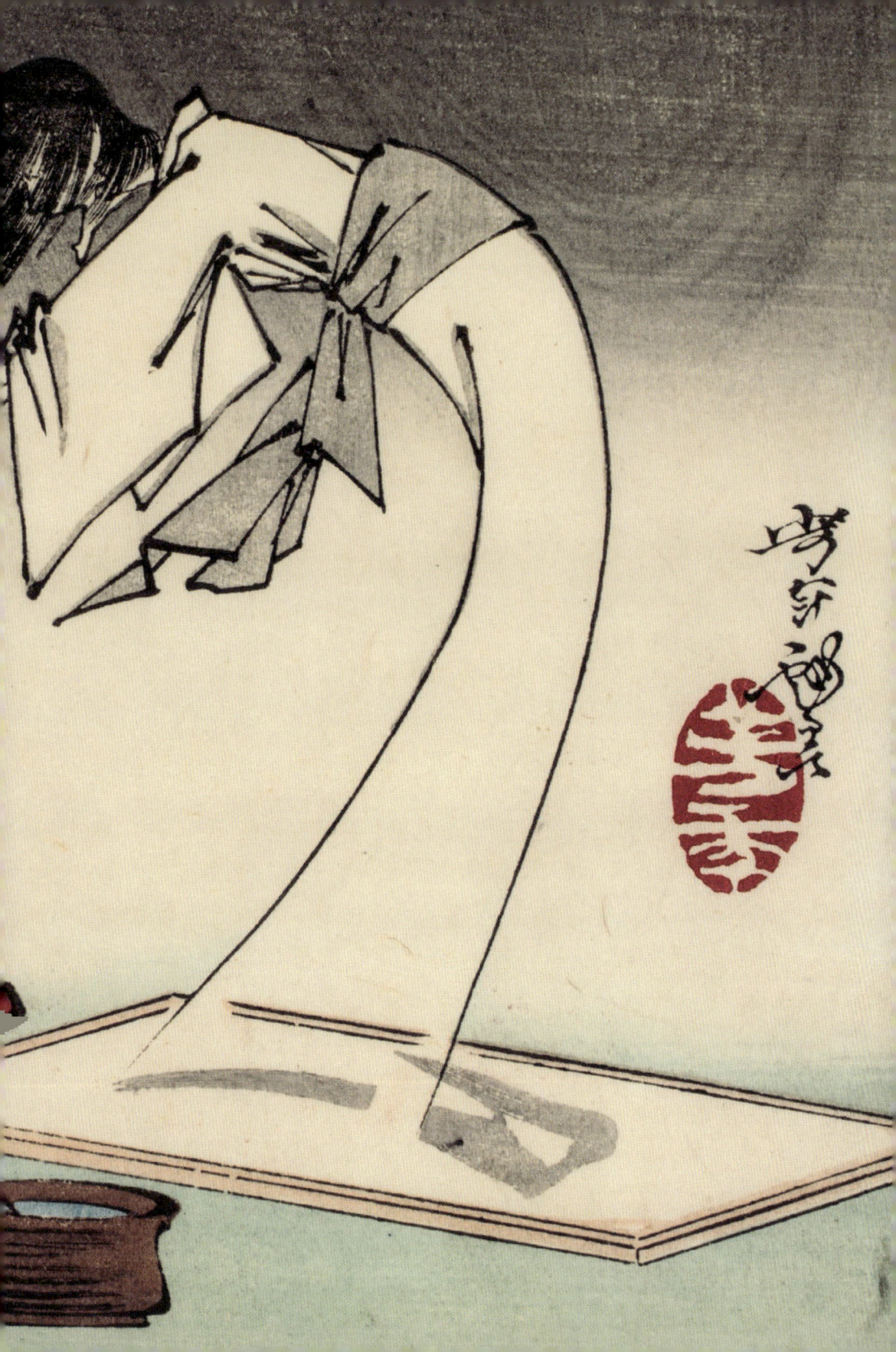

© Prestel Verlag, Munich · London · New York, 2025
A member of Penguin Random House Verlagsgruppe GmbH
Neumarkter Strasse 28 · 81673 Munich

2nd edition 2026

produktsicherheit@penguinrandomhouse.de
(The above information is mandatory information according to GPSR and should be used for all queries relating to the safety of our books)

First published in French as
Fantômes yokai
© Éditions Hazan, 2024

Editorial director Éditions Hazan: Jérôme Gille
Copy editor, image editor Éditions Hazan: Cloé de Lustrac
Graphic design: Paper! Tiger! (Aurélien Farina)
Editing and Proofreading Éditions Hazan: Katia de Azevedo
Production Éditions Hazan: Francis Verdelet, Justine Veillon
Separations: Hyphen Group, Italy

Project Management Prestel: Cornelia Hübler
Translation from French: Alexandra Cox
Copy-Editing, English Edition: Patricia Newman
Production Management Prestel: Martina Effaga
Typesetting, English Edition: Barbara Delius, Berlin

MIX
Paper | Supporting responsible forestry
FSC® C104723

Penguin Random House Verlagsgruppe FSC® N001967

Printed in China

ISBN 978-3-7913-7783-4

www.prestel.com